THE EDUCATION OF CHILDREN
IN
THE PRIMARY GRADES

The Education of Children in the Primary Grades

BY

JOHN LOUIS HORN

PROFESSOR OF EDUCATION
MILLS COLLEGE

and

THOMAS WHITE CHAPMAN

ASSISTANT SUPERINTENDENT IN CHARGE OF INSTRUCTION,
PUBLIC SCHOOLS, LODI, CALIFORNIA

NEW YORK
FARRAR & RINEHART, *Inc.*
1935

COPYRIGHT, 1935, BY
JOHN LOUIS HORN AND THOMAS WHITE CHAPMAN
ALL RIGHTS RESERVED
Published, January, 1935

372
H78e

PRINTED IN THE UNITED STATES OF AMERICA
BY J. J. LITTLE AND IVES COMPANY, NEW YORK

PREFACE

Three objectives have guided us in the preparation of this volume: to formulate an organized set of principles dealing with the first step in formal education; to cover systematically and completely the work of these primary grades; and to make our discussions so detailed and specific that the teacher may learn how to proceed and may have at hand definite criteria by which to judge the outcomes of her work.

There are three tasks which we have not attempted: Since we have taken it for granted, we have not undertaken to teach the content of the curriculum. The prospective teacher who has had no musical training will not learn in this volume how to teach music, and the teacher who herself has an unpleasant voice will not learn here how to teach the beauties of English speech.

Secondly, we do not wish to be understood as maintaining that, even granted a thorough training in content and a cultivated background, one may learn to teach by reading this book. Though its contents and plan should prove helpful to the young teacher in the practice of her profession, the volume has been prepared primarily for classes in teacher-training institutions where observation and directed teaching go hand in hand with theoretical instruction.

In the third place, we have referred to, but not dealt with, the technique of standardized tests and measurements. It is no longer necessary to testify to the importance of these procedures. We believe, however, that they deserve extensive and independent treatment.

PREFACE

While we have endeavored to present our own point of view in organization, content, method, and emphasis, we can lay little, if any, claim to originality. Too many specialists have devoted years of labor to every subject taught and to every type of activity carried on in the elementary school to entitle any one to claim originality for all of them. So far as specific procedures are concerned, ours has been frankly a work of compilation in accordance with a plan and a relative weighing of our own. We have endeavored to be scrupulous in indicating our sources and to give credit where credit is due. That we have not fully succeeded in this we know; it would be impossible in a field where so many have worked and where no one can make an independent beginning.

If we appear to have quoted at greater length than seems necessary, it has been done with two intentions: we have used the quotation as a method of acknowledgment, and we have thought in this way to lure some of the readers of this book to more extended reading in the particular fields that attract their interest.

We must acknowledge our special obligation to Professor George H. Hilliard of Western State Teachers College, Michigan. Dr. Hilliard read the manuscript and made a number of valuable suggestions which we were happy to adopt.

J. L. H.,
Mills College, California
T. W. C.,
Lodi, California

January, 1935

CONTENTS

	PAGE
PREFACE	v

CHAPTER
I. THE SOCIAL HERITAGE AND EVERY CHILD . . 3
The Meaning of Education. The Significance of Speech. The Significance of Reading and Writing. The Significance of Quantitative Thinking. The Arts of Expression. Music and Drawing as Tools. The Art of Speaking. The Non-Skill Phase of Early Education. References for Further Study.

II. EVERY CHILD AND HIS SCHOOL . . . 13
Home or School? The Place of the Nursery School. The Place of the Kindergarten. The Beginning of the Primary Unit. The End of the Period of Primary Instruction. References for Further Study.

III. BEFORE FORMAL SCHOOLING: A PERIOD OF TRANSITION 24
Children Are Variable. Pre-Elementary Education. Contrast. The Need for Transition Classes. Procedures in Transition Classes. Determining Readiness for Primary Work. References for Further Study.

IV. CURRICULUM AND METHOD 36
General Principles. The Meaning and the Function of the Activity. Organizing Instruction. References for Further Study.

V. READING: THE PRE-PRIMER PERIOD . . . 51
Basic Principles. Before Books. Translating Theory into Practice.

VI. READING: THE BEGINNING OF BOOKS . . 64
Discovering Reading. Variability of Response. Children Who Are Not Ready for Reading. The Child and His Primer. Testing and Remedial Procedure.

VII. READING: THE PERIOD OF RAPID PROGRESS . 75
Preparation for Independent Reading. Phonics as an Aid to Recognition. Reading at Sight. The Non-Reader. Desirable Outcomes. References for Further Study.

CONTENTS

CHAPTER		PAGE
VIII.	HANDWRITING AND SPELLING: GENERAL PRINCIPLES	87

Basic Principles Governing Penmanship Instruction. Basic Principles Governing Spelling Instruction. Tests and Desirable Outcomes.

IX. HANDWRITING AND SPELLING: THE FIRST SCHOOL YEAR 100

The Beginning of Writing. From Blackboard to Desk.

X. HANDWRITING AND SPELLING: PERIOD OF AUTOMATIZATION 110

Second School Year: Spelling. Second School Year: Penmanship. Third School Year: Spelling. Third School Year: Penmanship. References for Further Study.

XI. NUMBER: LAYING THE BASIS FOR COMPUTATION 122

Concepts of Quantity. Reading and Writing Numbers. Extension of the Number System. Concepts of Measurement. Organizing the Work in Computation. Addition-Subtraction Combinations. Desirable Outcomes

XII. NUMBER: INTRODUCING THE FOUR OPERATIONS WITH WHOLE NUMBERS 135

Addition and Subtraction. Multiplication and Division. Some General Principles of Procedure. Desirable Outcomes. References for Further Study.

XIII. SPEECH—INFORMAL COMMUNICATION . . 152

The Influence of Environment. The Task of the Teacher. Voice. Articulation. Phonetics as an Aid. Pronunciation. Aids toward Good Speech. Correct Usage. Good Conversation. Desirable Outcomes. References for Further Study.

XIV. SPEECH—FORMAL EXPRESSION . . . 168

The Story. Dramatization. Written Composition. Literature. Desirable Outcomes. References for Further Study.

XV. MUSIC 185

The Four Elements of Music. The Aims of Music in the Primary Grades. Procedure. Desirable Outcomes. References for Further Study.

XVI. ART—PRINCIPLES UNDERLYING INSTRUCTION . 203

The Four Elements of Art. The Aims of Art in the Primary Grades. Procedure. References for Further Study.

CONTENTS

CHAPTER		PAGE
XVII.	ART—INSTRUCTIONAL PROCEDURES	215
	Drawing. Construction. Color. Design. Appreciation. Desirable Outcomes.	
XVIII.	THE NON-SKILL OBJECTIVES	229
	A Brief Preface to Three Chapters.	
XIX.	TRAINING FOR CHARACTER	233
	Child and Adult. Character and the School. Course of Study. Method: Conviction or Habit? Desirable Outcomes. References for Further Study.	
XX.	TRAINING FOR HEALTH	249
	Scope of Primary Health Work. Desirable Outcomes. References for Further Study.	
XXI.	INTRODUCING THE CHILD TO HIS SOCIAL AND NATURAL ENVIRONMENT	261
	The World of Things. The World of Men. The World of Nature. Desirable Outcomes in Nature Study. References for Further Study.	
XXII.	ABOUT OUR PROFESSION	278
INDEX		289

THE EDUCATION OF CHILDREN
IN
THE PRIMARY GRADES

CHAPTER I

THE SOCIAL HERITAGE AND EVERY CHILD

The Meaning of Education. All the intricate mechanism of thinking and doing, of philosophy, knowledge, and the numberless skills that we call civilization, depend for continuance on their being relearned generation by generation. This relearning, in the largest sense, constitutes education. Children are born with nervous predispositions that enable them to master their environment, but this equipment probably differs little, if any, from that of their ancestors in the unknown past. Generation by generation, our religion and our philosophy, our manners and our ethical and social ideals, our accumulation of theoretical and practical knowledge, our skills and the operation of our structures of steel and stone, must be artificially transmitted.

The Significance of Speech. This, then, is the rôle of education: to add the social to the physical inheritance of man. But how is this aim of education to be achieved? How is man to transmit this social heritage to youth, born with none of the habits, skills, or knowledge essential to comprehension, to participation, and to the carrying forward of this civilization?

Man is the only animal to whom this problem of education is presented. The rest of the living beings in this world have been willing to leave the universe as they found it. By the processes of survival, other animals have developed behavior patterns suitable to existence and these they transmit through heredity as instincts. These instincts, as they unfold, suffice to repeat in each generation the round of living.

The non-human inhabitants of this planet create no problems for themselves. They do not improve their conditions. They do not devise means for enabling the unfit to survive. Above all, they have no means of introducing to their progeny the improvements or comforts on which they may have accidentally stumbled. Until such time as any new pattern becomes part of the physical inheritance, that which is discovered, no matter how precious, must vanish with each generation.

Man alone is the exception. In a world so utterly changed from its original state of nature that his instinctive equipment has become almost valueless, man provides his children with the greatest comforts. He teaches them all that he has learned. He gives them the advantages of all the experiences that all the preceding generations have lived through. He gives to the entire race the benefit of the achievements of the comparatively few geniuses, inventors, and creators.

What is the method by which man achieves all this? If he has changed his natural environment, nullifying the instinctive equipment which is the most essential possession of the rest of the animal world, he has also differentiated himself from this world by devising a means of obviating the need for inherited patterns of living. He has invented speech. "We have recent important anthropological evidence," states Stinchfield,[1] "which seems to indicate that speech probably began as far back as a million years ago, in the first glacial period, when the oldest known representative of humankind lived."

But the origin and development of articulate, learned communication, dim at best, are less important to us

---

[1] Stinchfield, S. M., *The Psychology of Speech*. Boston, Expression Co., 1928.

than is its incalculable usefulness. Without language, which enables us to remember and to transmit that which we have learned, there could be no civilization, no culture. Language is the treasure house in which we store the nuggets of experience; it is language that enables each generation to begin where the preceding one left off. Language is the repository which enables us to retain for the benefit of all the generations of man those things that the creative genius of every generation adds to the comfort, the happiness, and the elevation of the race. It is the use of words that makes man human. Because he is without articulate speech and must confine himself to images as a method of thinking, the chimpanzee cannot attain even the smallest beginnings of cultural development.

The Significance of Reading and Writing. As a learned method of communication, speech is invaluable. But, looking back at the evolution of society from our vantage point of the present day, we see that speech has distinct limitations. It places a strain on memory beyond the capacity of man. So long as remembering is the only method of preservation, the quantity retained must, in the nature of things, be held within quite definite limits. Oral language alone gives us only an illiterate society And illiterate we were for many, many generations. Man's culture resided in his memory. It was transmitted from mouth to ear. Indeed, the variability of people in the matter of memory and in the talent for telling what was remembered brought about a specialized or professional class of rememberers and narrators among early peoples.

"These bards,' Mr. Wells tells us, "existed among all the Aryan-speaking peoples. They chanted or recited stories of the past or stories of the living chief and his people. They were the first great artists of the ear. They mark a new step forward in the power and the range of the human mind. They sustained and developed in men's minds a sense of a greater something than themselves, the tribe, and of a life that extended back into the past. They not only recalled old hatreds and battles, they recalled old alliances and a common inheritance. In their hands language became as beautiful as it is ever likely to be. These bards were living books, man histories, guardians and makers of a new and more powerful tradition in human life. When first the art of writing crept into Europe, it must have seemed far too slow, clumsy, and lifeless a method of record."

But writing did, of course, prevail over oral tradition. "With the invention of writing, human tradition was able to become fuller and much more exact. Men separated by hundreds of miles could now communicate their thoughts. An increasing number of human beings began to share a common written knowledge and a common sense of a past and a future. Human thinking became a larger operation in which hundreds of minds in different places and in different ages could react upon one another." [2]

Man's memory, at best relatively inaccurate and certainly limited in scope, was released. Accuracy and permanence became assured. Literature, speculation about nature, theories of government and ethics, began to develop. Continuity and extensive development became a certainty. Written language now became man's repository. The arts of reading and writing became indispensable to education.

The child, an illiterate, finds that man is rich in the accumulation of the ages. Born primitive, with nothing to guide him but instinct, he is heir to a great legacy.

[2] From *Outline of History*, by H. G. Wells, copyright 1920, 1931, reprinted by permission from Doubleday, Doran & Co., Inc.

The adult world is willing and ready to guide him and introduce him to his own. But there are certain preliminaries of initiation. Since all that he would know is locked in writing, he must, at the very outset, be given the key. He must learn to read.

We have arrived at the first of the skills, without which no one can penetrate far into the human heritage. Man invented writing. What has been written must be read. Reading as an art demands much more than mere recognition of individual words. We do not read unless we at the same time comprehend. From this it immediately becomes evident that the content of true reading must consist of matter readily within the maturity and the experience of the child. In the widest sense, pupils cannot master the skill of reading in the primary grades or perhaps even in the elementary school.

Reading in the sense in which we employ the word in the primary grades is confined to that degree of efficiency which, to borrow a phrase from Professor Morrison, will enable the child to study. He ordinarily enters school as an illiterate. The world of books is closed to him. His information and contact with people have hitherto come through speech. The road to his mind has been through his ear. He has been barred from communication with all those who have written, except when he has listened while others read. The first task of the school is to give him enough skill in reading to enable him to help himself, to study directly from books insofar as these are adjusted to the degree of comprehension that goes with his years and his experience.

The Significance of Quantitative Thinking. We must not assume that verbal thought is man's only method of thinking and that the writing of words is man's only means of making records. Important as language and the language arts may be, there are great sections of the human heritage that would have remained undiscovered but for man's venture into the abstractions of quantitative thought. To reading and writing we must add a third tool, the use of numbers, leading to the concept of quantity.

We are so accustomed to number that we take it for granted as something obvious. But our methods of calculation and the further development of mathematics, made possible by our system of numbers, were slow in developing. The completion of the system that we now know dates back a very short time indeed. The Roman pupil was taught arithmetic by means of a device called an *abacus,* or by the use of the fingers. In the *abacus* pebbles were moved about, or knobs were made to slide in grooves which represented different values. In finger reckoning, amounts were indicated by the finger joints and by touching different parts of the body. These methods had their obvious limitations, and little of permanent value in calculation has come down to us from the Romans. On the contrary, their system of notation interfered with the progress of arithmetic.

The growth of writing has a long and interesting history into which this book cannot enter; similarly, the story of the development of our method of notation is too long to be told here in detail. Besides the Roman system of notation, systems were created by the Egyptians, the Babylonians, and possibly other peoples. Our present system was not spontaneously invented, but developed slowly. It was not until the Fifteenth, Sixteenth, and Seventeenth Centuries that most of the common symbols now in use were evolved. Our present, or Arabic system of notation is a Hindu system disseminated by the Arabians. With its comparatively recent adoption in Turkey, China and Japan, the use of Arabic numbers has become universal in the civilized world.

From the foregoing paragraphs it is clear that the first step in education is a preliminary one. The first task of the school must center about teaching the mastery of those tools or skills without which no one can study. Until such time as the child can meet the primary tests of ability to read and write and use the number symbols comprehendingly, he is not studying in the strictest sense of the word. Instead, he is merely engaged in learning to read and write and cipher for the purpose of employing these implements in beginning the next stage of his education. It need hardly be added that we employ the word *study* here in its narrowest sense. Naturally, in its broader use, all life, all observation, all effort, is study.

The Arts of Expression. Reading, writing, and calculation, the three skills to which we have just referred, are necessary for the carrying on and the recording of thought processes. They are the tools of reflective or formal thinking. But, and this applies somewhat more to writing than to calculating, their use is broader than that. Man also has need for, and has devised means of, expression. Besides history and philosophy, government, law, and science, man devotes himself to poetry and to fiction. He has moods as well as thoughts, emotions as well as theories.

In his need to express exuberance and sorrow, happiness and tragedy, his reaction to beauty and grief, to nature and to the infinitely variable color and rhythm of life, man has found the verbal form of expression insufficient.

The majority of us are destined to appreciate rather than to create masterpieces of literature. But that need not bar us from expressing ourselves in a poem, an essay or a short story, or even from writing interesting letters. Whether these be published or not, the delight of self-expression is ours. In the same way, while few of us will attain to the excellence of the composers who have permanently enriched the race, all of us should know how to use this means of self-expression. We have too long regarded music and art as something to appreciate and have too long neglected the possibilities for self-expression. Music and graphic expression may well be regarded as tools. They should be taught in such a way as to enable the child to "write" as well as "read."

Music and Drawing as Tools. "It is my belief," says Mrs. Coleman in her stimulating book,[3] "that improvisation, like singing and other powers, which many people consider as special gifts, is the outcome of early habit. The child who begins in the earliest stages of his musical development to improvise songs and dances and instrumental melodies, will grow as naturally into it as flowers turn to the sun. It is not difficult, when one begins at the natural beginning. It is much easier for a very young child to improvise than to learn a set melody. All children love to do it, and it is a very simple matter to guide their haphazard experiments into tuneful form. Like all their other powers, this power to create also grows and becomes more refined, and their compositions gradually take on more pleasing forms and greater variety."

The foregoing paragraph is not intended to imply that all of us are capable of creating works of art. As will be made amply clear in the chapters on music and art, most of us must, in the end, depend for our enjoyment on appreciation of the works of others. But this indisputable truth has persuaded us too easily to give art an esoteric place in the scheme of things. We must look at the graphic arts and at music as we do at literature. Only the few are creative, but all of us can command the tools —we can read and write. Both for creation and appre-

[3] Coleman, S. N., *Creative Music for Children.* New York, G. P. Putnam's Sons, 1922.

ciation, literature depends on fundamental literacy. In this sense of literacy art and music belong to all.

"We did not regard art in terms of sculpture, drawing, printing, literature, dancing, music, or acting," says Elizabeth Byrne Ferm in describing the work at the Modern School in Stelton, New Jersey. "We recognized art as self expression, as a revelation of the spirit projected outwardly. Every object made from an inner impulse, no matter how insignificant or useless it may appear, is a creation and bears the hallmark of the creator upon it."

The Art of Speaking. Unfortunately speech has hitherto been neglected by the school on the theory that it is acquired incidentally, and that the acquisition is, in fact, complete when the child enters school. As the chapter dealing with language suggests, much remains to be done if the school is to meet its full obligation of introducing every child to his social heritage.

The Non-Skill Phase of Early Education. At this point the student might conclude that the sole function of the preliminary step in education, ordinarily referred to as *the primary grades,* consists of the teaching of six skills. But a visit to the first few grades of any good school, or an attempt to recall one's own early school experience, will indicate the contrary. Mastery of skills is an important and indispensable part of the task. Without such mastery the school is a failure. But skills do not represent the whole task.

The child's education does not begin with school. Long before he comes to school the world is his to be comprehended so far as it lies in his power to do so. Through play, through relationships, through numberless subtle elements of his environment, through experiment and through accident, through the efforts of parents, and even through attempts to keep him from learning, life, as it is lived by man in his time and place, opens up to the young child and is absorbed by him. This sort of education is incidental, and in contrast with the formal education that begins later. It is life. It gives rise to that true and frequent statement that "education is living." Speech, the amenities of social life, religion, morals, habits of health, and much else that defies listing, have become his before his formal schooling begins.

Naturally, this aspect of the child's education does not cease with the beginning of school. His education must be broader in scope than the mere acquisition of tools. This growth through living is not only recognized by the school, it is facilitated and advanced by conscious and careful preparation. A conscious effort to develop it is another phase of the work of the primary school. Even in the beginning, the school cannot afford to concentrate exclusively on the acquisition of skills and thus defer the child's aesthetic, social, moral, and civic development. This is another and different phase of education. It is a part of the child's growth and must be approached with a different technique than that involved in the mastery of skills. After the six skills have been discussed in detail, this second but concurrent phase of the preliminary task of formal education will be elaborated.

REFERENCES FOR FURTHER STUDY

Bode, B. H., *Fundamentals of Education*. New York, The Macmillan Company, 1921.

Horne, H. H., *Philosophy of Education*. New York, The Macmillan Company, 1905.

Nunn, T. P., *Education: Its Data and First Principles*. London, E. Arnold, 1921.

Thorndike, Lynn, *A Short History of Civilization*. New York, F. S. Crofts & Co., 1926.

CHAPTER II

EVERY CHILD AND HIS SCHOOL

Home or School? In a general way the last chapter discussed the first or preliminary task that every child, and therefore, every child's school, must face. The last paragraphs of the chapter indicated, however, that the child does not wait passively for the formalities of the school. While the several skills discussed have not yet been mastered by him at the time he enters school, these skills are not co-extensive with education. If he cannot read, he has been listening for a long time. If he cannot write, he has been speaking for a number of years. Even the concept of quantity is in all likelihood not entirely unknown to him.

We face this question: When should the one kind of education, the informal, give way in part to the other kind of education, the institutional? At what age shall children be sent to school? How long should it take to complete the first instructional unit outlined in the last chapter? It is not enough to say that at the present time elementary education actually does begin at about the age of six for most children. This practice derives from tradition rather than from educational theory. It probably rests on convenience more than it does on technical considerations.

Children have not always been sent to school. For a long time the parental instinct sufficed to induct the child into the simply organized social group in which he was to live, and to teach him the few tasks which he was to perform. Without specific intention on the part of parents, the education of the child went on as a part of the general business of child rearing. It is, comparatively speaking, only recently that the general instinct for child rearing was found inadequate for formal education and this phase of training was entrusted to a specialized group which now takes the responsibility for the child at the age of six. But there is nothing permanent or unalterable about the age at which the child was originally taken from the general parental care and entrusted to the specialized care of the school. A great part of the business of educating was still left to the home. Our present practice of beginning institutional education at the age of six has no basis in pedagogical theory. It is more likely that the school has put the cart before the horse, determining first the age of admission and discovering later what the central group in an unselected aggregation of six-year-olds was capable of achieving.

Mr. Bertrand Russell, who has recently been interesting himself in this field of early infancy, thinks that "by the time the child is six years old, moral education ought to be nearly complete."

While the reality is not nearly so simple, this mode of approach does help us to realize that education as such does not begin at any particular point in the life of the child. Varying aspects of education begin successively along a series of stages of development. Conscious training for certain ends may quite properly begin at the beginning of the second year, if not at birth; vocational training, on the other hand, must obviously be deferred for a number of years beyond the conventional age for entering school.

The Place of the Nursery School. We are really facing the question of whether our present accumulation of professional skill in the hands of trained persons warrants a more extensive replacing of the home by the school. Has the school developed for the earlier years, hitherto left to the home, a specialized technique sufficiently superior to that of the average home to justify the removal of another level of nurture from lay to professional care?

Parents, say those who would answer this question affirmatively, cannot be expected to possess the skill or the leisure required for the art of dealing with young children, nor can they command the requisite medical and psychological knowledge. Moreover, children need the companionship of other children of the same age, and few homes can provide the space and the environment that best suit young children.

But these more obvious considerations are not comparable in importance to the intensely interesting assertion of Dr. Gesell, on the basis of studies of pre-school children at the Yale Clinic, that individual differences do not affect "the dynamic organization of the individual or his personality make-up." The "traits and trends" of the baby's personality depend more on conditioning environment than on specific inheritance. "It is almost dismaying," he says, "to note how promptly and how relentlessly the conditioning process begins. It begins literally at birth."

If, then, we can distinguish between instinctive and cultural behavior in earliest infancy, and if conditioned behavior may be regarded as the mechanism by which personality grows and takes its being in a matrix of social relations, if the "first outlines and the very tenure of a personality are laid down in infancy," is not the importance of sound pre-school guidance and development made clear?

When the elementary school was established, it was the first contact of the child with institutional education. It was the first step from the home into the outer world.

Children were gathered in schools and entrusted to professional educators to supplement and, indeed, to replace the home, so far as a part of their education was concerned. Today there is a growing demand to give the younger child the benefits of institutional opportunities and to permit trained professional workers to share still further with the home in his education. The demand is not, indeed, to teach the fundamental subjects of reading and writing earlier. It is a desire to control other elements of growth and development. As a result, the nursery school, which takes children as young as eighteen months, has made its appearance.

"Why should it appear to us reasonable," asks Dr. Woolley, "that public responsibility with regard to the education of children should suddenly be enforced at the age of five or six? The probable reason is that five or six represents the youngest age at which the techniques of reading, writing, and arithmetic can be profitably taught. Modern theory is laying greater stress on the development of character and personality as equally important phases of education."

And this phase of education must evidently become effective at a much earlier age than we have hitherto associated with school. "One can make or break the child, so far as its personality is concerned, before the age of five is reached," says Dr. Watson, who thinks that "by the end of the second year the pattern of the future individual is already laid down. The questions as to whether the child will possess a stable or unstable personality, whether it is going to be timid and beset with many fears, or subject to rage and temper tantrums, whether it will exhibit tendencies of general over- or under-emotionalism, have already been answered by the end of the two-year period."

It is these first few years of the life of the child, physically as well as emotionally, socially as well as in the more restricted sense of education as learning, that the nursery school undertakes to guide. Forest,[1] in an endeavor to indicate some of the features of the developing American nursery school, names health care and health education, psychological testing, and the study of personality. The educative activities provided for the children in these schools are naturally playful in character. Toys for indoor and outdoor play are provided in great variety; music and informal rhythmic activities are included in the procedure of all the good schools.

The nursery school is the beginning of a new first school for the child, which makes the elementary school, with which we are to deal in this volume, the third classification. Between the nursery school and the primary grades we have the kindergarten.

The Place of the Kindergarten. While not universally established, the kindergarten is in theory the second school of the series. Like the nursery school it is "preschool" in character, in that it refrains from teaching the formal or "school" subjects, and undertakes to supplement the home by providing the child with opportunities for development. Instruction is incidental. The kindergarten provides the child with an environment rich in educational possibilities, suitable for his intellectual, social, and physical development. It is interested in the child's happy and rounded development. Toward this end it provides activities and informal procedures of interest and calculated to advance his physical, social, emotional, and intellectual needs. It aims to make him a cultured, civilized individual, with the ability to live in a group of equals in contrast with his rather self-centered and self-important life in the home. Music, dancing, stories and poems, pictures and conversation, all have their place

[1] See references at end of chapter.

in the "curriculum," along with all of the sound habits that contribute to health and happy relations with one's fellows.

The Beginning of the Primary Unit. Institutional education is, in our day, being forced downward to an age so much earlier than that heretofore in effect, that the elementary school is no longer the first. But the questions with which this chapter opened still remain unanswered. At what age shall formal elementary instruction begin? How shall we establish the boundary line between the pre-elementary training which has been described and the work of the primary school? At what age can the preliminary step in formal education be regarded as complete?

While it is probable that the elementary schools have pragmatically discovered the type of achievement possible for a fairly large proportion of six-year-olds, there are almost as many exceptions as there are typical instances, the exceptions operating in both directions. Some of the children are, at the conventional age, far from ready to begin formal work; others have been ready for it for a long time.

Kindergartners have discovered that it is possible, with their materials, to teach arithmetic in the form of counting and measuring quite effectively and happily to some children well under six years of age. Some kindergarten children are capable of making excellent progress in reading. Terman, on the other hand, has found that a fourth of all first-graders are, mentally, on a par with the median kindergarten child.

The methods and the content of the first grade have, in the best school systems, recently tended to shade into the kindergarten. The movement for unified kindergarten and first grade instruction brings the study of social life through play up into the first grade, and carries similar

EVERY CHILD AND HIS SCHOOL

methods of studying the essential social skills, such as reading, down into the kindergarten. Today we see the nursery school enter still earlier into the life of the child and, while it has primary tasks of its own, it doubtless will soon be shading also into the sphere of the kindergarten.

It is unreasonable to demand clear boundary lines. We cannot impose uniformity where conditions are essentially variable. After all, schools and boundary lines and age-range divisions are *administrative conveniences*. The child has a certain pre-secondary task to master. The average child can do so by the age of nine. The highly endowed child will probably not be permitted, for several reasons, to enter on secondary work much before this age. The poorly endowed child will take longer.

At what age shall children be sent to school? As early as practicable, perhaps at the age of two. What types of activity shall they engage in on entering school? They should be provided with those types of activity that seem best adapted to them at any particular age. In general, the trend will be to provide for the youngest children the activities which are being developed in the nursery school, for the older children those activities which have long engaged the kindergarten, to be followed in due course by the established first-grade type of instruction.

At what age shall these several types of educative experience begin and end? No answer to this question is possible because none is conceivable. Children vary in the amount of native endowment which they possess, in the rate at which they mature, and in the progress they make. The first fixed point in formal educational development will be determined for a child when he is found to have those skills which are necessary for the beginning of the secondary type of formal education. Children can read, write, and use numbers when, to a certain degree, they have ceased trying to learn these tools and are ready to begin to use them for purposes of study. When they have ceased, like illiterates, to depend on others for their reading and writing, when they can begin to secure content from books and express their ideas in writing, when they can "put two and two together" with the conventional symbols in the realm of quantitative thought, when these conditions have been met, the primary unit of formal education has been completed.

In view of the need for attention to individual differences in ability and in rate of development, the soundest principles of organization and procedure would seem to call for grouping young children on the basis of maturity as determined primarily by chronological age, and treating them as individuals rather than as groups.

The End of the Period of Primary Instruction. How much time should the average child require to complete primary education? Most of us attended eight-year elementary schools which, on examination, appear to include in their curricula little more than has just been outlined for the primary grades. This traditional school is the American common school, the school of the three R's. It is the school in which the child ordinarily makes no advance toward the so-called "higher education," toward the acquisition of foreign languages, the sciences, mathematics, or, in any serious sense, literature and the social studies.

The reason for all this is found in history rather than in pedagogical theory. There has been, in other words, no particular and, certainly, no technical reason for the traditional duration of the American elementary school. The elementary school in which American children who attend the public schools begin their education was borrowed from abroad. This school, in the older countries of Europe, has always been a special, separate school for the masses of the population. In these countries there exists a double school system, frankly differentiating between class and mass, and limiting the educational opportunities of the latter arbitrarily on the basis of wealth or rank.

In these "folk" schools children remain to the age of thirteen or fourteen, after which they are apprenticed to a trade. The work in these schools is deliberately rudimentary, and never leads to higher education. The European system of schools is parallel, not sequential, as is the case in the United States. The secondary school stands side by side with, not following after and beyond, the elementary school. The few children who attend this school enter at about the age of nine, *after a preliminary three-year period in a preparatory school.*

The closing words of the last paragraph indicate a possible answer to our question of how long the average child should require to complete the first step in preliminary education. This first step, as indicated at length in the last chapter, must consist of preparation for study. Study, in this sense, is equivalent to the next, or *secondary* step in education with which the following paragraphs are concerned. In Europe, centuries of experience in the education of those children with whom the greatest care is taken would seem to indicate that the primary school should be a three-year unit. We are at the present time engaged in a re-organization of the American school series, shortening the eight-year school to six. Probably we cover in six years more than any school could achieve in three. But the question is whether, in any technical sense, a six-year school can be a single unit of instruction, facing one unified and describable task in the education of the child. After all, one might get further in a ten-year than a six-year school.

It isn't sound pedagogical thinking to determine the number of years before outlining the task. The question of duration must be stated in more realistic terms. "It seems to be sound reasoning," says one student, "to hold that higher or secondary education should begin for the child as soon as he has the tools with which he may profitably gain this higher training. Looked at in this way, the main function of the elementary school is to give the child the training necessary for participation in higher education as early as possible." *As early as possible* is not age fourteen, nor is it age twelve. "Experience," says Professor Morrison,[2] and most students of this field will fully agree with him, "seems to suggest that most children under effective primary teaching reach this point and master these primary adaptations not far from the age of nine."

The preceding evidence indicates a definite point in the educational development of childhood, a point which represents the termination of the first step in formal education. We must not, however, over-emphasize the average age. While it is true that mastery of the tools is reached at about the center of the present six-year elementary school, the attainment in question need not be described in chronological terms. On the contrary, the expected achievement prerequisite to effective secondary-school work can be designated in true pedagogic terms. It represents achievement of a clearly definable set of skills, the possession of which is definitely determinable for each child by test.

The American elementary school will, in all likelihood, remain a six-year institution. It will probably not be re-organized to conform to the conclusions of educational theorists. These considerations need not, however, prevent us from recognizing the fact that at about the center of the present six-year school period there does come a

---

[2] Morrison, H. D., *The Practice of Teaching in the Secondary School*. Chicago, University of Chicago Press, 1926.

EVERY CHILD AND HIS SCHOOL

point of technical differentiation in content and method. This is, the student is now aware, the point at which the effort to master the fundamentals has so far succeeded that the pupil may begin to use them—in other words, to study. The character of the aims and of the teaching processes on one side of the line must be distinctly different from those on the other. It is the first of these units, primary education, that engages our attention in this volume.

REFERENCES FOR FURTHER STUDY

Forest, L., *Pre-School Education.* New York, The Macmillan Company, 1927.

Yearbooks of the National Society for the Study of Education
  Vol. 6, Part II, *The Kindergarten and Its Relation to Elementary Education.*
  Vol. 7, Part II, *The Co-Ordination of the Kindergarten and the Elementary School.*
  Vol. 28, *Pre-School and Parental Education.*
  Bloomington, Public School Publishing Co., 1907, 1908, 1929.

CHAPTER III

BEFORE FORMAL SCHOOLING: A PERIOD OF TRANSITION

Children Are Variable. The laws of every State specify the age at which children must be admitted to the first grade. Such provisions go counter to ordinary practices outside the school. Children are variable. They do not walk at a given age, or talk at a given age, or enjoy foods in a precise series adjusted to the months of their growth. Children vary in maturity, in physical development, and in mental growth. Yet in this important matter of school readiness the law is uniform. A child who has reached an age within three or six months of six years at the time that the school opens is, according to most statutes, prepared to learn to read, write, and cipher.

On the basis of theoretical considerations it is probable that, taking 1,000 six-year-old children as they present themselves for instruction at the opening of school, some are mentally younger than 4.2 years, while others are mentally older than 7.8. This represents a difference of three and a half years of mental development in a group of children whose chronological ages are identical. Terman [1] reports a series of studies in which psychological tests were applied to whole groups in typical public schools. It was discovered that among one hundred and twelve kindergarten children there was a mental age range from three years four months to seven years seven

---

[1] Terman, L. M., *The Intelligence of School Children.* Boston, Houghton Mifflin Co., 1919.

months. The range in I.Q. was from 61 to 152, or "from feeble-mindedness to very unusual superiority."

In the case of one hundred and fifty first-grade children there was found a range in mental age from three years to practically eleven years. "The highest mental age among these first grade pupils considerably overlaps the lowest we have found in the eighth grade," says Terman. The range in I.Q. was from 45 to 145. Among the 79 fifth-grade children studied, the mental age ranged from 7¾ to 15 years, and the I.Q. ranged from 60 to 148.

These findings have been most interestingly confirmed in a study by the Reading Readiness Committee of the International Kindergarten Union in 1926. In replying to the question whether they felt that they were "expected to teach some children to read before they are ready," ninety per cent. of five hundred and sixty first-grade teachers answered affirmatively, and only nine per cent. responded in the negative.

What happens in the first grades where children are grouped in conformity with statutes rather than with professional judgment? Every term and every year, in every section of the country, in every school where an effort is made to have the class attain standard first-grade achievement, from one fourth to one third of the children enrolled fail of promotion. These children were unable to do the prescribed work at the time of admission.

This lack of readiness for the work of the school is ascertainable by psychological test. Children are, year after year, allowed to face failure in a task to which they should not have been subjected. On the other hand, always present in these first grades are children to whom the standard set for accomplishment is far too low. These are children who, without formal instruction, have mastered the content of the course of study long before they were, according to the laws, old enough to be enrolled.

Some Children Require Pre-Elementary Education.
Readiness for formal school work is discernible and determinable for any particular child. But children vary in individual endowment and in general development. Therefore they reach this point of school readiness at various ages. It should be axiomatic that, prior to their attainment of that point of development, all efforts to teach them the fundamental skills are destined to fail. No such efforts should, therefore, be attempted. In view of the fact that children must, in accordance with law, be admitted to school on the basis of evidence which has little to do with pedagogy, i.e., a certain period of elapsed time since birth, every school should maintain a pre-primary division.

Children should be treated in terms of their stage of development. They should be happy in their growth and should not be allowed to meet failure. They should be given tasks adapted to, not beyond, their capacities. In this division a technique should be developed for the discovery of readiness to go on to formal instruction. When children, in terms of reality and not in terms of the calendar, give evidence of their ability to begin formal work, they should be advanced to the regular primary grades. The central concept advocated here, and which should guide procedure in the pre-primary division, is that the child's life and development should shade and imperceptibly grow from one educational level into the other. Sudden breaks and abrupt changes should be avoided. Such changes from the home or the kindergarten to the first grade, involving, in addition to a change of environment, a marked change of attitude toward the child and demanding a change of attitude on his part toward his world, are not desirable.

The child, during the years which have preceded school, has been growing from within outward. He has been

A PERIOD OF TRANSITION

taking in the world and life as fast as his development would allow. He has been an experimenter, an explorer in a fascinating land. He has been active. His development, urged on by his deepest impulses, has been rooted in and responsive to his instincts, his naïve emotions, his physical needs.

There are certain dangers for the child in an abrupt break that tends to turn him from a self-active and partly self-directing individual into the receptive first grader, member of a large group directed by a teacher. He has, as we have said, been growing from within outward. A method of teaching that implies passivity on his part is difficult for the child to adjust himself to, since hitherto he has been in charge of his own education. His teacher, the environment, has allowed him to take the lead. Others may now take too sudden and too complete charge of his further growth. He may give up too much of his initiative, become too receptive, and much too "good" a pupil.

There should be no abrupt change. Life and activities should shade from home or kindergarten into school. The child should not be permitted to realize that there are tasks beyond his capacity. He should not be urged to attempt things which may lead to failure.

Contrast. The kindergarten which, unfortunately for American childhood, has not been as extensively developed as it deserves to be, has always exemplified the point of view advocated in the preceding paragraphs. Froebel's three fundamental conclusions regarding education in early childhood follow:

> (1) Children are usually intensely interested in playfully imitating the activities of their elders, and in this way they acquire many useful social ideas, attitudes, and habits.

(2) They are commonly interested in building and constructing, in modeling in sand and clay, in drawing, singing, skipping, and in motor activity. Through these activities they may acquire useful information, artistic taste and skills, practice in thinking and designing, habits of enjoyment.

(3) They are commonly interested in the traditional or conventional plays and games of childhood, and these interests may be systematically modified to attain much of the knowledge, skill, enjoyment, and moral development that may be appropriate to their age.

These principles sufficiently illustrate the phrase *development from within outward*. Conversely, the objection to imposition *from without inward,* abruptly turning the child into a receptive, passive being who must "learn" is illustrated in the extreme by the following quotations from The New England Primer, the earliest American first book for school children. It is one thing to learn by growing as he has been learning during the years before school, and quite another to find the teacher in command, prepared to "instill" the ready-made point of view of an adult world.

> He who ne'er learns his A, B, C,
> Forever will a Blockhead be;
> But he who to his Book's inclin'd,
> Will soon a golden Treasure find.

> He that ne'er learns his A, B, C,
> Forever will a Blockhead be;
> But he that learns these Letters fair
> Shall have a Coach to take the Air.

A PERIOD OF TRANSITION 29

In Adam's Fall
We sinned all.

Thy Life to mend,
This Book attend.

The Cat doth play
And after slay.

The idle Fool
Is whipt at School.

Young Obadias
David, Josias,
All were pious.

Peter denies,
His Lord, and cries

Queen Esther sues
And saves the Jews

Rachael doth mourn
For her first-born

As runs the Glass
Man's life doth pass.

My Book and Heart
Shall never part.

Job feels the rod,
Yet blesses God.

Kings should be good.
Not men of blood.

Time cuts down all,
Both great and small.

Uriah's beauteous Wife
Made David seek his life.

Whales in the Sea
God's Voice obey

Xerxes the great did die
And so must you and I

Youth forward slips
Death soonest nips

Zaccheus he
Did climb the Tree
His Lord to see.

If the idle fool is no longer whipt at school, it is still too true that the first grade remains to a large extent an instrument for the transmission of skills that are beyond the present capacity of some of the pupils. There is more than one way of being whipt. If the teacher, facing the need of going forward with her course of study, finds certain children unable to do the work, and of necessity gives them the definite feeling of failure which is ultimately capped by non-promotion, they are very clearly whipt.

To teach the basic skills, to help the child master the course of study, to lead his first steps toward finding a place in society—these things are clearly necessary. But to begin this work before the child is ready, at a stage in his development when failure is predictable,—that is to whip him.

The Need for Transition Classes. There are, as has been noted, three problems: Just when is a child ready for formal elementary instruction in the skills? How may this readiness be determined? What shall the school do with those children who are not yet ready for such instruction, but must be retained in school?

Were the school permitted by law to refuse to admit children until they are ready for instruction in the skills, it might be comparatively easy to organize the work of the primary grades. It has been well established that mental age six is a minimum for this work, and we know how to determine mental age by the Binet-Simon test of intelligence. In addition to this highly reliable test of general intelligence, there are available a number of group tests for young children to determine school readiness, among them the ingenious Detroit First-Grade Intelligence Test.

But the problem is not so simple. Children must be admitted to school regardless of attained mental age or determinable school readiness. It is, furthermore, highly desirable that they should be admitted to partial institutional nurture and care at as early an age as possible. But the school should not use attained chronological age as an index to the kind of work to be undertaken. The school activities should be adapted to the aptitudes and interests of the child. Techniques should be developed to enable the teacher to occupy the child in an educative manner and to discover by observation when he is ready to begin the work of the first grade. It is with these two objectives in mind that the subhead of this chapter has been entitled A Period of Transition.

To deal with the situation which exists in all school

A PERIOD OF TRANSITION

systems, we must organize transition classes which will provide older children with experiences like those made possible in the kindergarten. All children who are not mentally ready to take the first definite step in formal education belong in this pedagogical classification, regardless of chronological age. This transition class might well be an extension of the kindergarten. It might be an independent pre-primary unit, or, in accordance with a certain current movement, a unified kindergarten and first grade. The important thing is that its particular function should be understood. Its emphasis should be on the child rather than on achievements in terms of subjects of instruction.

The contrast in atmosphere and attitude between the older traditional school and the newer kindergarten procedure is very well expressed by Miss Vandewalker,[2] one of the American historians of the kindergarten.

"The primary teacher who visited a kindergarten could not fail to be impressed by the kindergartner's attitude toward her children—by her co-operation with them in the spirit of comradeship, and by her sympathetic insight into their interests and needs. She was impressed no less by the children's attitude toward their work, by the spontaneity of their interest, and by their delight in the use of the bright-colored material. The games were a revelation to her, since they showed that there could be freedom without disorder. The interest which the children took in the kindergarten songs made her own drill on scales and intervals seem little better than drudgery. The attractiveness of the kindergarten room gave her helpful suggestions concerning the value of beauty as a factor in education."

There are those who, taking this point of view too

---

[2] Vandewalker, N. P., *The Kindergarten in American Education.* New York, The Macmillan Company, 1908.

literally, would solve this whole problem rather easily by turning the entire primary school into a kindergarten and replacing all formal instruction with "activities." That is rather too simple a solution. Much as the needs of undeveloped children require attention, we cannot forget those at the other end of the scale. The bright children require instruction. For their future a solid foundation must be laid. They do not require far-fetched projects. They have no objection to work; on the contrary, they enjoy it.

Activities have their place in the primary school. One can hardly imagine children in these early grades without visualizing the many activities and life situations that make the scene such a happy one. But the acquisition of skills depends on the organizing of habits. Where activities fail to lead in that direction, as they so often do, we must resort to drill.

Procedures in Transition Classes. The appropriate techniques for pre-primary education are still in the making. The following quotations from the tentative program of activities of the Los Angeles public schools are an example of the research and the experimentation now going on in advanced city school systems:

A SUGGESTIVE CURRICULUM OF ACTIVITIES FOR THE TRANSITION GROUPS

 1. *LANGUAGE:* Conversation; rhymes and verses; listening to stories; telling stories and playing them; learning words of songs, talking games, language games; asking and answering questions.

 2. *CONSTRUCTION:* Block building; bench work; toys and manipulation; playhouse; social plays; organizing games with things; cutting, pasting, modeling; book making; sewing; costume making; pageantry.

A PERIOD OF TRANSITION

3. *ART:* Drawing; large brush work on easels; crayola work; poster work; cutting out and mounting pictures; color work in cutting and pasting; designs for costumes; book borders, book covers; hearing stories about pictures; arranging flowers and selecting vases for them; arranging books; the finer aspects of modeling; interpreting and dramatizing pictures; observing line and color.

4. *RHYTHMS:* Singing short songs, the words of which the child comprehends and enunciates well; making up new songs; tone work; interpreting rhythms; recognizing fine pieces of music; participation in rhythmic games; learning dance steps; walking and standing properly; cultivating a sweet speaking voice; participating in a baby band; imitating animal sounds, whistles and calls.

5. *HEALTH:* Learning about his weight, food, teeth, cleanliness, bathing; acquiring and discussing good health habits.

6. *NATURE STUDY:* Getting acquainted with living things, trees, plants, and flowers; cultivating an attitude and sense of responsibility toward them; having his own garden or own flower box or flower pot; watching things grow; learning about the sun and moon, sky, weather, rocks, soil; knowing animals by name, their use, their homes, habits and character.

7. *PLAY:* Play with materials, with each other, with stones, with the language and with anything that is in their environment. First reading growing out of plays and games.

Determining Readiness for Primary Work. So much for the program in general. What about the specific problem of determining school readiness? The authors of the Los Angeles Bulletin take the position that the first grades

34 EDUCATION IN THE PRIMARY GRADES

are so organized and equipped that reading is one of the big activities of the first year's work. The children in the transition groups are, therefore, largely those who are not yet mature enough to learn to read. For this reason the Los Angeles Bulletin furnishes the teacher with the following detailed aids in determining which children may safely be sent forward from the Transition Group.

The child who is ready to begin reading shows recognition of a reading situation by

1. Curiosity as to signs; advertisements; labels in and out of school and at home;
2. Looking at picture books, and asking about the names and stories;
3. Associating words with actions, objects, pictures, music, writing;
4. Beginning to read, wanting to be read to, and listening when others read;
5. Following thought sequence and being able to
    a. carry general idea of a story in mind;
    b. fit new words into thought;
    c. get new words from content;

6. Ability to recognize a few words with certainty;
7. Ability to get words from positions at beginning or end of line and in word group;
8. Ability to get words from capitals;
9. Ability to find names several times on page;
10. Ability to find other words or word groups several times;
11. Ability to remember word which has just been called.

While reading-readiness is probably as reliable a single index of school readiness as any other, there are other "signs." Some indications of readiness to begin the formal work in number should be noted. The child who is ready to begin the work of the first grade will show that he has

1. Some conception of counting, showing this in a practical way by being able to determine the number of children or objects in a room, and by recognizing, without counting, groups of three or four.

2. The comprehension of a fraction, such as a half.

3. The beginning of a sense of measurement, showing itself in the ability to understand the distinction between long and short, wide and narrow, thick and thin.

4. Some conception of time, expressing itself practically in a sense of duration, of the difference between long and short periods of time, and a realization that there are several days in the week.

References for Further Study

Parker, S. C. and Temple, A., *Unified Kindergarten and First Grade Teachings*. Boston, Ginn & Co., 1925.

Pickett, L. H., *Early Childhood Education*. Yonkers, World Book Co., 1923.

CHAPTER IV

CURRICULUM AND METHOD

GENERAL PRINCIPLES

Curriculum Construction. The first chapter of this volume referred to six essential elements of early education: reading, writing and spelling, number, music, graphic art, and speech. These essentials are so obviously a part of early education that no theoretical considerations of curriculum are necessary to explain their place as the backbone of the structure of the course of study. But primary education extends beyond the mastery of skills.

There is no space in this volume, nor is there need, to enter into the history of the development of modern curriculum theory. It will be sufficient to state that the contemporary approach to curriculum construction consists of the formulation of aims, sometimes called objectives, or goals, to be achieved as the result of formal education. Since the publication of the Report of the Committee on the Reorganization of Secondary Education there has been quite general agreement that these are the main objectives that "should constitute the principal aims in education: health, command of the fundamental processes, worthy home membership, vocation, citizenship, worthy use of leisure, ethical character."

The student will note that the objectives do not belong to any particular phase of education, to any particular maturity level or school, but are single for the entire educational process. All of the schools, from the nursery school to the college, undertake to work toward the same set objectives. Since these objectives envisage the good life as the result of the whole of education, each school must in turn represent one step toward the ultimate outcomes. So far as the individual child is concerned, all of the schools have one and the same set of aims, each in turn advancing him further toward the ultimate achievement of all of them.

What, then, is the character of the task of the primary grades in this general work of helping children to become educated within the terms of the specified goals? Of the seven objectives listed, it will be clear without further discussion that the primary school will not concern itself specifically with direct vocational training. The fundamental processes, on the other hand—reading, writing and spelling, number, music, graphic art, and speech—belong in a special way to this period of schooling. They represent the groundwork for the future, the foundation on which all further training is to be laid.

What of the other five objectives? It is obvious enough that the primary school, like every other that precedes or follows it, must carefully plan to do its share toward their growth. To these we would add the established practice of introducing the child to the social community and the phenomena of nature. We may, therefore, visualize the whole task of primary education structurally as it is outlined below:

The Task of the Primary School

Fundamental Processes	The Other Objectives
1. Reading	1. Health
2. Writing and spelling	2. Worthy home membership
3. Number	3. Leisure
4. Music	4. Citizenship
5. Graphic art	5. Ethical character
6. Speech	6. Introduction to nature and society

We have selected as belonging to primary education six of the seven objectives, and emphasized one of these in particular. What is the meaning of this emphasis? Do we desire for the "fundamental processes" more stress, greater effort, more time to be devoted to a mastery of the basic skills, and less time, perhaps merely incidental treatment, casual attention or even neglect for the other objectives? To the extent that training for the other six objectives depends on books, on study, and on personal effort these objectives must remain a closed world to the children of the primary grades. Later, when the pupils have acquired the fundamental tools of study, the schools may approach these objectives by way of "subjects." At this stage, it is of necessity the direct approach or none. Experience and living are the only methods of growth available in these directions. Assignments, texts, and recitations are out of place. It is the supreme opportunity for the project, for living, and for experience.

The tools, on the other hand, do represent the need for direct attack, for genuine, intentional teaching. They must be mastered. The several tasks to be achieved are clear, definite, and measurable. The objectives for the primary grades have been separated into two grand divisions because there are in the work of early education two principal methods of instruction. The fundamental processes should be taught, as indicated by the chapters which follow, directly by organized and habit-forming drill. The other objectives should be approached incidentally, by means of the indirect method currently known as the *activity*.

Method in Education. The foregoing paragraphs present the need of a brief discussion of the principles of method as applicable to primary education. There are three general or basic methods. Whatever may be the exercise of the moment, one, two, or all three of these general methods are involved.

(1) One of these methods appeals primarily to the intellect. In it is included the securing of information and knowledge, the learning how to think, the forming and improvement of judgment.

(2) The most frequently employed general method is based on the laws of habit-formation and is used whenever we try to help the child achieve basic skills. Skill is a word broader and more inclusive than the motor co-ordination necessary in swimming, handling tools, or playing an instrument. All forms of habit response such as good manners or sound health practices, knowledge of the multiplication tables, or word recognition, are achieved by means of this general method, most frequently referred to as the method of drill.

There is, finally, the general method which aims at the development of the emotional life, tending on the one hand to influence the pupil's attitudes and ideals in the fields of ethics, civic life, social relationships, and, on the other, building up his aesthetic appreciation.

Reflective Thinking. Of the methods referred to above, the first is frequently described as training in reflective thinking. Sound reasoning can hardly be taught directly at any level, and must certainly be left for indirect and incidental instruction during the early years of education. The able teacher will find opportunities for such incidental use of this method during the numerous class discussions that accompany the work in oral English, social studies, and other phases of the course of study. Here she can see that her children bear in mind the central topic, remain relevant, examine various possibilities of solving a problem, and otherwise gain experience in sound thinking.

Drill. The second of the general methods is the procedure to be advocated in these pages for teaching reading, writing, and numbers; for the basic work in music, art, and, partially, for the acquisition of habits of good speech.

There is a movement in contemporary education—the progressive, or new, or child-centered school—which would minimize the use of drill. This school of thought either directly or by implication holds that there is no need for drill. Drill, they feel, implies that the child is having something imposed on him by the teacher. Therefore he is, to that extent, not free. This school of educational thought interprets the doctrine of Rousseau to the effect that if the child is left entirely free, and if the school is wholly organized in terms of his present interests and needs, there will be no occasion for drill. Whenever, in the course of the numerous activities that are continually occupying children, the need for knowledge or ability arises, the children can be led to master such knowledge and to acquire such ability. Being then highly motivated, and facing the need for the information or the skill, the child will naturally master these essentials of the curriculum, and will do so more thoroughly and more quickly than when the school imposes the work on the child.

The educational doctrines of this school cannot be outlined in a paragraph or two, but its attitude toward drill has been briefly summarized. It is, however, the function of the mature to train the young and there should be no hesitancy in imposing on the next generation the knowledge and skill which we know to be essential. We have not found that the typical American school enslaves children or that children dislike the school.

Although it does not seem advisable to enter here into the established psychology and general theory underlying the drill method which the inexperienced teacher should

CURRICULUM AND METHOD 41

study in detail elsewhere, a brief summary of some of the best known principles of procedure follows:

1. Bear in mind that the drill lesson is based on the formation of the desired habits and that acquisition of any desired skill is the acquisition of a habit or set of habits. The most essential of the several aspects of habit-formation is the one stated by James in these words: "Permit no exception to occur." In other words, see that the correct response is made every time, so as to avoid having to undo wrong habits wholly or partially formed.

2. Since it is essential to insure that the right response be made every time and that the wrong one be prevented, all practice should, in the beginning, be carried on under the immediate supervision of the teacher until such time as she is assured that no wrong or partially wrong actions will be taken when the child is practicing without supervision.

3. Repetition is the heart of the drill lesson. Where interest and pleasure accompany the repetitions, the learning will proceed faster.

4. In beginning the teaching of a new skill, proceed slowly. In dealing with a complicated skill, analyze it into a series of habits and automatize these singly before attempting the entire performance.

5. Attention is necessary in drill, but attention soon wanders when we are engaged in monotonous repetition, particularly in early childhood, when the attention span is brief at best. It follows that the available time for drill had best be divided into a number of periods; that each period should be only as long as it appears effective; that the periods should not be so close together as to give the same impression as single periods of too great length, or

so far apart as to necessitate beginning all over again at each session.

There is one aspect of the drill lesson which we would emphasize particularly. Drill is essentially an individual, not a group matter. Let us direct attention to a group of pupils starting to learn to swim, play baseball, or play the violin. How long can this group be held together, or taught together? Soon after the beginning of the instruction the individuals will have scattered in achievement all the way from no ability to great or complete ability. Under this method, necessarily individual, each pupil masters each preceding step before undertaking the next one. Whenever the ability has been mastered, the instruction ends. Under the method of group instruction and group promotions, many children are unnecessarily retarded and, on the other hand, many go forward to complex tasks without the necessary foundation for them, a defect that cannot be remedied later.

Children make the most satisfactory progress in the skills through individual instruction. The child of less than average intelligence should set his own pace in proceeding toward complete mastery, rather than face failure and grade repetition. The child of better than average intelligence should be permitted to complete the primary phase of education earlier than the allotted three years, and go forward to the work of the upper grades when he is ready for it.

Concerning the theory underlying the individual method of instruction in effect in Winnetka, Illinois, the superintendent writes that, "If a certain bit of knowledge or skill is necessary to practically every normal person, every child should have an opportunity to master it. There should not be excellent grasp for some, fair for others, and poor for still others. . . . There should be real mastery for every child. The wide differences that are known to exist among children make it obvious that this mastery cannot be obtained by all children in the same length of time and with the same amount of practice. Hence it is necessary to provide varying amounts of time and varying amounts of instructional material for different children."

Appreciation and Attitudes. It has already been indicated that the teacher who is endeavoring to further the child's emotional development is doing so with one of two major objectives in view. She may be presenting experiences and opportunities calculated to enrich his aesthetic life and growth. This aim, usually referred to in educational literature as worthy use of leisure, deals with music, art, literature, and the love of nature. Or the teacher may be dealing with emotions in the moral, ethical, or civic sense, motivating the will to be a good citizen, neighbor, friend, or member of the family group. This aspect of emotional growth is sometimes referred to in educational literature as the development of sound attitudes and ideals.

In the evolution of pedagogical procedure, we have thus far done better in the first two of the three divisions of general method than in this third. While it is conceded that in a well-rounded education there should be developed aesthetic appreciations, the detailed technique for the achievement of these ends still remains to be created.

Possibly one of the reasons for slow progress in the discovery of this technique is to be found in the traditional conception of the school as an institution in which to learn; of the teacher as one who imparts knowledge; of the pupil as one who masters facts; in short, an overemphasis of the intellectual aspects of education. The conception of education as a process of growing, living, and experiencing, is still making its way slowly.

With its tradition of appealing exclusively to the thinking processes, the school has treated the more recent additions to the curriculum in its old and well-established manner. It has dealt with music and literature as if they were arithmetic, grammar, and penmanship. It has intellectualized them. The lesson devoted to music or poetry ordinarily differs too little from the procedure during the lesson in arithmetic. Data regarding the biography of authors; careful examination of a novel or drama for the purpose of mastering the plot; noting the fact that the composition in hand is considered good literature—these are all non-emotional processes little related to the response which would make the pupil appreciative of literature. Objectives primarily emotional cannot be reached by the tried methods that have been found useful in helping the pupil to attain objectives primarily intellectual.

The fundamental psychology underlying emotion, and specifically the aesthetic and moral-civic emotions, is too little known, and the pedagogic procedures for the development of these emotions in school are too little understood to warrant the outlining here of any specific techniques. Rather should the teacher be urged to take an experimental attitude, and to keep in the foreground of her consciousness the fact that there are fields such as music, graphic art, and literature in which, while skills and knowledge are essential as a basis, the ultimate aim is not fulfilled by comprehension or technical competence but by delight, pleasure, and happiness.

It may, however, be stated with some degree of certainty that the desirable outcomes are more likely to be attained when the following conditions are established:

CURRICULUM AND METHOD

1. The general atmosphere, carefully prepared, should be one in which such enjoyment is possible.

2. The teacher herself must appreciate and sincerely enjoy the particular experience. Otherwise it had better be avoided.

3. Compulsion, formality, and pretense must be absent. Each child should be allowed to enjoy or not to enjoy the experience as he may.

4. The possibility of enjoying the experience must be well within the maturity, the basic skills, and knowledge of the group.

5. Teaching in the sense of direct instruction is out of place except as explanations to enhance enjoyment seem in order and are desired by, not forced on, the class.

THE MEANING AND THE FUNCTION OF THE ACTIVITY

The Project. The foregoing section which deals with emotional growth should serve as excellent preparation for the discussion of the activity in primary education. There are times when teaching is out of place, and living is in order. "The project," according to Professor Kilpatrick, one of the foremost proponents of the method, "is any unit of experience dominated by such a purpose as sets an aim for the experience, guides its process, and furnishes the drive for its vigorous prosecution." "The project," says Stormzand,[1] after a careful survey of the field of progressive education, "is a definite and clearly purposeful task, and one that can be set before a pupil as seeming to him vitally worth while, because it approximates a genuine activity such as men are engaged in in

[1] Stormzand, M. J., *Progressive Methods of Teaching.* Boston, Houghton Mifflin Co., 1925.

real life. The project method is the solution of problems on the real plane of activity."

Besides being interesting, well motivated, appearing to have been originated by the group, and dealing with a real activity, the project will be useful *only when it is educative in character* and produces definable, measureable and clearly envisaged outcomes definitely related to the course of study. It should, in addition, have incidental superiorities over direct instruction. It should be demonstrable that, motivated by the project, the children have actually achieved the knowledge, skills, and emotional growth which would otherwise have been sought for by direct instruction.

Rather than attempt a statement of the project technique when the fundamental philosophy of the project method holds that technique is out of order and that each group each semester in each locality should be a law unto itself, the following quotation from Professor Adams [2] is submitted: "We have always had the new art, and lately we have added the new theology, the new nationalism, the new psychology. Now we have the new education with its variant, the new teaching, not to speak of the *new children.*"

Rousseau, he says elsewhere, can "be justly claimed as a precursor of the new educators who fix their attention upon the pupil as the center of their interest." When we recall that *Emile* was published in 1762, it may not be amiss to note the words of Professor Monroe who says that its author is "the forerunner of many who, all unconscious of their indebtedness to the despised revolutionist, have followed in the trails he blazed through the forest."

"*Creative Education.*" While it will not be possible to

---

[2] Adams, John, *Modern Developments in Educational Practice*. New York, Harcourt, Brace & Co., 1922.

follow the advocates of the complete activity program into the various avenues of their effort, there is one line of thought to which the student must be introduced—"creative education." There are several modes of approach in education that may be called creative. In the first place, the old adage that we learn by doing, is one. In many instances, the effort to create something, whether it be a poem or a magazine rack, will result in enhanced skill. In the second place, it has long been known that the creative method is an excellent approach to appreciation. Only those who have tried their hand at it can fully appreciate great achievement in any field. For that reason, good teachers have always induced students to compose in music, the graphic arts, and in the literary forms. It is an excellent means of helping the pupil to appreciate more keenly the work of the real masters in the several arts.

Finally, there is the creative work of the relatively few persons in each generation to whom nature has been particularly generous. It is not the purpose of these paragraphs to imply that "genius will out" and that creative work has always been done by children in spite of the alleged stupidity of the schools. Certainly the school should discover and foster all the creative ability developed by each generation of children. Society can little afford mute inglorious Miltons, or roses that blush unseen. The advocates of the creative education movement take the extreme view that all children are creative and that therefore all education should be creative. To them creative effort seems to come first, and the skills can take care of themselves. Since opportunity for creative effort is not based on a solid foundation of previously acquired skills, it almost seems as if these educators would sponsor a diffused creativeness in lieu of skill.

The work of the artist is based on highly developed

technical abilities, secured by hard labor. One cannot conceive of a great actor whose enunciation is faulty, whose voice is badly placed or undeveloped. It may well be that creativeness is a gift of God. Skill is the result of effort. Without underlying skill, creative imagination may prove of little value.

The proponents of creative education put the cart before the horse and hurry creativeness along because they fear that in the effort to master the skills, the child will become imitative and lose the creative faculty. Surely skill should not hinder, but free creative expression. That composer would never leave a record of his dreams who is without the skill of writing down his melody and harmonizing it. Inspiration will not always wait on a faltering technique. Frequently it will be balked by it. William James believed that the more we "hand over to the effortless custody of automatism, the more our higher powers of mind will be set free."

Organizing Instruction

1. *For the Skills, Drill, and Individual Progress.* It should be sufficiently clear from the foregoing and indeed, it has frequently been pointed out by educational historians, that the "new" education and the "child-centered" school do not belong exclusively to any single group of teachers.

The following paragraphs, stating the point of view of the present authors toward activities at the primary level, serve as a preface to the remainder of the book. Earlier in this chapter the objectives of primary education were divided into the fundamental processes and the "other objectives." So far as concerns the skill part of the curriculum we are opposed to reliance on incidental learning as the principal method. We believe in the straight attack on mastery, and in drill where necessary. We would, when possible, individualize instruction in the skills. One of the principles of educational differentiation, the easiest of all to apply, is the rate of progress toward the achievement of a particular goal. When, as at the primary level, an educational objective means the acquisition of a number of skills, differences in rate of progress are particularly in order.

Two facts make this clear: In the first place the primary level is the easiest point at which the school can, by sending them forward to "study" earlier, save time for the brightest of the pupils. In the second place, children differ in the age at which they are prepared to begin to learn to read, write, and calculate. Individualization of instruction to conform to individual variation in educability is far superior to the current practice of skipping and repeating grades.

2. *For the Other Objectives; Group Projects.* Coming now to the "other objectives," (health, worthy home membership, citizenship, worthy use of leisure, ethical character) we must in the nature of things become vague so far as concerns content and measurable achievement. Here, we believe, is the ideal place for an activity program at the primary level.

Toward the attainment of these "other objectives" the child should go forward in school as he has been going forward for the years before entering school. By means of activities which provide him with interesting and educative experiences he should grow and develop. This is the supreme opportunity, perhaps the best that the school ever has, of putting into practice the maxims that education is life, that experience is the best teacher, that the school is effective only as it results in changed conduct, in growth, and in development. Here is the opportunity for the school to demonstrate that education is more than knowledge, more than skill.

The school may best proceed in this direction by continuing the means which the child has so far employed to adjust himself to his environment. Children's lives are full of activity. They are constantly carrying out projects and solving problems of their own. Why should not the school adopt this natural method, organizing experiences and purposeful activities which will carry the child in the direction of achieving or making progress toward the achievement of the formulated objectives? "The project method," says Professor Bonser,[3] "holds that the desirable and interesting life activities in which children spontaneously engage or the activities in which they may be led to engage wholeheartedly and enthusiastically should be the basis of all educational endeavor. Having purposes of their own which furnish drive for their activity they will, if given opportunity, plan and execute whatever is necessary to realize their purposes."

References for Further Study

Columbia University, Teachers College, Lincoln School, *Curriculum Making in an Elementary School*. Boston, Ginn & Co., 1927.

Davis, S. E., *The Technique of Teaching*. New York, The Macmillan Company, 1922.

Melvin, A. G., *The Technique of Progressive Teaching*. New York, The John Day Co., 1932.

Parker, S. C., *General Methods of Teaching in Elementary Schools*. Boston, Ginn & Co., 1919.

Stevens, M. P., *The Activities Curriculum in The Primary Grades*. Boston, D. C. Heath & Co., 1930.

Washburne, C., *Adjusting the School to the Child*. Yonkers, World Book Co., 1932.

Yearbook of the National Society for the Study of Education. Vol. 33, Part II, *The Activity Movement*. Bloomington, Public School Publishing Co., 1934.

[3] Bonser, F. G., *The Elementary School Curriculum*. New York, The Macmillan Company, 1920.

CHAPTER V

READING: THE PRE-PRIMER PERIOD

BASIC PRINCIPLES

Learning to read is the first and the most important task before the child entering school. Teaching him how to do so is, fortunately, one of the professional procedures best understood in modern educational practice, and one in which possibly the greatest advances have been made. As an introduction to the discussion of these procedures the following paragraphs are a brief statement of the history of teaching reading and of the psychological processes which underlie reading and learning to read, as these processes are understood today.

Logic. Perhaps the prettiest example of the contrast between logic and "psychologic" so frequently pointed out in the theory of educational method, is to be found in the history of the development of the method of teaching reading. The first step of the untrained person facing the task of teaching is likely to be an analysis of the material into its logical elements, to begin at the beginning and go forward from the simple to the more complex. Long experience has, however, taught the educational profession that the psychology of the learner is a safer guide than logic in organizing teaching.

Reading, for example, appears to consist of recognizing words, one after the other. Words, it appears, are made up of letters. The way to begin teaching would, on the basis of this analysis, be to teach the child his A, B, C's. The average layman today thinks that he learned to read in this way and, if asked to teach reading, would doubtless proceed in the historic manner.

Until well into the middle of the last century and, it is to be feared, in some remote places today, the alphabet method reigned supreme. It was a slow, joyless, and essentially ineffective method of teaching reading. Those who became excellent readers, and many did, learned in spite of the method. Some children learn to read without any one's knowing how it happened. In this synthetic method, the child slowly and arduously learned his letters. Then he learned to read these in combinations of meaningless syllables of two or more letters. Some of these monosyllables were words. Others were eventually put together into two- and three-syllable words. In the end, if he persisted long enough, the child read *words*. Sentences took care of themselves, so to speak, since they were collections of words. The whole process was one of laborious drill, and the end of the process was likely to be reading *as word recognition* rather than reading *as comprehension*. If the text became meaningful, as to most persons it eventually did, that was in spite of the method.

We come to the next step, little, if any, in advance. This step, equally disregarding the psychology of the learning child, did improve the logic of the process. Shortly after the middle of the last century, the phonic method made its appearance. The contention was that sounds, not letters, are the elements of the language, and therefore of reading. Instead of the letters these teachers presented the phonic elements. As there are more sounds than letters, the leaders of this movement invented a phonic alphabet which the children learned as a means of word recognition. An improvement, but no fundamental change, was brought about. The children continued to sound their way through syllables and words.

Toward the end of the last century, American teachers

READING: THE PRE-PRIMER PERIOD

began to abandon the synthetic methods which have just been described in favor of whole words as the unit of learning. It was discovered that, without preparatory drill on letters and sounds, children could learn to associate words with objects or pictures and learn to recognize them independently with ease and rapidity. The idea itself was old, having been enunciated by Comenius and maintained by Horace Mann. It represented the beginning of our present conceptions of the process of reading and learning to read.

Psychology. It is neither the letter, the sound, nor even the word, that is basic in language. The unit of thought, and therefore the unit of reading, is the phrase or the sentence. As one does not think of the letters that compose the word, so competent readers ordinarily do not think of the words that compose the phrase or the sentence. Furthermore, one does not read in order to call out words, but silently, to secure meaning from the printed page.

Perhaps the best commentary that can be made on the synthetic methods of teaching reading is that even now, when we have abandoned the attempt to tell children how they ought to learn to read and have been trying to discover how they actually do learn to read, we have not yet found the answer. We know a number of things about reading and the process of learning to read, of which our predecessors were unaware. Indeed, we know enough to convince us that they were wrong in their methods. But we do not know with precision or certainty what the processes of learning are. We know that children learn to read. Precisely how they do so is still obscure. Some children learn to read without instruction. They do not know when or how they learned to read. Most intelligent persons became good readers under the old, and obviously wrong, methods of teaching. There is probably no one way of learning to read. We possess experimental information that indicates the conditions under which children learn most readily.

The fundamental error in the old methods of teaching reading lay in the assumption that we read by recognizing the elements of the matter of the text as the eye passes evenly across the line, letter after letter, syllable after syllable, word after word. The truth is that the unit of perception in reading is not the letter, but rather the word; the best readers frequently take in phrases, and there are some who read sentences. Furthermore, the eye does not cross the page at an even pace. In mature reading the eye moves across the page in a series of rhythmic sweeps and pauses. It is during the fixation pauses that reading takes place. No reading is done during the interfixation movements, when the eye goes forward from one span of perception to the other. The good adult reader makes from four to fourteen fixation pauses in crossing the line when reading silently. When reading aloud, the pauses are more frequent and longer in duration, since the eye must wait on the voice. The faster reader is the one whose span of recognition is greater. The more inclusive the recognition span, the less the number of pauses and interfixation movements. The duration of the pause is also of importance in effective reading. The better the reader, the briefer the pause. The interfixation movements, during which no reading takes place, are briefer in duration than the pauses.

Certain aspects of ineffective reading are important. Their recognition will enable us to prevent the child from acquiring these bad habits. The poor reader makes what are known as regressive movements. He interrupts the sweep of the eye across the page by going back to get another look. The poor reader is sometimes retarded by inner speech. This vocalization, essentially oral reading

READING: THE PRE-PRIMER PERIOD

though no sounds are made, has the disadvantages of oral reading. The fixation pauses, for example, are more frequent and longer. Finally, one who has learned to read single words will have a narrower recognition span at each pause than one who has learned to read phrases or sentences.

Oral and Silent Reading. There is an aspect of teaching reading which is of vital importance and which was overlooked by teachers until recent years—the distinction between silent and oral reading. Most of the reading of adult life is done silently. All of the teaching of reading in school has heretofore been carried on orally. The transition from learning to read, an oral process, to actual reading in later school work and in adult life, which is a silent process, was left to take care of itself. The student may well ask what harm there is in this procedure, why silent reading should have to be taught or emphasized when the child has demonstrated by reading aloud that he knows how to read.

Instruction in reading naturally begins as an oral exercise. This is the only means the teacher has of getting the child started, and of testing the effectiveness of her instruction. When oral reading is carried on exclusively and for too long a period, the reader may, when the transition is finally made, suffer from the habit of vocalization or inner speech. Because of this habit, very many adult readers proceed slowly, hesitantly, and with reduced ability to comprehend. Again, the "speech unit" in reading is far narrower than the unit of visual perception. When we have accustomed the child too long to oral reading, the fixation pauses will be too frequent and too long; the eye-voice span, unnecessary in silent reading, will tend to persist; the return sweep to the next line will not recur with the smooth regularity that is desirable; and the "hearing" of the words will tend to hamper comprehension.

The test of oral reading is the enunciation of the words, phrases, and sentences. But the true test of silent reading is comprehension. The modern teacher has available for use numerous means of training the child to comprehend without repeating the words, and of testing this comprehension. This procedure is training for "reading" in the effective sense of that word, in the way that reading will be later employed. It is preparation for study.

Silent reading, to name another important use, gives the teacher the opportunity of meeting the problem of variability among children. Where oral reading is employed exclusively, the period is taken up by the slow method of having one child at a time read to the group. In the case of many children this represents boredom and sheer waste. Where silent reading is encouraged some children may, at the end of the first year, have read ten times as much as others in the same class. While recognizing and emphasizing the distinction between oral and silent reading, we must not overlook the importance that still belongs to reading orally. Although most reading is, indeed, necessarily silent, we do occasionally read aloud for the pleasure of others and, even more important, some reading matter can be enjoyed only when read aloud.

Before Books

In spite of all that has been said above about the relative unimportance of oral as compared with silent reading, it is with the former that we begin our instruction in this skill. Oral reading is the most natural transition from speech to print. The problem before us is to teach the eye to aid in the task that has hitherto been carried exclusively by the ear, i.e., to comprehend language. The page replaces the voice and we begin by teaching the eye to tell the ear. Slowly, but inevitably, as the mastery of the skill increases in effectiveness, silent reading increases and oral reading decreases in importance. Oral reading must, nevertheless, retain a place in life and, therefore, instruction. Much of poetry must be heard to be fully enjoyed and there are still those who enjoy the delight of reading aloud together.

Reading Readiness. The child does not, however, begin at once with reading. The first step in the process must consist of laying plans for reading later. The teacher endeavors to create a situation of reading-readiness. She does not begin with books, but prepares the way for their later reading. As has been said before, however, this preparation implies no certain knowledge on our part of how children learn to read.

How do children learn to speak? A comparison of this process with that of learning to read should be useful. As with the latter, we are not sure of the precise manner in which they learn to speak, but we assume that, by imitation, during the plastic period of infancy, they put forth efforts to speak. Living in an environment of language, hearing words, phrases, and sentences, the child does not at first understand them. His own first sounds are meaningless. Slowly but surely he begins to gather more and more meaning from what he hears, to put more and more meaning into what he says, and ultimately it is obvious that he can speak.

The best teachers of reading take their cue from this observation about speaking. They create an environment of reading. The child finds himself in the midst of printed matter such as books, papers, and notices. It is the same sort of environment he has been noticing at home for many years. The content, he finds, is within his ability to understand. He is motivated by the careful teacher.

It is interesting and important to learn "what it says." He is curious and he makes efforts. Gradually the eye begins to learn to tell the ear. He is beginning to read.

Pre-Primer Procedures. The first period, sometimes called the pre-book or pre-primer period, is devoted to precisely the task which we have just described. It marks for the child the beginning of reading by setting up a reading environment. Put in technical terms, the teacher faces the task of teaching her pupils or, better, of seeing to it that they learn to associate visual symbols with words and phrases *which they already know orally.* The last phrase refers to an essential principle. The child does not read who has learned to repeat words with which he is unfamiliar. In that way one might learn to "read" a foreign language without understanding a word of it. Reading and comprehension are indissolubly connected. The eye must tell the ear and no telling is telling unless it is meaningful.

This being the task, the teacher must next ask herself this question: What are the exercises or experiences that will most effectively help to build this bridge between the printed symbol and the word, phrase, or sentence that the child already understands? Here are three answers to this question that are probably indisputably true.

1. The greater the interest, the speedier will be the process of learning to read. The teacher must make every effort to induce the children to want to read. She must create a child-like, happy atmosphere, in which reading seems natural, important, and worth while. Undoubtedly the teacher's personality, a pleasing voice and manner, are of greater importance at this stage than later in the child's development.

2. The greater the exposure to printed symbols under conditions where the child gladly and eagerly makes efforts to read, the sooner will he learn to

READING: THE PRE-PRIMER PERIOD

read. When the exposures are numerous, varied, and meaningful, and it appears important and worth his while to know what it all means, he will learn to read.

3. Skill in reading is a habit and habits are formed and permanently fixed by drill. There will be no genuine reading skill for most children without drill. Let it be borne in mind that in the end the test of reading ability must rest on the ability to recognize the word regardless of context, and to do so with ease and rapidity.

How can these desirable ends be brought about? Here are some methods the usefulness of which has been demonstrated:

Bulletin Board. The bulletin board is one excellent means of stimulating a desire to read. On it the children find pictures with printed descriptions and explanations. There is something about the pictures that urges the children to want to know what the printed matter says. Anyone who has seen the average American child pestering grown-ups to read him the Sunday comics will understand that there are circumstances under which children may be induced to want to read. The bulletin board contains directions for the day, requiring different children to do different things. It contains important announcements, telling the children what is to happen, where, when, and how.

The bulletin board is, of course, constantly changing. It is, further, of vital importance to the members of the class. They need to have the information that it conveys. If some of the children who learn faster tell the others what it says there is no harm done. If the children, aided by the context, guess rather than read some of the words, again there is no harm done. It is better if the context assists in the recognition of the word. The test of reading the word without any context, a definitely essential ability, may come later, as will the remedy where such an ability has been imperfectly developed.

The Blackboard. The blackboard is an invaluable aid in teaching reading. Here, before the very eyes of the children, appear in print the sentence that has just been spoken, the answer to the question that they have asked. Who is it that will be the heroine of the dramatization? Is the answer *yes* or *no* to the question whether the teacher will read a story? What is the teacher asking us now? On the blackboard, changing continuously, appear directions, announcements, the names of the different children who are to participate in various activities, the teacher's questions and her answers to questions, the news and information that the children may want.

The Chart. The chart is a more permanent form of summarizing an activity, winding up a project, describing some of the important outcomes of extensive concerted efforts. The chart is best made of tag board, clearly printed in large black letters, the lines three inches apart. The chart should never contain entirely new material. The great pleasure of reading it will come from recognition.

The chart is really the beginning, and the best beginning, of extended reading. It should sum up recent familiar and delightful experiences, tell these in the language that the children themselves use, characterized by repetition and brevity of sentence. It should contain only words which the children understand, and largely words which they have already learned to recognize. Experiences which the children have told should be presented on the chart in their own words, phrasing, and sentence structure. They should be read both orally and silently. This is the teacher's opportunity to observe the beginning of good reading habits.

READING: THE PRE-PRIMER PERIOD

Translating Theory into Practice. Thus far the treatment in this book has been confined to general principles rather than specific, detailed procedures. There is no other way of presenting the matter. The children, the place, the other elements of the situation, vary far too much to do otherwise. There are, it is true, writers who propose rules of thumb, telling the teacher just what to do, step by step. These specific "methods" of teaching reading which deprive the teacher of personality, resourcefulness, and therefore maximum effectiveness, are numerous. There are those who present sample lessons reported stenographically. But surely the probable difference of conditions under which the lesson was observed and those where the work is to be done make such samples hardly worth the while. To the teacher who, because of lack or inadequacy of opportunity to observe in a good teacher-training institution, finds the foregoing paragraphs rather vague and difficult of application, this counsel is offered: Find out the teachers in your section who are admittedly able in the work of the receiving class, and visit them. Such visiting, conscientiously and earnestly carried on, accompanied by intelligent questions, will not fail to illumine what heretofore seemed elusive and difficult to apply.

There is another matter to which reference must be made. No teacher should do all of her beginning work with ready-made materials. These will help, but the best motivation will come where the teacher deals with the particular children in the particular place at the particular time, and creates the reading material out of their activities and interests. This involves writing or printing on bulletin and blackboard. It involves the making of charts.

Many writers fear that this task is too difficult for the teacher and counsel her to use script. We do not believe that this is necessary. The sample which we here present was taken from an actual classroom. It is not perfect. Possibly the teacher would have been more accurate in the details had she known that it would appear in a book. It is, however, entirely adequate and not at all beyond the average teacher.

Note carefully that while this is print, not script, it is not "lettering." This teacher has not followed the printed letters absolutely, as will be seen in her a's and g's. These deviations are desirable, simpler for the teacher, and we believe, make more interesting copy.

Jim is an airplane pilot.

He has a bi-plane.

The bi-plane is in a hangar.

The hangar is in an airport.

Jim is an air mail pilot.

His airplane carries mail.

In preparing individual reading booklets out of the class experiences, as some teachers do, a typewriter with very large type, such as is used in sight-conservation classes, will be found useful. In preparing charts for class use the teacher may find it desirable to employ a rubber stamp print set.

One other suggestion may interest the teacher. The plate which follows is manuscript writing, a subject dealt with at some length in the chapter on handwriting.[1] It was prepared by a teacher who, at our request, had practiced for six hours, following the directions of the manual. There is no need to confuse the young reader with script. Every professionally ambitious teacher should be able to add this to her other skills.

Jim is an airplane pilot.
He has a bi-plane.
The bi-plane is in a hangar.
The hangar is in an airport.
Jim is an airmail pilot.
His airplane carries mail.

[1] See Chapter VIII for a further discussion of manuscript writing.

CHAPTER VI

READING: THE BEGINNING OF BOOKS

Discovering Reading

In every first grade classroom some space should be found for a browsing table. At first a few enticing pictures make their appearance. Some picture books soon follow, and from these the teacher is occasionally induced to read interesting stories. Sometimes the teacher and the children sit at the table together, recognizing, commenting, and, in general, enjoying the pictures and the books. Some of the children begin to bring books from home, and leave them on the table for a while if the other children ask them to do so. The books on the table are changed quite frequently. In time some of the children go to the table independently, and enjoy their reading. Later they may tell the others what they have read. Ultimately there appear on the table books that vary in difficulty and books that vary in content, giving scope to the variety of the interests of the young readers. Gradually more and more of the children resort to these books for information and for pleasure.

The blackboard, the bulletin board, the chart, and the reading table—these are some, but by no means all, of the ways for creating the environment that will induce children to begin to read. Their contents had best be local and immediate, arising from the children's own interests and activities, and the habits and customs with which they are familiar. The teacher should be careful to include the simple words which she knows the children

READING: THE BEGINNING OF BOOKS

will meet in their primer. She should also bear in mind that the content of all of this reading must be meaningful. A child is not reading when he recognizes a word which he would not understand if he heard it.

In this beginning of his reading experience the teacher will not introduce the child to letters or phonic elements. It is content, context, meaning, reading, that are important, not the mechanical makeup of the word. Adult readers are never aware of these mechanics. It is only in the case of the few children who do not learn to read naturally that mechanical aids to recognition should be resorted to.

Variability of Response to Reading Opportunity

What response may be expected to come from the teacher's efforts to create for her pupils this reading environment, these motives and opportunities? Children will vary greatly in the ways in which they meet the opportunity to learn to read. They will differ in mental age, the outstanding index of reading readiness, and in the possession of certain environmental elements that prepare for reading, notably the character of the home background. Children who come from homes where there has been reading and conversation and a certain social atmosphere of culture will, undoubtedly, have the advantage over others who come from homes where communication is limited to the daily routine of concrete things or from homes of foreign parents where they have missed the linguistic heritage of the ordinary American child.

The teacher, realizing the inevitableness of this variability in response, will not try to hold her class together as a group. Where individual instruction is not possible, as it is not in nearly all American public schools, the teacher will soon divide her class into a number of sections, providing useful occupation for some while she is working with others. Unless the class has been highly selected, coming either from a very excellent or a very poor neighborhood, or has been classified by psychological tests, the teacher may find that some of the children have a certain degree of ability to read on entering school; some are definitely ready to learn to read—and this will usually include a majority of the children who are six years of age or older—and some are not yet ready to begin to learn to read.

CHILDREN WHO ARE NOT READY FOR READING

While the reasons for children's lack of readiness to begin reading are numerous, the principal one, where we are dealing with a typical American group, is a mental age distinctly below six. This problem has already been dealt with in another chapter. It would be better if these children were not placed in the regular first grades. They will not respond to the beginning reading procedures that were outlined in the last chapter. Where, as in most American schools, they have been included in the first grade, these children should be offered the opportunities which will help get them ready to learn to read.

For the time that may be allotted to these children toward reading readiness the following desirable lines of activity are suggested:

1. Help build in their minds concepts of words in speech. We cannot read until we understand spoken language. Read to them, and in other ways give them experience with language and with words as representing meanings.

2. Endeavor to enlarge their experiences. Point out to them and help them to make the observations in their environment that the other children, perhaps, make spontaneously. Excursions into the garden, the park, the neighborhood, will help.

3. Lead them into the habit of expressing thoughts in sentences. Encourage them to enlarge their vocabularies.

4. Endeavor to arouse their curiosity about the world they live in. Lead them to wonder what pictures mean, what signs and labels tell them. Answer their questions on the board with a single word such as *yes* or *no,* and otherwise let them become aware of the world of print.

THE CHILD AND HIS PRIMER

The period of preparation is followed by the introduction of the child to the primer, his first book. Attempts have been made to formulate tests for determining just when the child is ready to take up his primer, but the teacher who is doing her work intelligently will know when the time has come without the need of following any rules of thumb. When the child has learned what it means to read, he is ready to begin to secure content or meaning from print. It may be of assistance to know that in typical situations there are sometimes children who reach this point quite early: somewhere between the fifth and eighth week of school. Most children, however, can continue for a much longer period profitably and happily with charts and pre-primers.

The most essential bit of psychology to bear in mind at this point is this: Do not let the child have the primer until you know when he does get it he will read it with rapidity and with pleasure. It is more important to understand that the child should not undertake to use the primer *until he can read it.* In discussing the work of the pre-primer period this principle was proposed: Do not let the child meet a word for the first time in print. He should previously have fully understood and used it orally. The teacher will find another principle useful for this period: *Do not let the child meet a printed symbol for the first time in the primer.* He should have mastered all of the words he meets in the primer during the preparatory stages on charts and on the blackboard.

This careful preparation will assure the formation of good reading habits of rhythmic eye movement, large units of perception, and the absence of regressive movement. The matter being already familiar in other forms, there will be no need for the child to struggle to interpret otherwise meaningless symbols. Instead, the child will read with confidence and pleasure. Adequate preparation of this sort makes beginning book reading smooth, meaningful, and effective.

Preparatory Drill. We have already called attention to the fact that reading is a skill and, as such, ultimately rests on the formation of sound habits. The method of teaching skills is most frequently called the drill lesson. During this period, as a preparation toward helping the child enjoy his primer and actually to read it when it comes into his hands, the following drill lessons are offered. The object is to make sure that the children have learned to read on charts all of the words they will later meet in their primers.

1. After the children appear to be reading a chart, sentence by sentence, and recognizing the sentences in the order in which they occur, the teacher should point out single words, phrases, and sentences, to test whether the children recognize them without the assistance present when the chart is read right through.

2. The next test of recognition involves reading the words, phrases, and sentences away from the chart where they are known in a certain order. The teacher presents these on the blackboard or on pre-

READING: THE BEGINNING OF BOOKS 69

viously prepared cards. The children recognize or match with the chart.

3. The final test comes when, the chart put away and no context present to help them, the words and phrases are listed on the board not as sequential reading but for independent recognition.

Qualities of a Good Primer. While the teacher will only rarely have the privilege of selecting the primer that the children will use, there may be occasions when she will be consulted. At any rate she should be in the position to pass professional judgment on the character of the tool that she uses or is asked to use.

The content should, above all things, be interesting and familiar. The construction should be idiomatic, and the material should be reasonable and suited to the age for which it is intended. Familiar content and idiomatic construction will induce word recognition and lengthen the span of recognition. These qualities will make for regularity of the movement of the eye across the page, the sweep back to the next line, and, by holding attention, eliminate regressive movements. That failure to observe these conditions will have the contrary, detrimental effects may be easily seen from the fact that the best adult reader will slow up the process and lose the rhythm of his reading when subjected to a page of place names, nonsense syllables, or other matter that lacks flow and continuity. Familiar content presented in short units, interestingly and idiomatically expressed in the brief sentences suitable to childhood, with a certain carefully planned continuity, will not only win the child's attention and *pull his eye along,* but reduce the number of pauses and shorten the duration of each.

In order to provide needed drill in recognition, the primer must be limited in total vocabulary, present new words at relatively long intervals, and be repetitive in form. Yet the text should not be organized with the need for drill too exclusively in view. Content so organized might consist of a number of unrelated words or, indeed, phonic elements, systematically repeated. Such a procedure would over-emphasize recognition and under-emphasize meaning. When a few words are tediously repeated, even under the guise of a reading lesson or story, and all the possible variations are elaborated in connection with an idea that seems trifling, even to the child, there is an absence of forward-impelling sequence, and therefore no real reading.

We now have available many primers which prove that it is possible to repeat without loss of literary value; to use language to which the child is accustomed, and yet observe sequence and consequence of events. To obtain the best results for permanent good habits, the matter must go forward, not round and round or backward and forward.

From the point of view of mechanical construction, the book should be light enough to be held easily in the hand, minimizing the temptation to place it on the desk, which presents a poor angle for reading. The pages should, preferably, be white, and opaque rather than glossy. The ink should be black. The illustrations should be so placed as not to interfere with the full length of the lines. The type should be clear, twenty-four point size and the lines should be of even, uniform length ranging from 2.5 to 3.5 inches. Short lines prevent, as long lines may induce, regressive movements.

Presenting the Primer. The transition drill which was outlined above, carefully planned and executed, will furnish splendid preparation for books. The teacher will, by anticipation, heighten the children's pleasure in beginning to read in books. She may have the books on view;

READING: THE BEGINNING OF BOOKS

she may show the pictures; she may anticipate the nature of the stories.

In addition to the foregoing, there are certain points that are universal in application:

> 1. Children of normal vision should hold the book ten to fourteen inches from the eye. Each child should be provided with a marker and taught how to use it, line by line.
>
> 2. This first reading should be oral, since the child is learning to read and the teacher must observe whether he is doing so. *The child should be given time to go silently over the matter that he is about to read orally.*
>
> 3. The child should be taught to read for *meaning, not for expression*. He is learning to read, not reading for the pleasure of an auditor. He should, therefore, not be interrupted with pronunciation or any of the other elements of oral speech.
>
> 4. Wherever possible, several primers should be used concurrently. Where this is done, progress is made gradually. When the primers are used one after the other, the child is continually going backward and retracing his ground.

TESTING AND REMEDIAL PROCEDURE

Locating Reading Difficulties. We have dealt with two stages of reading method, the pre-book, and the initial stage. The third step is most commonly referred to as the rapid progress stage of reading. Before deciding that the children are ready for this final phase of learning to read, the teacher should take stock of the accomplishments so far achieved. She will nearly always find that some of her pupils, while they have not entirely failed to hold their own, have certain difficulties. This is the point at which to discover and to remedy these faults of reading, if the children are not to be sent forward permanently hampered as poor readers. For these reasons we shall, in this section, deal with testing, seat work, and remedial work.

For the purpose of a thorough evaluation of the child's reading capacity at any particular stage of primary instruction, there are available several excellent tests. These tests are cleverly arranged for rapid administration, and are standardized for comparison with established norms. They are commercially available, accompanied by directions for administration and scoring. They are, without question, very useful and highly reliable.

As this book is written for teachers rather than for supervisors, methods of attaining results by instruction are more important than the measurement of outcomes. The suggestion is made, therefore, to the teacher that she frequently use informal tests devised by herself. These tests should be based on the material in actual use, and employed with sufficient frequency to determine the effectiveness of the instruction and the progress of the pupils. It should not be difficult to determine whether a particular child is reading or remembering, guessing, bluffing, or just dazed. The simplest principle to bear in mind is that the method and materials of instruction can be turned around and used to test.

Possibly the most convenient and simplest test for checking silent reading ability is the completion or direction type. The teacher provides the child with cards which may omit the last word and direct him to indicate comprehension by drawing in an object that represents the missing word. Again, she may ask him to do something like coloring a tree or finishing a drawing by putting in some obviously missing detail. The silent reading may be followed by an exercise containing questions with ready-made answers for the child to underscore, such as *yes-no* or a choice of three or four possible answers—in technical terms, the true-false or multiple choice type of response.

The most important question after a test is the question of diagnosis. What does the test disclose? The usual outcome is the discovery that the children of the class differ so widely in ability as to require grouping and variation of work. The slower children require more drill, the brighter children more scope. In order to supply more drill and occupy them while the teacher is caring for her faster pupils, there should be provided seat work, sometimes referred to as work-type reading. Another discovery that may be made as the result of the test is that many of the children still have difficulty in word-recognition, and confuse certain words. Finally, there may be disclosed an individual who is failing to read for reasons so elusive that he represents a special problem. This individual, distinguishable from the child of low mental age, has been called a non-reader. The problem of the non-reader will be discussed in the next chapter. Remedial measures for the other two types of difficulty will be offered in the following paragraphs.

Seat Work for Additional Drill. It would be possible to list a dozen principal seat work drills and a score of variations in these procedures. There are available so many and so excellently conceived procedures for seat work that no home-made devices should be expected of the teacher. The teacher who has in her class the large number of children of varying ability ordinarily found in American schools should not be required to spend many hours preparing materials for individual supplementary work. All of her efforts will be needed not only for the preparation of charts for her own particular group, but for keeping her teaching a stimulation to her class.

Recognition and Other Difficulties. Tests will disclose various difficulties which obstruct the path to effective reading. One frequently discovered cause of trouble is the confusion of simple, short words in oral reading, such as *saw* and *was, in* and *it.* Since children will confuse these words when they actually recognize others of several syllables and of apparently greater difficulty, one suspects that, since it has been so easy to guess them by context, and they have so little specific character, they have been overlooked.

If one source of confusion is the lack of specific character in words, another is too much similarity in such words as *how* and *now.* Other errors, particularly in oral reading, are the substitution of one word for another, repetition, insertion of words not on the page, and omission of some that are there. The remedial procedure is obvious enough: Present these words with sufficient frequency to fix the recognition once and for all.

The breaking up of sentences without regard to proper word grouping, and the wooden reading whereby the child pronounces one word at a time and all on the same tone level, are errors brought about by poor instruction which could have been forestalled. The remedy is indicated: better instruction.

CHAPTER VII

READING: THE PERIOD OF RAPID PROGRESS

Preparation for Independent Reading

Speaking for most of the pupils, we may say that the preparatory period will occupy six weeks or more, the primer period will occupy the rest of the first term, and the transition period, which we are here calling "preparation for independent reading," will extend to the end of the first year. The compilers of the Twenty-fourth Yearbook of the National Society for the Study of Education furnish an interesting set of criteria to determine when the child has satisfactorily completed the initial or primer period and is ready to begin independent reading. When ready for this next step, he

1. Becomes completely absorbed in the content of interesting selections when reading independently;

2. Reads silently with few or no lip movements;

3. Asks questions about and discusses intelligently the content of what is read;

4. Reads aloud clearly, naturally, and in thought units rather than by individual words;

5. Handles books with care, opens and turns pages properly, knows the order of paging, and is able to find readily what he is looking for.

A basic procedure during the initial stage of reading which was described in the last section was this: Do not let a child meet a new word for the first time in his book; prepare him for it. In this way, the best teachers give their children a reading vocabulary of several hundred words. But we cannot teach reading a word at a time. The English vocabulary is extensive, the child matures, and his interests expand. He reads for information as well as for pleasure. The new words he encounters increase rapidly. Besides being new, the words gradually become longer. The time has come for independent reading. The time has come for sight reading. Can the pupils read?

The answer is that, faced with unfamiliar and difficult words, some of the children read them with ease, while others find them stumbling blocks. The first group needs only the experience and opportunities with which we shall deal later. The children who find it difficult to read need specific help to serve as a transition to sight reading. Such an aid is instruction in phonetic analysis.

Phonics as an Aid to Recognition. One point should, however, be noted before the teacher decides which are the children who really require the aid of phonics. The more familiar the words, the less likely is the child to find them difficult to read. Trying to read unfamiliar words is comparable to trying to read a foreign and unknown language. Many teachers find it expedient to extend the vocabulary of their children. This may be begun by discussion and then followed by the preparation and reading of charts which contain the new words that the children have learned to understand and to use.

We discussed and discarded phonics as a method of instruction. Reading should begin as reading, not as word recognition. It has, however, been satisfactorily demonstrated that at this stage phonics may serve in helping children toward independence in reading. This method is one of analyzing words into their constituent sounds.

In the English language the letters in a particular word

READING: THE PERIOD OF RAPID PROGRESS

may not all represent sounds. Furthermore, single sounds are frequently represented by a group of letters. For these reasons there would be little value in calling the child's attention to the individual letters. We analyze words for him into the several sounds of which they are composed, teach him to recognize the letter groupings that represent the sounds, and then train him to realize that these sound-symbols constantly recur in different words. When all is said and done, we teach pupils to sound their way through unfamiliar words by recognizing phonograms, i.e., combinations of letters that are pronounced together.

It will be seen that one might make a complete analysis of the language, discover all the phonograms that it contains, range these experimentally in order of the frequency of occurrence or in order of difficulty in learning, and then teach the system. While work has been done along these lines it is not necessary for the ordinary teacher to make an extensive study of it. It is not possible, necessary, or desirable to teach children phonics as a system. It might, in fact, turn out distinctly harmful, leading to pronunciation rather than comprehension.

Too many big words have been used in the literature of phonics. Controversies rage over the composition of the phonograms. Some teachers insist that phonograms must begin with a consonant, as in *ma-n*. Others reverse the process and join consonant sounds to the initial vowel, as in *m-an*. The teacher is advised to commit herself to neither the initial or final blend method,—in fact, to adopt no method.

We all know the pronunciation of the consonants and consonant combinations. We all know the pronunciation of the vowels and the vowel combinations. We all know that some of the vowels and diphthongs have several pronunciations, depending on the place in the word and the relation to consonants. Indeed, there are rules of pronunciation which might be an aid to adult foreigners learning the language. None of this systematic information is, in our opinion, necessary for little children. Phonics should be used as an aid where necessary, as necessary. Once her attention has been called to the desirability of having children recognize phonograms wherever they occur, the teacher may be left to devise her own methods.

It is quite likely that, when he meets printed matter containing new words, the child who reads them readily at sight does so because the phonograms of which they are composed are familiar. The child who finds it difficult to read unfamiliar matter probably fails to recognize the phonograms which he has actually read before. He, therefore, needs special instruction to recognize the phonograms. An excellent principle in his case would be this: Do not let the child meet new words until he has been taught to recognize the phonograms of which they are composed. This represents a true transition from the reading of familiar matter in the initial stage to the independent reading of the rapid progress stage of the second and third years.

The following suggestions in teaching phonics, based on experience and common sense, may be found of use in organizing this work.

1. Do not begin by teaching sounds. Begin with words which the child already knows, and lead him to *discover* the phonograms. Do not, in other words, put sounds together into words, but analyze familiar words into their constituent sounds. After sound combinations have been discovered in familiar words, they can be recombined into new words, not hitherto recognized.

2. One excellent procedure is to list a number of words that the children already recognize, all of which have a similar phonogram, such as *sh*e, *sh*op,

READING: THE PERIOD OF RAPID PROGRESS

*sh*ort, *sh*all. Call attention to the *sh* combination, and the similarity of the sound in all of the words. The children have heretofore recognized these words without making this observation. In order to give them the experience of discovering and sounding the phonogram, the teacher has the children isolate it in familiar words, i.e., sh-e, sh-op, sh-ort, sh-all. She then proceeds to present new words, possibly polysyllabic ones, in which the children find and recognize, and pronounce the phonogram.

3. Never interrupt a reading lesson to sound out words or teach phonograms. Give this aid to those who need it as a separate exercise. The effectiveness of the drill will be increased if it can be made pleasurable by plays and games and rivalry. The attention span will be lengthened and fatigue minimized if the teacher begins with simple and obvious sounds, such as the single letters *b* or *m*, and if she can devise a playful approach, such as rhyme or alliteration.

READING AT SIGHT

What is to be the work of the second and third grades? This period has been distinguished as one of rapid growth in the fundamental attitudes, habits, and skills on which intelligent interpretation, speed of silent reading, and fluent, accurate, oral reading depend. By the end of this period pupils should be able to read independently and intelligently, either orally or silently, simple content material such as is usually assigned in the fourth grade.

There is nothing essentially new to teach. This is a period of progress, a period of consolidating the habits that have been formed and making them permanent. As there are no essentially new steps to be taken, there are no additional principles of procedure to be mentioned. The desirable outcomes listed at the end of the chapter will indicate to the teacher the aims toward which to direct her instruction.

While oral reading should be retained during this period, silent reading must gradually increase and outweigh it in importance. As much as three quarters of the time allotted to reading should be silent reading in the second grade, and an even greater portion in the third. The point to bear in mind is that in these grades opportunity must be given for growth in independent reading, and scope must be provided for the various degrees of aptitude among the pupils. Independent reading on the part of the child should be fostered. This reading may be quite unrelated to school exercises, or it may be related to nearly all of them, for example, to history, nature study, and literature. More advanced children are by no means limited to the school texts and the school library. The public libraries and many homes supply books. In a later chapter concerning speech, literature available for children will be discussed.

During the first year the child learns to read in the sense of becoming acquainted with symbols as a means of conveying meaning. During the second two years he learns to employ reading as a tool for his purposes. What are these purposes? The child reads silently for information and for pleasure. He reads orally in order to provide information or pleasure for others. One further end to be sought during this period should be an extension of the child's vocabulary by his meeting the new word, understanding it, gaining experience in using it. That is what reading does for all of us. It broadens the horizon.

Silent reading and provision for individual differences are not conceivable without a classroom library. Every primary room should be the possessor of at least fifty carefully chosen books. A daily period should be provided for free reading. The books should be of both types, those primarily literary in character and those that are informative. The wise teacher will find ways and means to motivate reading by such methods as failing to finish an interesting story she is reading aloud and by providing an audience for those who wish to read aloud or to narrate what they have read.

The Non-Reader

Definition. The careful teacher who tests as the instruction proceeds will ordinarily be safeguarded against the unpleasant surprise, after her class has been launched into semi-independent reading, of finding a pupil who cannot read in any effective sense. Occasionally, however, such a child will turn up. Either his peculiarity has eluded the teacher in spite of all her efforts, or he has been transferred from another school where his deficiency was not fully realized. He is a non-reader who, for some reason, possesses a unique lack of aptitude, and must be distinguished from the slow learner who has possibly been pushed too fast. This latter child needs to be sent back to retrace his steps. The former, however, requires a careful diagnosis to discover the particular defect that hinders his development of the reading skill.

The non-reader is no general type, since the causes of non-reading are numerous and frequently elusive. For this reason, no single specific procedure can be prescribed. In fact, the non-reader, as distinguished from the backward reader, presents a baffling problem which really belongs to the educational psychologist rather than to the classroom teacher. In well-organized cities these children are segregated for instruction by teachers who are especially trained for the work and are under supervisors who understand the difficulties. Even in rural schools the county or the state authorities should provide the teacher with technical aid and directions for teaching the non-reader.

Diagnosis. It is not possible here to enter into the extensive literature of this problem. For the teacher who may have no access to expert assistance, a rather brief statement is presented here, but with the warning that there is an excellent literature in this highly specialized field to which the interested student should resort.

In beginning her study of one particular non-reader, the teacher's first step is an endeavor to discover why he is having difficulty. The child should be given an individual intelligence test. We cannot expect children to make any progress in reading if they begin this work when they have a mental age of less than six. Where there is no attraction toward or desire for reading, they should not be mentally younger than six and a half years. For these same reasons we cannot expect children, even where the instruction has been excellent, to meet the later grade standards unless they are of corresponding mental age.

The next step in diagnosis is a reading test. The best procedure is to employ only standard tests, and as many of these as possible, in order to locate the specific trouble. No one is prepared to list all of the defects that may be disclosed as a result of careful diagnosis. The following may, however, be found:

1. Generally inadequate and slow silent reading.
2. Oral reading that is slow and laborious.
3. Oral reading that is rapid and careless.
4. Reading in the sense of pronouncing words without understanding the content.
5. Difficulty in recognizing words.

Remedial Procedure. A discussion of methods of dealing with these children will follow the order in which possible causes have been indicated.

(1) The slow silent reader may be suffering from poor vision which can be discovered and corrected, from naturally slow mental processes and time-reaction, which brings it about that meanings "dawn" slowly; from disinterestedness either in the particular material or in his own progress; from inability to give attention for extended periods; from too little experience and practice in silent reading; from vocalizing, and the consequent undesirable eye-movements, narrow recognition span, and other bad reading habits. The remedial work for any of these particular defects is obvious.

(2) When the child reads slowly and laboriously, plodding along, a word at a time, it is at least possible that he has been driven too fast, so that the material is beyond him. This in turn narrows his span of recognition, and forces him to concentrate on the words one at a time. It is also possible that in his previous instruction there has been too much emphasis on word recognition and on phonetic elements. Such over-emphasis on small units tends to narrow the recognition-span and interfere with phrasing. Some teachers insist on clear articulation and precise pronunciation. This insistence is certainly justifiable. When, however, it is carried into the reading instruction instead of being dealt with during oral speech work, where it belongs, and the child is continually interrupted for particular words, he will concentrate on words which he will carefully articulate and pronounce one at a time.

(3) Conversely, the rapid and careless reader may be suffering from the result of well-intentioned instruction in which emphasis on large units was laid too early in the learning, making for fluent superficiality.

In the case of the slow and laborious reader, the mistakes of teaching which we have indicated may have annoyed and discouraged the child and caused him to lose interest. In both instances, if any of the possible explanations we have offered happens to fit the case, the remedy is obvious: Go back to simpler material and retrace the steps of teaching reading.

(4) The child who "reads" without comprehension may well be suffering from too much oral reading instruction, too little silent reading experience. His habit-reactions may be too much motor, too little mental. In the case of this child it may be well to go back to material entirely within his capacity, have him read silently, and give continuous evidence of comprehension.

(5) The child who has difficulty in learning to recognize words even with the aid of phonics, is obviously the most baffling of the non-readers, perhaps the only non-reader in the technical sense. In his case vision, as well as intelligence, should be tested. If these two possibilities are eliminated, we must consider the experiences which help or hinder all children when they begin to learn to read. Is the child's background such that he has had experience with language, has heard conversation, has acquired an oral vocabulary of some dimensions? Does he, when he *hears* them, understand thoroughly the words which he cannot read? Can he listen to a story and repeat it? Can he narrate an incident he has observed or an experience which he has had? Has his training, step by step, been what it should be, or must we retrace the whole process?

If all of these obvious possibilities have been eliminated, and the child still remains a non-reader, the teacher must ask herself whether the child's method of recognizing words is correct. As stated earlier in this chapter, we do not really teach reading. We place children in situations in which they ordinarily learn. Just how they learn to recognize words and phrases we do not know. The methods are probably numerous. Just as they vary in nearly every trait, so children vary in methods of recognizing visual symbols. Just as every capacity is possessed in varying degrees from very much to very little, so we find occasional children who are non-readers. The final solution to this baffling pedagogical problem has not yet been discovered.

Desirable Outcomes

At the End of the First Year. The pupil has satisfactorily completed the work of the first year if he

   1. Has read twelve books in class and at least ten at home or at the library table;

   2. Takes pleasure in reading, and reads with rapidity and accuracy;

   3. Reads silently without lip movements, with rhythmic eye sweep, wide recognition span, and no regression;

   4. Reads aloud clearly, naturally, and with good eye-voice span;

   5. Cares for books properly and knows how to look for needed information;

   6. Concentrates for short periods, working promptly and efficiently, and understands the directions for seat work.

At the End of the Third Year. Pupils who have mastered reading as a tool for use in later work

   1. Have thoroughly established the habit of reading independently;

   2. Interpret effectively the reading materials assigned in connection with the other school activities and are able to discuss or make use of the content;

   3. Inquire about or independently seek reading

materials which relate to the problems or activities in which they are interested;

4. Read more rapidly silently than orally;

5. Are able to read orally at sight with ease and effective expression, provided the materials assigned do not contain word difficulties or difficulties of meaning.

REFERENCES FOR FURTHER STUDY

Dougherty, L., *How to Teach Phonics*. Boston, Houghton Mifflin Co., 1923.

Gates, A. I., *The Improvement of Reading*. New York, The Macmillan Company, 1927.

Gist, A. S., and King, W. A., *The Teaching and Supervision of Reading*. New York, Charles Scribner's Sons, 1927.

Klapper, P., *Teaching Children to Read*. New York, D. Appleton-Century Co., 1926.

National Society for the Study of Education. Twenty-fourth Yearbook, Part 1. Bloomington, Public School Publishing Co., 1925.

Patterson, S. W., *Teaching the Child to Read*. New York, Doubleday, Doran & Co., 1930.

Pratt, C., and Stanton, J., *Before Books*. New York, Greenberg, 1926.

Storm, G. C., and Smith, N. B., *Reading Activities in the Kindergarten-Primary Grades*. Boston, Ginn & Co., 1928.

CHAPTER VIII

HANDWRITING AND SPELLING: GENERAL PRINCIPLES

Writing is the complement of reading. Just as reading extends the scope of communication beyond the possibilities of the ear by employing the eye, so writing, by means of a conventional system of symbols, extends the scope of speech beyond the possibilities of the vocal organism. Subsidiary to, but inevitably connected with writing, is the ability to write accurately, i.e., the ability to spell. Penmanship and spelling both represent skills, the one largely motor, the other resting on automatized associations. In both cases, instruction must follow the well-trodden avenues which lead toward the establishment of habits.

There are few schools in which the individual teacher will be permitted to choose her system of writing. There is, therefore, little need for theoretical discussion. Yet the student's attention must be called to the fact that there are now available two general handwriting modes: the cursive, which is the traditional method that nearly all of us use, and the manuscript, a method which antedates our present penmanship and which has recently been revived in England.

Since "testing the pudding" has some advantages over argument about it, two samples of fourth-grade writing are presented here. One of these is taken from a school that teaches the most commonly accepted method, the other from a school that teaches manuscript writing.

Ideal fourth-grade writing could have been reproduced from the manuals of the publishers who sponsor the methods. Such material, however, is more theoretical than practical.

No unusual efforts were made to secure representative work for use as illustrations. These specimens are what the statisticians call random samples. It is possible that some schools would make a better, and some a poorer, showing for each method. For the classes from which these samples were taken, the writing represents the best. Some of the children in each class wrote a poorer hand. Few, if any, wrote a better.

> At the time of the Revolutionary War, a brave little American girl named Anne Randolph lived on a farm not far from Philadelphia. Her father and her two brothers had joined the American army under the command of George Washington. Anne and her mother were left alone to take care of the farm.

> At the time of the Revolutionary War, a brave little American girl named Anne Randolph lived on a farm not far from Philadelphia. Her father and her two brothers had joined the American army under the command of George Washington. Anne and her mother were left alone to take care of the farm. *

The outstanding arguments in favor of manuscript writing are its beauty and its legibility. There are addi-

* These two examples of handwriting have been reduced one-half in size from the originals.

GENERAL PRINCIPLES 89

tional points in favor of this form of writing: Many students of education advise deferring the teaching of handwriting because the muscular co-ordinations required are too fine for the child in the primary grades. Yet the child, to keep pace with his general development and the other aspects of his school work, does need a written form of expression. Since the movements used in manuscript writing very much resemble the larger movements of drawing, the child is not subjected to as much strain as in cursive writing. The letters being made individually, the fine co-ordinations necessitated by a running hand are eliminated. There are still other claims that impress us as less important: In effect, the reasoning is that as manuscript writing bears a close resemblance to print, the child learns only one alphabet and system of symbols instead of two, and his writing is associated with, instead of running parallel to, reading.

In our discussion of methods of instruction we shall, in view of the recent revival of manuscript writing, assume that the teacher will deal with the established script. It is, however, well to state here that the procedures would, in general, be much the same. The chief difference lies in the form of the letters, and the absence of joining them together. The fundamental habits governing position, arm movement, seating, rhythm, and paper, remain the same.

Basic Principles Governing Penmanship Instruction

In facing the beginning of the instruction in writing, the teacher should recall that the child does not come to school without experience. He has seen people write and, usually, he has pretended to write himself. In organizing the experiences and the repetitions that will lead the child to acquire this skill, the teacher must not analyze it into its logical elements and have the child begin with strokes or letters. Rather must she be guided by children's interests and allow them to write whole words, if possible, words they want to write.

There are other psychological factors involved that must be carefully borne in mind. Progress will be faster if the skill is taught through application, as one that can be used, than if it is taught without motivation as an end in itself. Writing is the goal, not handwriting; written expression, not penmanship. It is so easy to organize procedure in a manner that will enable the child to write something he wants to learn to write, as for example, his own name, that there is no need for unmotivated drill.

The teacher should consider it as her principal aim to make the learner see the word he is endeavoring to write, and to feel the elements as he writes. Fundamentally, writing is taught by the classic procedure that applies to all motor skills. It involves the instinct of imitation. The teacher sets the model, calling attention to the sequence of the movements as she makes them. The child endeavors to imitate while the teacher stands by with friendly aid, helping him to acquire good form. The task before him is to build up accurate and synchronated visual and kinaesthetic images. He should, at the same time, have before him a visual image of the word he desires to write, and by imitation endeavor to acquire the correct movements that will help him to achieve his object.

Since writing calls for muscular control and delicately co-ordinated movements, and since young children have difficulty in making small, finely controlled movements, instruction begins at the blackboard, not at the desk. Fortunately, most of the elements needed may be acquired through this preliminary large-scale writing, which avoids fine work and cramped muscles. From this beginning, the writing is slowly reduced in size; the child leaves the blackboard and crayon for coarse paper with widely spaced lines and a large soft pencil, which allow him to continue large free writing movements. There are competent teachers, probably in the minority, who do not begin the penmanship work at the blackboard. On the psychological principle that we should learn a skill as it functions in life, they consider this blackboard work wasteful. These teachers begin with large pencil and large rough paper—a procedure which many teachers who begin at the board consider a good means of transition from board to desk.

The Left-Handed Child. Before going on to details we must consider the inescapable question of left-handedness. The world is organized for right-handed people. The school room lighting and seating are arranged for right-handed pupils, as is the whole teaching procedure for perfecting the art of writing. The teacher should make tentative efforts to learn whether the child's tendency toward left-handedness is weak and can be easily redirected. In nearly all cases it will, however, be found that the child is essentially left-handed.

In such cases efforts should not be made to compel the pupil to work with the right hand. There is too much evidence of the grave danger of transference to warrant any teacher in being violent about this matter. The child who naturally does things with his left hand must be allowed to write that way. But he requires a great deal of special attention. To counteract the danger of writing toward, instead of away from, himself, he must be taught to place the paper on his desk in the direction exactly opposite to that demanded of the right-handed children. This done, he must be required to conform to the work of the other pupils in all respects. Failure to follow this procedure alertly and consistently will lead to the formation of a "back-handed" style of writing.

BASIC PRINCIPLES GOVERNING SPELLING INSTRUCTION

The Committee on Spelling of the Department of Superintendence of the National Education Association presented a statement of the aims of the instruction in spelling here quoted for two reasons: As an excellent statement of aims it should be useful to the teacher as a goal. On the assumption of the accuracy and inclusiveness of the formulation the following discussion of the teacher's work will be based, topic by topic, on this statement of aims:

1. To make automatic the accepted sequence of letters in words most commonly needed for expression of thought in writing;
2. To develop the meaning and use of the words to be spelled;
3. To develop what is termed a "spelling consciousness";
4. To develop a "spelling conscience";
5. To develop a technique for the study of spelling.

The first of these implies two major tasks: the discovery of the words that are most commonly needed for expression of thought in writing, and making automatic the accepted sequence of the letters in these words.

Which Words Shall We Teach? The second half of the first aim provides for learning to spell those words that are "most commonly needed for expression of thought in writing. "We cannot teach all the words in the dictionary. We must not teach spelling as an end in itself. But which are those words that are most commonly needed? Fortunately for the present generation of teachers, much important work has been done in the endeavor

GENERAL PRINCIPLES

to answer this question. There are available numerous word lists, most of which are reasonably reliable.

This volume is no place to detail the researches. It must be sufficient to say here that in the endeavor to locate the words whose spelling should be definitely taught in school, students of education have examined themes written by pupils at all stages of development; studied family correspondence; tabulated the words used in current newspapers and magazines; and listed the words employed in business correspondence and in literature. In each instance, there was naturally an enormous number of "running" words, but when duplication was eliminated there remained a surprisingly small number of "different" words comprising the actual vocabulary for the particular type studied.

In addition to all this, research workers have compared one another's studies to discover the extent of agreement; they have sampled the dictionary by taking every word that occurred in a predetermined place in a series of predetermined pages; and, more specifically pedagogical, they have searched out the common words which for one reason or another are difficult to learn to spell accurately.

One of the best known lists at present, and possibly the most reliable, is that which resulted from an extensive investigation carried on under the direction of Professor Ernest Horn of the University of Iowa, published in the Fourth Yearbook of the Department of Superintendence. It lists the 3009 words most commonly employed in adult writing, and is sometimes referred to as the Commonwealth List, after the name of the Fund that subsidized the investigation.

The sources of material used in this study were: (1) a compilation of all investigations made up to the year 1923; (2) the vocabulary of letters of twenty-six different types of business; (3) the vocabulary of personal letters from every State in the Union; (4) an extensive sampling of the letters of eight noted English writers and eight noted American writers; also all of the letters of E. V. Lucas's "The Gentlest Art"; (5) the vocabularies of letters printed in magazines and metropolitan newspapers; (6) the vocabulary of letters of application and recommendation; (7) the vocabulary of minutes, resolutions, and committee reports; (8) the vocabulary of excuses written by parents to teachers; and (9) the vocabulary of a single individual over a period of eight years. The total number of "running" words in these investigations was more than five and one half million. Over thirty-eight thousand different words were found.

In Which Order Shall Words Be Presented?

We must now face the pedagogical challenge of the first aim of the Committee on Spelling, i.e. training children to the point of automatically using "the accepted sequence of letters in words." This challenge presents two major questions: (1) In what order shall any total list of words be taught? (2) By what methods can the "accepted sequence of letters in words" be made automatic?

In what order shall the words be presented in spelling instruction? What proportion of the total of three thousand to be mastered shall be presented, grade by grade? The list referred to above, like all lists that result from research, is presented in alphabetical order. But obviously the words cannot be taught in that order. The words in this list are marked to indicate their frequency of occurrence. But frequency is no indication of ease of mastery and therefore no index to the order of presentation. What we need to know is the order of the difficulties met by the child in his effort to learn spelling. We also need to know the number of words to be assigned to each grade. The answers to these questions can be found only by experimentation.

Which of the words are appropriate to the several grades from the point of view of immediate use in the spoken, written, and reading vocabulary? In providing for repetition, as must inevitably be done, which words present peculiar obstacles to mastery, peculiar temptations to mis-spelling? To indicate the need for careful investigation it should be pointed out that some of the words which are easiest to mis-spell because of inherent difficulty or easy confusing with other words, are those in actual daily use at the lowest age levels. To advise the teacher to conduct the investigations that will provide the answers to the questions that have been raised would be the height of folly. In the first place, the task requires far too much time and covers too much ground. In the second place, it has been quite adequately done. The administrative authorities or the teacher will select one of a number of modern "Spellers" which are based on investigations and experiments calculated to answer these questions. In these manuals the presentation and the repetitions are carefully planned and soundly organized.

The Method of Presentation. What are some of the ways to automatize the accepted sequence of letters in words? The third and fourth aims must necessarily form part of this discussion. The Committee recommends the development of a "spelling consciousness", which it defines as the ability to recognize almost instantly the correct and incorrect spelling of words, and a "spelling conscience," which it defines as an ardent purpose or desire to spell correctly. In effect, all three aims emphasize the necessity of establishing as a habit invariable accuracy of letter sequence. Naturally, as much motivation as possible should be back of the formation of these habits. All teaching which aims at skill and habit-formation is based on the well-known principles of the drill lesson—repetition, avoidance of inaccuracy, provision for motive, the avoidance of fatigue which diminishes attention. Nonetheless, each specific skill presents peculiar aspects of its own. There are particular procedures that have been found useful in teaching spelling.

The ability to spell words is, essentially, the ability to hold in mind the forms of words for the purpose of written reproduction. This is an exact contrast to reading, where the ability called for is recognition. In each of these abilities one needs to recall word forms or letter combinations, but in reading, the need is for *recognition*, in spelling, for *reproduction*. Whereas in reading one needs ready recognition of the total form, in spelling one must recall the detailed make-up.

(1) *The Words Must Be Meaningful.* The first essential to the decomposition of a word is the recognition of the word in its most complete sense. It is wasteful and confusing to teach spelling in the narrowest sense, as an end in itself. Words to be spelled must be meaningful. The word must first be known and recognized for what it is. Never teach a word which the child cannot easily employ in expression.

(2) *The Approach Must Be Visual, Auditory, and Motor.* The ability to spell depends essentially on the ability to recall the correct sequence. That which is to be recalled is an image. But we must not be misled by the apparent relationship of the word image to that which is visual. The recall may be visual, a picture of how the word looks. It may be auditory, an echo of how the sequence runs when we spell the word out loud. It may be kinaesthetic, a recall of how it feels to write the word. It is quite conceivable that a child who cannot "spell" a word in class will write it accurately; that one who "spells" it correctly in oral recitation will write it inaccu-

rately. The teacher must employ every avenue toward the goal of establishing the image. She will soon find that there is no one road. Children differ distinctly in the matter of the usableness of the several kinds of imagery in learning.

(*3*) *Spelling Must Be Taught in Association with Use.* Spelling, as all else, should be taught functionally in application, not as an end in itself. We learn to spell in order to write and express ourselves with accuracy. Spelling should not be dissociated from writing. Insofar as possible, it should be correlated with it.

Tests and Desirable Outcomes

This volume does not deal in detail with the matter of standard tests; the emphasis is on instruction rather than on supervision and the measurement of the outcomes of instruction. It must be assumed, however, that every teacher will become acquainted with the modern movement which makes achievement tests available which are accompanied by manuals of directions for administration, and norms that will enable her to compare the work of a child, a class, a school, or a school system, with the standards that prevail generally in the country.

Penmanship. Handwriting is particularly suitable for the establishment of standard tests and a number of these have been constructed, some dealing with handwriting in general, some dealing with details. In each instance the teacher secures a sample of the work of the pupils in her class, compares it with the graded standard test, which is marked or "scaled" to enable her to determine the number that indicates the quality of any particular paper.

Among the best known handwriting tests, all of them made available by educational publishers, are the Ayers, the Thorndyke, and the Houston Scales of Handwriting. In each of these scales are norms established for each of the grades. All of them aim at the measurement of handwriting as a whole, the principal point being its legibility. The Freeman Scale, on the other hand, is of the more detailed type. This last test enables the teacher to analyze penmanship into its elements and to diagnose the pupil's writing and compare it with grade norms for alignment, slant, spacing, letter formation, and quality of line. In view of the fact that the teaching of this skill is not fully completed in the primary grades and refinement is deferred to later years, it will probably be wiser, as a rule, for the primary teacher to employ one of the first three scales mentioned. On the other hand, the ambitious teacher, particularly interested in the perfection of this skill, may find the Freeman Scale of value during the third year of school.

A statement of desirable outcomes follows in the list of grade norms on four standard tests, together with the speed at which such norms must be attained.

Grade	Ayers	Thorndyke	Freeman	Houston	Letters per minute
II	35	8.5	11	40	30
III	39	9.5	12.5	45	44

Spelling. The spelling scale almost appears to have outlived its usefulness. When spelling books selected their words in every which way, the scales were organized methodically by educational investigators who endeavored to determine in numerous ways the most commonly used words. The test then indicated whether the pupils were able to spell these words. When, however, this technique was taken over for curriculum purposes as a method of listing the words to be learned, there remained little to say except that the words assigned to any given grade and to all the grades preceding it should be spelled accurately by the pupils of that grade. Furthermore, any other test the teacher might be required to administer would simply be used by her as a word list to coach the children, and quite properly so.

There may be occasions when the teacher desires to make a test of spelling ability as such, rather than of ability to spell the particular words studied. It is very questionable whether any such test can be made with any degree of validity. Students of language instruction question it. However, superintendents, supervisors, principals, and "surveyors" frequently do attempt to test spelling ability. For this purpose there have been published a number of scales. The World Book Company, Yonkers, N. Y., and The Public School Publishing Company, Bloomington, Ill., are among the most active publishers of tests. A representative spelling test of the former is the spelling section of the Stanford Achievement Test, and the latter may be well represented by Monroe's Timed Sentence Test. Other tests have been published by Columbia University and the University of Iowa.

CHAPTER IX

HANDWRITING AND SPELLING: THE FIRST SCHOOL YEAR

The Beginning of Writing

Work in writing usually begins at the blackboard. Speaking for the class as a whole, one may safely say that this first step should occupy the better half of the first term in school, or about three months. As is the case in every other subject, the teacher must be assumed to possess the skill which she is about to teach. Teachers who have been so unfortunate as to miss adequate training in a well-conducted teacher-training institution should secure the aid of their fellow teachers in the effort to make good the deficiency. To those who must work alone we heartily recommend a small pamphlet of advice entitled "Blackboard Writing," distributed by Zaner & Bloser Company of Columbus, Ohio.

In making her preparation for this work, the teacher should rule the blackboard so that small letters will be written at a height of two inches, capitals and loop letters at twice that height. Between the written lines there should be left a space of four inches.

The actual work begins with a model written by the teacher, preferably something that will hold attention. The most obvious thing to do is to select some child whose name will be written on the board. This the teacher writes slowly several times, erasing and writing it again and again, so that the children may observe the movements and the form of the word as it develops.

THE FIRST SCHOOL YEAR 101

The object of this procedure is to try to reach the child's mind through as many avenues as possible—the eye, the ear, the hand—in an endeavor to insure a mental image. Pupils are asked to watch the teacher closely as she writes the word. She writes very slowly, and as she writes she calls attention to her movements saying, "Push—pull, over—under," as the case may be. The word is erased and written again and again. Next the pupils in their seats trace in the air with the teacher the word that she has been writing on the board. When they seem to have acquired the visual image, one child is asked to go to the board and write the word. By degrees more and more children are sent to the board, while those in their seats make comments.

As her next step, the teacher writes and asks the children to watch her position at the board. She breaks a piece of chalk in half, and shows them how to hold it in the palm of the hand, with four fingers on top and the thumb underneath. She then stands erect about a foot from the blackboard and writes with the side of the chalk. She calls attention to the fact that she writes directly in the field of vision, not too high above her head, nor too low. As she writes with large free movements, she walks along the blackboard to the right, always standing directly in front of the word she is writing.

Children may now be called to the board in larger numbers and given individual models to copy. From the first, the teacher must be careful to see that they face the board at arm's length from it, write directly in front of the face, and not to the right of the body. The pupil should hold the chalk as described above. When the writer is too close to the blackboard he will not be able to see his work quite as well as otherwise, and will find it difficult to make free arm movements because of the temptation to rest his hand against the board. At the proper distance he will not press too heavily on the blackboard, and will be safeguarded against chalk dust.

In addition to the details mentioned above, which will help establish large arm movements, swing, and right direction, the teacher should note this warning: Do not have more children at the board than you can observe all of the time. Teachers frequently have a whole class at the board. Under these circumstances the teacher is unable to watch the actual work, but comes to each pupil in turn and comments on the result. What happens too frequently under these circumstances is that the product which seems acceptable, and which the teacher commends, has been attained by drawing rather than by writing. The standard practice appears to be to allow the child to hold an eraser in his left hand "behind his back." How often he erases part of a word, corrects and keeps on correcting until he attains a satisfactory end-result by entirely inappropriate methods! We would allow the child no eraser, cleaning the board only at fixed intervals. *Since the process is the essence of building the habit,* and the outcome valueless unless attained in a certain manner, the pupil at work should be under observation all of the time.

Some teachers have children trace before they write, going over the model several times with the chalk almost touching. There is no need to have all of the children writing the same word. The child's own name should be interesting to him, and this is written on the board for him by the teacher. As the children work, the teacher remains on the alert to see that they are practicing the proper form she pointed out when they were observing her. It is well to let the children practice writing their names until they can do so without a model.

The business of learning to write must, however, now be organized in an effective manner. The teacher begins with words, but she selects short ones, preferably words of two or three letters. The writing should begin with the simplest letters, requiring either a push or pull stroke, such as the letter *i*. This may be followed with the letter *u* which is very similar in its make-up. The letter *i* should not, in the beginning, be followed by letters like *m* and *e* which are made with different strokes. The teacher must try to avoid confusion and to present a minimum amount of difficulty at each step. The following order of presentation of letters is suggested, with the reminder that it is best to write words. There should be no difficulty in combining the letters in these groups into words of gradually increasing complexity.

1. One-space letters: i, u, w, e, r, s, n, m, v, x, a, o, c.
2. Letters with upward loop: l, b, h, k, f.
3. Letters with downward loop: y, g, z, j.
4. Letters which are a little shorter than loop letters: t, d, p, q.

Rhythm. The very beginning of work at the blackboard is not too early to pay attention to rhythm in writing. All questions of writing efficiency aside, rhythm is a worthy end in itself. There are those who would center the whole educative process about rhythm. Not only are the arts based on rhythm, but all of life has rhythm. Since we cannot do anything with perpetual motion, but must rest, the rest had best be at regular intervals, making for grace and poise.

In writing, all of us break the whole movement into units or strokes. The units are, obviously, not separated by complete pauses, but rather by a slowing down which makes writing a "succession of alternate flights and rests." These units may as well be regularly recurring as jerky. The teacher is advised, when the children have learned to write certain words, to have them "write in concert," rhythmically, and guided by her count. In this work the unit may be made to correspond to a double stroke, either upward and downward or in reverse order. When well done, each unit will represent a gradual increase in speed toward the middle, and a gradual decrease toward the end.

In rhythmic writing, the teacher will be careful to adjust her count to the letter forms that are being made and, naturally, to the present ability of the pupils. Preceding each exercise, the teacher should carefully explain the relation of the count to the strokes in the particular words. It is necessary to do more than count. The child must be instructed how the count is applied to the letter. The writing, in other words, should be in concert. Indeed, enough preliminary work should be done to assure the correct response when the rhythmic writing begins. Ordinarily, one unit of the count will correspond to a double stroke, upward and downward, the beat coming on either. The teacher who engages in this work conscientiously and consistently will be amply repaid, when the children begin to work on paper, by noting how naturally they organize their writing movement into units, how rapidly they develop free and fluent writing with a minimum of fatigue and a maximum of effectiveness.

Drill. Blackboard writing will ordinarily proceed backwards from simple words to drill on certain letters which prove difficult and appear to need more practice. In this way, by means of suitable words and, when the need is demonstrated, by drill on particular letter forms, all of the letters will be mastered at the blackboard and again combined into words or brief sentences, bringing into play all of the combinations of letters. Toward the end of the first term most of the children under good instruction will be found ready to take the next step and transfer their writing activities to paper and pencils at their desks.

In parting from the blackboard, one piece of advice

THE FIRST SCHOOL YEAR

may be left with the teacher: *Whenever a child at any stage of the progress of learning to write appears to need more drill, send him to the blackboard for practice.* It happens quite fortunately, says the author of the booklet referred to on page 100, "that the same muscles are used in writing on the board with chalk as upon paper with pencil or pen and precisely the same movement or movements are employed in writing upon the board as upon paper."

FROM THE BLACKBOARD TO THE DESK

Paper and Pencil. At their seats the children should be furnished with large-sized pencil or crayons and rough paper with lines ruled an inch apart. The child should be taught to write the small letters three eighths of an inch high, the capitals and loop letters just twice as high. During the early stages of seat work the teacher should station herself at the blackboard, carefully setting the model and calling attention to her movements. The individual correction and guidance will follow later. Before the details of instruction for this second step are discussed, there are several fundamentals to be dealt with, all of which will affect the child's future writing activities.

Position. The same principles apply to mastery of writing as to the mastery of any other motor skill, such as tennis. All the elements that go to make up the whole act of writing must be in the best form. It should be obvious that certain positions at the desk or table will be good and certain positions poor. The matter of position will govern ease and fluency of movement which are essential for excellence in writing; it will govern fatigue and the ability to stay at work a longer or a shorter period. The habitual position acquired may have some influence on the child's eyes, posture, and general health. The following directions for position follow Freeman.[1]

The writer should sit facing the desk squarely. His seat should be of such height that his feet may rest flat on the floor and the thighs be parallel to the surface of the seat. The desk should be of such a height that when the child is sitting erect and the arms rest on the desk, the elbows will be two or three inches from the body. The feet should project under the desk slightly in order that the child may sit back in the seat without being compelled to lean forward in order to rest his arms upon the desk. The child should sit back in the seat in a reasonably erect posture. The head should be held moderately erect and not inclined much to the one side or the other.

With the hands on the desk, palm turned down and the wrist almost rigid, the hand resting on the third and fourth fingers, the pencil is held in a natural position between the thumb and the first finger. It will be found useful to draw a diagonal line with chalk from the lower left-hand corner of the desk to the upper right-hand corner. The paper may then be placed directly in front of the child, with the bottom edge parallel to the chalk line.

The arm should rest lightly on the desk, with only part of the forearm actually on it. The left arm should rest at the top of the paper to hold it, supporting the weight of the body. In this way the right arm will be free to move easily across the page. The right arm should be maintained at right angles to the paper, with the palm face downward, the tips of the third and fourth fingers gliding across the page. While it is possible to make the upward and downward strokes with the hand turned over, it is impossible to move sidewise after a few letters have been written without lifting the hand and then

---

[1] See references at end of next chapter.

sliding it along. As the writing progresses along the page the pupil shifts the paper to the left and upward. The teacher should guard against a natural tendency of children to slide along in their seats instead of shifting the paper.

Arm and Fingers. In the literature on this subject there is much erudite discussion of movement in writing. For many years the schools have held it as an ideal to write with arm movements and not with the fingers. Freeman now finds that the fingers are naturally adapted to the formation of the letters; that the arm movement carries the hand across the page but is impractical for the formation of the details of the letters; that the most carefully trained children still use their fingers to form the details of the letters; and that even expert writers use the finger movement to a certain extent.

Primary teachers have known all this for a long time, having found it an almost impossible task to have the child write exclusively with the arm movement. In spite of all theoretical decrees from above, they have done what Freeman now advises, i.e., that the child be allowed to use his fingers as much as he is inclined provided he maintains the proper position, the freedom of sideward movement, and ease of grasp. Fluent lateral movement and rhythm will bring the arm into use to the maximum extent that is possible in good writing. In the finer details the fingers must be allowed to have play.

The Period of Transition. From this discussion of mechanics we come to the principles of procedure during the first weeks of desk work. The preceding extensive discussion of form may easily mislead the teacher to concentrate, as some do, at the beginning of the work, on dreary exercises calculated to teach the child position, movement, rhythm, and other elements of form. Such procedure, which eliminates the element of interest, goes directly counter to what is known about the laws of learning. The components of form should be in the foreground of consciousness of the teacher, not the pupils. They should be engaged in writing, not in gymnastics. The teacher should set the stage. By instruction that is organized and direction that is incidental she should lead to improvement in form. Let the teacher concentrate on the appropriate movement and the other details of form. Let the pupil address his attention to the words that he is writing, the beauty and the legibility of his product.

The matter that is being written will, of necessity, be much the same that the child has been writing at the board. This is a period of transfer. While he is unconsciously becoming habituated to good position and a smooth lateral movement, and is adjusting his hand and fingers to the somewhat finer work demanded by pencil and paper, he should be learning to write all of the small letters in various relations to one another, many of the capitals, selecting those that are most common in his reading, and the numbers from 1 to 50.

We must not expect too great accuracy in the detail of the form. Only gross errors should be pointed out. Improvement should come through experiences provided by the teacher rather than through direct and specific effort. Rather than concentrate on the way the individual letters are made, let the teacher aim at excellence by controlling the rate of writing. The child who has a tendency to write too fast while learning will form his letters carelessly. The child who has a tendency to write too slowly while learning will tend to draw rather than write, and retard the acquisition of fluency. The best way to control speed and to contribute to ease and fluency is, to follow the advice given for blackboard writing—to have the children write in rhythm. It is better to begin with rhythmic movements and poor writing than with well-formed letters made so laboriously and slowly that the pupil fails to achieve the desirable muscular co-ordinations and well-controlled fluency of writing.

The teacher's best procedure is to write on the board while the children work at their desks. She will, in advance, have thought through the details, the fall of the beat, and the other elements discussed earlier in the chapter. Preliminary explanations and instruction are given the children. The teacher counts as she writes at the board, cultivating rhythm and controlling the speed. Some teachers use rhymes and jingles instead of counting; some make use of the phonograph. Many employ the metronome, which can be set with precision for any rate that it is desired to maintain. Just as the size of the writing during the primary period is gradually reduced, so the rate of the count slowly increases. Toward the end of the first school year, twenty letters a minute, written rhythmically, represent an ideal form of drill exercise which should be enjoyed by most normal children. Ten or fifteen minutes a day will be found quite long enough for penmanship practice. The wise teacher will provide frequent rest periods during the writing to prevent fatigue and to insure continuous freedom of movement.

CHAPTER X

HANDWRITING AND SPELLING: PERIOD OF AUTOMATIZATION

The Second School Year—Spelling

Point of View. The child has no need for spelling during his first year. In teaching reading, we avoid analysis into letters, preferring to have the child learn to recognize units of expression, such as words and phrases. In teaching writing, we do analyze words into their constituent forms for purposes of practice, but the analysis frequently is into movements and structural combinations rather than into letters. Many adults still think that the school is governed by a traditional ritual which demands that the child learn to spell "c-a-t" the first day. It is quite true that until fairly recent years the spelling books contained thousands of words selected, one suspects, for their contrariness, and the child was required to gird himself for battle at the very outset of school life. Ultimate victories and defeats on the field of combat came in the course of the spelling match.

Spelling today is taught with a view to function—for the purpose of writing one's language accurately. Because of the comparative rarity with which the average adult or school child is called upon to write the ancient jawbreakers, modern children are early taught how to find out the spelling of words by consulting the dictionary, while effective spelling instruction is limited to the actual vocabulary that serves the needs of daily life. During the first year the child writes, and writes accurately, with-

PERIOD OF AUTOMATIZATION 111

out being made aware of the sequence of the letters that form the words. At the beginning of the second year, with the inevitable increase of the vocabulary soon to come, he must be made aware of the need to learn and habitually to employ the only correct sequence of the letters in every word that he uses.

Planning the Instruction. Beginning with the second grade, it is customary to set aside a daily period of fifteen or twenty minutes to be devoted to spelling. The word list, the number of words, the sequence of presentation, including repetitions, should be one selected from the best available publications. No teacher will slavishly follow the words found in the speller. She may eliminate some that seem to her inappropriate for her particular class and she may add some that seem essential. Above all things, she should adapt the work to the individual spelling abilities and needs of her children.

In general, the teacher will find it advisable to progress at the rate of from two to five new words a day, always bearing in mind the need for continuous repetition, review, and employment of the word in written form as *an instrument of expression*. The teacher should not be satisfied with approximate ability in spelling. The ideal to work for, and one that is practicable to set for all normal children, is perfection. Children will not reach this desirable goal at a uniform rate of progress. To assist her class in achieving it, the teacher may assign other tasks to those children who have mastered the spelling list to date, while she works with slower learners to perfect their spelling ability.

Method. The teacher should determine whether every child in the room can pronounce each new word as it is presented. She will then endeavor to make it each child's own by understanding and frequent use. Unless this aspect of the work is carried on during the oral language periods, too little of the spelling period will be left for actual drill in spelling.

We all know that one may look without seeing. In working for the child's recognition of the visual image the teacher will help the pupil to look at the word. In building the visual image, the child must learn how to analyze the word into its component parts and to see the letters. An excellent procedure is one whereby the teacher writes the word on the blackboard in the presence of the children, spelling it as she writes. Where the oral use of the word has hitherto been in connection with speech, it will be well to pronounce it again, associating the sound with the visual image. At the same time its meaning may again be taken up while the children are looking at the word. Where possible, it is well to present the word or words of the day on the printed page and to have the children note the letter sequence again.

The teacher now writes the word on the blackboard once more, and, where it consists of more than one syllable, she divides the syllables, helping the children to pronounce each syllable in turn and to visualize their sequence in the formation of the word.

Next the pupils are asked to shut their eyes and visualize the word, or else the word is erased and the children are asked to visualize it, spelling silently or aloud in unison, in order to build the auditory recall. When the visual and auditory images seem on the way to being established, the children proceed to write the word from recall, without copy. To avoid the danger of establishing the wrong habit, the child should not write the word more than once before the teacher has passed on its accuracy. Thereafter he should write it a number of times, preferably in short sentences, to establish the habit in the connection in which it will function. In accordance with the well-known laws of drill, the teacher will not regard the word as "learned" until many repetitions have established the habit and many tests have shown that it functions invariably in practice.

The Second School Year—Penmanship

In view of the comparatively short period of experience provided during the first year in school for writing with pencil and paper, the work in penmanship during the second year consists largely of continuation of the effort to master the art. Unlike arithmetic and some other subjects, penmanship progress cannot be made by proceeding from the simple to the ever more complex. Instead, all of it must be learned and steadily improved as the pupil goes forward from his first crude attempts to ever greater refinement. The method is called spiral, since no material introduced after the child has written all of the letters is new. Although the actual task is the same in grade after grade, the level of desirable quality is continually being raised.

During the second year, then, the teacher's principal objects are the continuance of the effort to establish the motor co-ordinations essential to writing. She will aim to make definite progress in ease, fluency, and rhythm; to continue the habituation of placing and holding the paper, and maintaining the desirable bodily position.

For content, she will demand that the child write words independently from recall, carefully drilling on difficult combinations such as *br, on, wi,* and *wr.* She will assure herself that the child has finally mastered all of the capital letters, knows when they should be employed, and can write the numbers to 100.

In the second year the child continues the use of a medium soft pencil and unglazed paper. As part of the plan of gradual reduction of the size of the writing, the ruling is reduced from the full inch of the first grade to five eighths of an inch. By habitually having the children write sentences rather than words from her dictation, the teacher will assure increasing independence on the part of the children. The dictation of sentences will also provide definite mastery of capitals and will tend to develop smoothness and rhythm in writing. In the matter of standards, the aim is to write small letters not higher than a fourth inch at a speed of thirty letters a minute.

The Third School Year—Spelling

The beginning of the third year represents the time when spelling attains real importance as one of the elements of the curriculum. Reference has already been made to the selection of the general list of words to be learned, the grade location of the list, and the need for repetition of words that are generally known to be difficult. Specific suggestions for desirable procedure are presented in this section.

Planning the Instruction. Having before her the list of words to be mastered during the term, the teacher may well divide the total number of words by the number of full weeks of school in the term and lay her plans to master the allotted unit week by week. Next, let her recall the most fundamental rule of drill—that mastery is an individual, not a class matter. We cannot expect the members of any group to make equal progress in learning to drive an automobile, play tennis, swim, or spell words. Because the mastering of skills depends on the establishment of associations, each person must be allowed to attain each step at his own rate of progress within the terms of his own nervous organization.

Applying this general principle to the specific instance of spelling, the teacher may find any or all of the following conditions: (1) Some of the members of her class already know how to spell some of the words, varying in both the particular words and in the number they can spell. Conceivably the range may extend from the child who already spells all the words to those children who can spell none of them. (2) A rough test will show that some of the children learn almost instantly, others seem unable to achieve permanent mastery even after the most arduous effort. (3) Some of the children may know how to pronounce all of the words, others none of them. (4) The same conditions may be found in the matter of understanding the meaning of the words. (5) Some of the children may have greater visual or greater auditory imagery. For that reason it is highly advisable to employ two distinctly different modes of emphasis in the process of instruction.

An excellent plan would be to discover some of these differences. On Friday of every week, dictate to the class the words that have been assigned for mastery during the next week. Most writers advise the teacher to have the children write the words in columns after they have been properly pronounced and their meaning has been made clear. We would advise her to test the ability to spell in the only way in which the ability is ever called into use —by writing sentences.

For each word to be tested prepare a brief sentence that can be written by the child on one line. Let the sentence read so that the word to be tested occurs at the end. This will not only provide a list for the teacher's convenience in correction, but, without the child's knowing it, test the spelling in the only way in which it is employed. After correction the teacher will have at hand for the following week a list of the words that each child needs to master. There is no need to waste time on words that he already knows how to spell. The teacher will also know the words that are difficult for most of the children and therefore need special attention. This list of generally difficult words will be the one that she will build up throughout the year. It will always contain the words that must be continuously drilled and repeated for permanent mastery. By degrees words should be eliminated from the list as they are mastered until none is left. It need hardly be pointed out that the dictation for spelling purposes may at the same time provide opportunities for penmanship drill and instruction in the elements of composition.

Procedure. In carrying on her daily work the teacher will find it useful once more to divide the weekly list, this time by five. A brief but intensive daily period should be devoted to spelling. Each day there should be presented some words that are new, some in review. Bearing in mind the general principles that have been discussed, the teacher will carry on her instruction by marching toward the goal of permanence of imagery along all of the avenues of approach. Put tersely, the procedure is to *hear, see, pronounce, write.*

Prior to the attack, the teacher will always assure herself that every child understands the word, as evidenced by his frequent and various use of it, not by the echo of definitions. The teacher should continuously test mastery by dictating the words in sentences without concentrating the child's attention on particular words. There can be no more compromise in spelling than in arithmetic. Only perfection is satisfactory. A child who cannot spell a word or words should learn to do so.

Teachers have discovered a number of specific devices that seem to be useful. Certain common words that must come early in school experience but present difficulties, such as *there* and *their, our* and *hour,* need to be isolated for specific perception and drill. It has been found useful

PERIOD OF AUTOMATIZATION

to teach some words in groups rather than individually. Sometimes words are grouped which have a similarity of meaning. More often words are grouped because of common phonetic elements. We cannot enter into the numerous inventions for learning to distinguish the different spelling of words that sound alike, such as *believe* and *receive,* many of which do prove helpful to some children.

The Dictionary. The fifth of the aims of the Spelling Committee of the Department of Superintendence was the development of a technique for the study of spelling. Although we teach a limited number of words, and although it is possible that as a by-product of this instruction our pupil will know how to spell others, there still remain numerous words that he may encounter and use later. It is true that excellent instruction will tend to habituate children to the close examination of new words and the unconscious mastery of their spelling. It is, however, unwise to rely on this aid exclusively. The Committee would have the school teach the child "how to use the dictionary in finding the pronunciation, meaning, and correct spelling of unfamiliar words, and what to do when in doubt concerning the spelling of a word."

While most of the children at the end of the primary period are too young to use the dictionary, some of them can make active use of it, and the opportunity should be available to them. There are, at this early age, just these points to learn: the alphabet and the ability to apply it in looking for a word in the dictionary or a name in the directory, letter by letter, as we proceed along the column. The spelling of the word is automatically discovered in the course of this hunt, but the child must be taught to note the definitions and to select the one that seems appropriate to the context that he has in mind. He should also be taught to learn the standard pronunciation as indicated.

Our elders were taught the alphabet as part of the business of learning to read and write. The methods of instruction having changed, our children pass through the grades without the ability to repeat the alphabet in sequence, and find themselves at a loss when looking for a name in the telephone book or for an author in the card index at the library. The need being pointed out, there should be no further discussion as to the methods of instruction. The only point that remains, and this is technical for the child, is the ability to understand the markings that indicate syllabication, accent, and pronunciation. The teacher who is herself shaky on this last point can easily master the symbols by studying the dictionary.

Even the most advanced children are too young to use the dictionary to learn syllabication, whether words are hyphenated, what part of speech a particular word is, its history or its synonyms. They may, however, be taught to look to the dictionary for authoritative information on other aspects. The spelling of a word or the preferred spelling if there are two forms in use, which words must be capitalized, the proper pronunciation or the preferred pronunciation, if more than one is in use, and the definition—this information is available. In addition to the formal guide found in the beginning pages of all dictionaries, we would refer the young teacher to a pamphlet published for distribution by G. and C. Merriam Company, Springfield, Mass.—*The Value of the Dictionary.*

THE THIRD SCHOOL YEAR—PENMANSHIP

During the first two years of work in handwriting we endeavor to establish all of the essential motor co-ordinations. During the third year the aim is to automatize these co-ordinations and the writing ability to the point where the child can give his undivided attention to content, free from awareness of the process of writing. No one has mastered the art of writing until, when he is engaged in it, he can devote all of his attention to the content he wants to express. To set him completely free, to make the ability to write fully his own, is the attainable object of the third year in school.

Pen and Ink. In the general trend toward ever improved quality, the child is, toward the end of the third year, introduced to pen and ink. This presents some mechanical difficulties that require attention. A fairly large wooden penholder, a pen with rounded point, and unglazed paper that takes ink well, with lines ruled half an inch apart, are advisable. It will take some time and care to teach the child how to hold the pen and dip the ink. It will be found useful at the beginning to work with pen and ink for only part of the period, using pencil the rest of the time. As he gradually becomes accustomed to them and masters the mechanical difficulties, pen and ink may completely replace the pencil during the formal penmanship period.

While the schools still go through the agony of pen, ink, penwipers, dipping and their sad consequences, it must be obvious that the whole procedure is obsolete. The time must soon come when manufacturers will supply the schools with inexpensive fountain pens and teachers will instruct their pupils how to fill, clean, and otherwise care for them. In cases where parents are willing and able to provide their children with fountain pens in the second term of the third or the first term of the fourth year, we strongly advise teachers to allow these pupils to substitute this modern writing instrument for the none too attractive inkwell-penholder combination.

Alignment, Slant, Spacing. Automatization is not the

only objective of this grade. The quality of the writing must be distinctly improved. Following the first two years in which attention was directed to the movement, the speed, and the form of the letters, and correction was limited to gross errors, the third year represents the beginning of attention to details. While attention must still be paid to the maintenance of speed, form, and fluency of movement, there are three elements of penmanship that demand emphasis during this year: alignment, slant, and spacing. We shall devote a brief paragraph to each of these elements.

Proper alignment calls for keeping the letters on the base line straight and the tops of the letters uniform at their several heights. It is most important to discover and to correct any tendency to write off the base line. Careful attention to placing the paper and maintaining it in proper position will be found a fundamental aid in staying on the base line.

Uniformity of slant makes the writing legible and pleasing to the eye. An acceptable slant is one that roughly approximates 25 degrees from the perpendicular. In attaining uniformity of slant, the child should be taught to keep all the strokes parallel to an imaginary main slant line. In the endeavor to show the child irregularities in the slant of his own writing, it will be found useful to draw straight lines through the letters that he has written, calling his attention to the variations from the main slant.

Even spacing makes the page pleasing and legible. Not only should the pupil learn to avoid crowding the letters, he should also realize the desirability of even spacing between words. A good mechanical rule is to assume that there should be one space between letters, two spaces between words, and three between sentences.

At this level, pupils should be required to write at the

rate of forty-four letters a minute. The size of the letters is indicated by the half-inch ruling.

REFERENCES FOR FURTHER STUDY

I Handwriting

Ayer, F. C., *Course of Study in Handwriting.* Seattle Public Schools, 1926.

Freeman, F. N., and Dougherty, M. L., *How to Teach Handwriting.* Boston, Houghton Mifflin Co., 1923.

West, P. V., *Changing Practice in Handwriting Instruction.* Bloomington, Public School Publishing Company, 1927.

II Spelling

Breed, F. S., *How to Teach Spelling.* Dansville, Owen Publishing Co., 1929.

Horn, Ernest, *Principles of Method in Teaching Spelling as Derived from Scientific Investigation;* Eighteenth Yearbook, National Society for the Study of Education. Bloomington, Public School Publishing Co., 1919.

Pryor, H. C., and Pittman, M. S., *A Guide to the Teaching of Spelling.* New York, The Macmillan Company, 1921.

Tidyman, W. F., *Teaching Spelling.* Yonkers, World Book Co., 1919.

CHAPTER XI

NUMBER: LAYING THE BASIS FOR COMPUTATION

In the realm of formal quantitative thinking, the primary teacher faces two main tasks. The first of these involves introducing the child to the concept of quantity. The second consists of giving him skill in computation.

It is difficult for the adult, habituated by years to habits of quantitative thought, to realize that the child has it all to learn. We suggest that the student select a child of five years or younger who has learned to count and carry out the following procedure of the Stanford-Binet Intelligence Test:

> Place thirteen pennies in a horizontal row before the child and ask him to count them and tell you how many there are. To make the instructions clear, add this direction: "Count them with your finger, this way," and yourself pointing to the first penny, say, "one, now go ahead."

It will be found in most instances that the child well under five years of age who can "count" is repeating figures by rote but has no concept of the meaning of his repetition. When given a chance to count objects, he cannot determine how many there are. He will not point to them one at a time. The test contains other interesting evidence of quantitative inexperience at various age levels as, for example, the problem of determining which of two objects that look alike is the heavier. Prior to a certain age the child will look at them and point one out arbitrarily. Length, height, weight, fractional parts of a

LAYING THE BASIS FOR COMPUTATION

whole, distance, time—all of these belong to man's concept of quantity to which the child is to be formally introduced.

Computation is the actual skill. So far as concerns the elementary school, this consists of the four fundamental processes of adding, subtracting, multiplying, and dividing whole numbers, fractions, and decimals. Work in the primary grades does not go beyond whole numbers. But it is not enough to limit instruction to the processes, lest the children master them as abstractions in the same way in which they learned to count during their pre-school experience. With the processes must go application to real problems which give continuous evidence that, in addition to the ability to add, subtract, divide, and multiply, the pupils also know when each process is in order.

Concepts of Quantity

The work must, obviously, begin with the effort to introduce the child to the realm of quantity. Fortunately he is no stranger here. During their years of living and learning, the environment introduces most children informally to all of the experiences that await them in school. It is so with concepts of quantity.

Rational Counting. The dangers of rote counting have already been indicated. We must now set ourselves the task of building up in the mind of the child the functional concept of number. Children choose groups at play, sort papers into groups according to size and color, and the teacher invents numberless opportunities to instill this first quantitative idea with which instruction begins, *the recognition of the distinction between one and several.*

The object is to have the child learn to recognize groups varying in number from two to five or six. He will first learn that groups differ in size. He has *more* or *less* marbles, pencils, or apples, than his classmate. Groups also may be the same in number. This row has as many boys as that row. Approaching this concept in still another way, the teacher asks a child to put the books on the second, third, or fourth shelf, to select every second object, and in other ways gives the idea of number grouping and sequence.

Not forgetting to keep the rote-counting ability active, we now test its reality by applying the numbers to objects, as three apples, four boys. We offer the pupil seven marbles—too large a number to recognize at once. To learn how many there are he points to each in turn and counts. We ask him to hand us a certain number of marbles. When he can select the correct number every time, we know that the child can count rationally.

Reading and Writing Numbers. We must now proceed to teach the recognition of the written symbols which represent the quantitative concept that the child has in mind. Procedures are numerous or easily invented. Here is a typical game:

> Have a board about 18 inches square upon which the numbers from 1 to 12 inclusive are printed. Fasten an arrow in the middle so that it will spin easily. A pupil spins the wheel and tells the number the arrow points to. If he does not know, he goes to the calendar, and counts until he comes to the number indicated by the arrow.

The best procedure is to teach counting, reading, and writing numbers at the same time. The child should be watched from the beginning to see that he makes the numbers correctly. The blackboard is the most economical and convenient means of teaching the entire class to write figures correctly, and should always precede the

LAYING THE BASIS FOR COMPUTATION

seat work with paper and pencil. The digits, about three inches in height, should be written on the blackboard as a model, between lines which show the tops of 4 and 6 extending above the upper line and the 7 and 9 projecting below the lower one.

1 2 3 4 5 6 7 8 9 0

Assign each pupil a permanent place at the board. Write the figures under instruction on the board about three inches in height at each child's place, on a level with the eyes. Direct the children to trace and retrace the figures being learned and then have them write rows of figures directly under the model. Care should be taken to have the pupils write the figures in the one accurate way. Left to themselves, children may painstakingly draw instead of writing the numbers, sometimes erasing and improving part of a figure. An excellent way to teach the numbers is in pairs in the following order: 1-4, 0-5, 7-9, 2-3, 5-8. Another order of writing the numbers, advocated by some teachers, is this: Group the numbers that are (1) made primarily by strokes, i.e., 1, 4, 7; (2) made by curves that go clockwise, i.e., 2, 3; made by curves that go counter-clockwise, i.e., 5, 6, 8, 9, 0.

Some competent teachers defer the instruction in writing numbers for some weeks after the beginning of school. They contend that it is wiser to let the child learn to read the numbers on the board. They consider that after the numbers have become familiar to the child in this manner, he will learn to write them more rapidly and with less effort. Thus he attains a feeling of accomplishment with a minimum of monotonous drill and unsuccessful attempts.

Extension of the Number System. When pupils can actually make use of the numbers from 1 to 10 in their everyday activities, they are ready for the extension of the number system. We should then proceed to have them count by 2's and 5's to 50. Next we teach the vertical "tens lanes" of the decimal system (10-20-30-40, etc., to 100) and each horizontal "lane" (11-20; 21-30; to 100) covering the number system in this way from 10 to 100.

Concepts of Measurement. The work in counting will inevitably include quantitative ideas such as how much, how many, more-less, short-long, longer-shorter, larger-smaller, higher-lower, heavier-lighter, nearer-farther. There are, however, other aspects of quantitative thinking which the child meets continually in life and which must be presented to him in the primary grades. There is no need to do this work in a formal manner by way of drill. Since he will not require these concepts in his actual computation in the primary grades, the child may be allowed to learn them incidentally in the course of his numerous activities and projects. But learn them he should.

The teacher who has before her a formal statement of the concepts of measurement with which her pupils must become familiar in the course of their experience during the first three years in school, will determine from time to time what the children know and what they need to learn. With this information in hand she will see to it that opportunities present themselves for learning and applying this information. A brief summary is given below for this purpose.

Time. Man measures time, and children should learn the names of the days of the week, the months of the year, the meaning of yesterday, tomorrow. A calendar on the wall, referred to occasionally, will be found useful for all of this and will, in addition, give the child the habit of knowing the day of the month. As they develop, chil-

LAYING THE BASIS FOR COMPUTATION 127

dren should learn that the years follow one another in a numbered series, and know in which year they live. They should learn that the day is divided into twenty-four hours which, in turn are divided into minutes and seconds. Ultimately they should grasp the relationship between the fraction of an hour and the corresponding number of minutes.

Units of Measure. Man measures distance, weight, and liquid quantity, and children should be given comprehension of certain of the units of measure. They should learn the meaning of an inch, a foot, a yard, a mile, and simple fractions thereof, such as a half and a quarter. They should likewise learn the meaning of a pint, quart, gallon, and their halves and quarters. They should learn about ounces and pounds, and simple fractions of the pound such as a half and a quarter.

Money. Man uses money in his daily life, and the child cannot wait for the work in decimals for his knowledge of the several coins, and the number of cents contained in each.

Parts of the Whole. While we do not apply the four processes to fractions in the primary grades, certain concepts are essential in daily living and are easily grasped. We should see to it that pupils secure true and basic concepts of the half, the fourth, and possibly other easily comprehensible divisions of the whole, such as a third and an eighth.

Symbols other than Numbers. There are, finally, certain written symbols and verbal usages which the primary child should learn. By this is meant such terms as a dozen, such signs as those representing the dollar and the cent, and the Roman numerals. It will be well to teach all of these symbols in practical application. In the case of the Roman numerals, for example, the child's attention should be called to the face of the clock, the method of numbering the chapters of a book, or the dating of a cornerstone.

Organizing the Work in Computation

Sequence of Skills. There are two warnings for the student or the inexperienced teacher beginning this work in computation, each of which has occurred in other portions of this book but cannot be overstressed.

The order in which the elements of computation, addition, subtraction, multiplication, and division, one after the other, will be discussed in this book is not the order in which they are to be taught to children. Insofar as possible they should be taught together. Even while we are teaching the very beginnings of addition the child may secure his first concept of division by learning the meaning of a half or a quarter. In general, however, the work should be taken up in the order in which we discuss it.

Need for Individualization. In a skill such as calculation, the value of class instruction is reduced to a minimum, the need for individual instruction is at its height. Consider a class in swimming or a class in automobile driving. Suppose that a certain number of days or lessons after the commencement of instruction the teacher were asked "where the class is." The only possible answer would be that the class is scattered all the way from *no ability* to *complete achievement*. A skill must be mastered by each individual at his own rate of progress. Insistence that the class go forward at a certain rate can have only one result: the rate will be too slow for some of the pupils and too fast for others.

At the educational level of the primary grades, too slow a rate is inefficient, but too fast a rate may be tragic. It may mean that certain children will be required to go

LAYING THE BASIS FOR COMPUTATION

forward before they have mastered the preceding step. This in turn will mean that for all the years of their further schooling these children will be handicapped by this lack of thoroughness at the beginning. In arithmetic, the term "class" should be interpreted to mean the group which the teacher is instructing, not the group which she is instructing simultaneously. Arithmetic is a drill subject and in drill each individual has his own set of habits to acquire. It is futile to teach "the class."

Work in this field should be individualized to the greatest possible degree. Fortunately for the teacher the American publishers of school books and teaching materials have developed a wealth of material for individual drill. This is one investment that no Board can afford to overlook.

The Addition-Subtraction Combinations and Facts

There are forty-five possible combinations of the digits from 1 to 9 and the first step in teaching addition and subtraction is to give the child habit-responses with regard to these so that he knows them *without the need of counting*. The response must be instantaneous, and come not as the solution of a problem or the comprehension of a situation or the result of a rapid count, but *as an arbitrary habit*. The combinations are presented on the next page for the convenience of the student.

The question is frequently raised as to whether teaching a combination one way, for example "8 and 7 are 15," automatically teaches the reverse, namely that "7 and 8 are 15." It is hardly worth while to enter this controversy. Rather than take a chance, it is the part of wisdom to teach the combinations both ways. Eliminating those which remain the same either way, as "9 and 9," we find that reversing the order provides us with 81 addition facts. Some would go so far as to combine each digit with

1	1	1	1	1	1	1	1	1
1	2	3	4	5	6	7	8	9

	2	2	2	2	2	2	2	2
	2	3	4	5	6	7	8	9

		3	3	3	3	3	3	3
		3	4	5	6	7	8	9

			4	4	4	4	4	4
			4	5	6	7	8	9

				5	5	5	5	5
				5	6	7	8	9

					6	6	6	6
					6	7	8	9

						7	7	7
						7	8	9

							8	8
							8	9

								9
								9

zero and have the child memorize the answer, thus producing (when used in each direction) one hundred addition facts. Our own opinion is that the child can be taught once for all that zero added to or subtracted from a number leaves it the same.

There are, finally, the *higher decade facts*. It is obvious that if the child is ultimately to add single columns whose total exceeds 10, he will need to form habits of instant

LAYING THE BASIS FOR COMPUTATION

response for combinations beyond the original 45. In other words, in addition to knowing the answer to "8 and 4," he needs to know the answer to "18 and 4," "28 and 4," "38 and 4," etc. There are 765 higher decade facts the sums of which are less than 100. There will be no need to teach every higher decade fact as such. Beginning with those that total less than 20, going on to those which total less than 30, etc., the teacher will continue the drill until such time as she finds that it is no longer necessary.

This topic of the higher decade facts is referred to here for the sake of logical organization. It is, however, not desirable to teach these facts at the same time as the original 45 combinations. The teacher will begin single column addition early, perhaps before all of the 81 addition facts are mastered, and possibly cover all of the work in the higher decade facts later as an incidental part of the work in column addition.

Some concrete advice on the addition-subtraction combinations follows:

1. Make every effort to prevent counting, and to secure an immediate, automatic response to every statement of a combination. One way to prevent counting is to give or flash the answer immediately. Any time allowed the child gives him a chance to count and defeats the purpose, *which is the formation of a habit.*

2. Teach the correlatives together: At the same time that you teach 8 plus 7, teach 7 plus 8.

3. Teach first those combinations whose sums do not equal more than 10, then the others.

4. The best time to prepare for subtraction is the very time when we are preparing for addition. At the same time that the child learns that 6 and 4 are 10, he should be learning that 10 less 4 is 6, and that 10

less 6 is 4. The addition and subtraction facts can be formed into natural units of *four* each; two of addition and two of subtraction, except the doubles: i.e., 3 plus 4 equals 7; 4 plus 3 equals 7; 7 minus 4 equals 3; 7 minus 3 equals 4. The missing number drill is an excellent device. Example: 7 and how many are 9? 5 is how many more than 3? 5 is how many less than 7?

5. The work just outlined requires a great deal of drill, and in drill, as indicated above, each child may have reached a different stage and require different work. No teacher can get around a class and give each child all of the work he requires. Flash cards and other useful devices for individual self-correcting work are essential. The teacher might, of course, prepare such materials. Otherwise she should avail herself of the convenient and ingenious devices available commercially.

Desirable Outcomes

As stated at the beginning of this chapter and, in greater detail elsewhere in this volume, we consider it best to view the whole primary period as a unit rather than as a series of units based on the calendar, and we consider progress in the acquisition of a skill an individual rather than a class matter. Under the best instruction, individual children will achieve the outcomes noted below at varying ages and after varying lengths of time in school.

It remains true, nevertheless, that averages can be discovered, and it will be useful to the teacher to compare with general practice the progress of her group and of the individuals that compose it. For these reasons we have prepared the following outcomes half-year by half-year, basing them on the literature, the courses of study, and the practice in American public schools.

LAYING THE BASIS FOR COMPUTATION

First Half Year
   Quantity
      A. Direction and relationship
        1. Right-left, behind-in-front, above-below, over-under, top-bottom-middle, high-low, up-down
        2. First-last, here-there
      B. Size and measurement
        1. Long-short, large-small, inch-foot, as many as
        2. How many, as much as, how much, more-less
        3. Whole-part, none-all
      C. Time
        1. Day, week, month
        2. Hour, minute
      D. Money
        1. Cent
        2. Nickel
        3. Dime
      E. Rational Counting
        1. Ability to count numbers to 100
        2. Ability to read and write numbers to 100

Second Half Year
   I. Quantity
      A. Size and measurement
        1. Large-small, big-little, wide-narrow, thick-thin
        2. Tall-short, pair, far-near, heavy-light
        3. Pint, quart, cup, dozen, pound
      B. Time
        1. The year
        2. The clock
      C. Money
        1. Penny, dime, nickel
        2. The meaning of buying, selling, paying, price and cost
      D. Fractions: meaning of a half

II. Computation
    A. Ability to count to 50 by 2's, 5's, and 10's
    B. Ability to name the number between two given numbers, before and after a given number
    C. Mastery of the 21 addition-subtraction combinations whose sums do not exceed 5

CHAPTER XII

NUMBER: INTRODUCING THE FOUR OPERATIONS WITH WHOLE NUMBERS

Addition and Subtraction

Single Column Addition. There is no need to put off formal addition until the child has mastered all of the 45 combinations and their reverse, the 81 facts. As soon as the children have learned the first 25 combinations whose total does not exceed 10, they should be introduced to column addition. We do not consider that it makes any difference whether the adding of the column is done up or down, but a habit should be formed and adhered to either way.

When children add columns of two or three digits whose total does not exceed 18, they actually have nothing new to learn except the form, and will enjoy the pleasure of applying what they know. This work in single-column addition should be going on while all of the combinations are being mastered, but the total should not exceed 18 until the higher decade facts have been learned.

This is the best time to teach the zero facts, namely that zero added to a number or a number added to zero does not change the number. The subtraction aspect of zero should be taught at the same time. Slowly, with the teaching of the higher decade facts, we may increase the height of the single column, adding a total of more than 18. This will, at the same time, teach the facts and prepare the child for two-column addition.

There are two useful drill methods that the teacher

may employ in introducing the child to the higher decades: She may use flash cards for drill like this, always placing the higher number above, $\frac{24}{3}$ $\frac{24}{7}$, or she may extend to five or six the single-column addition problems of three digits to which she should limit herself in the beginning.

Multiple Column Addition-Carrying. After extended experience with single-column addition, we come to two-column addition and the problem of carrying. Many devices have been used to explain this process. Our own opinion is that most children require no explanation, and few would grasp it if offered. We see no urgent reason for endeavoring to rationalize the process. In the comparatively rare cases where pupils demand a reason for the procedure, the teacher will find it easy enough to show the child that a number more than 10 is simply added to the column which represents the tens, and so with the higher columns. We do not favor writing down the number carried, a practice sometimes recommended.

The following specific advice is offered to the teacher so far as concerns multiple column addition:

    1. Bear in mind that computation is not a matter of explaining and understanding, but of fundamental habit-formation. A very large amount of drill, made as interesting and practical as possible, is essential.

    2. In preparing your examples in two- and three-column addition, provide blank spaces in the second, third, and fourth columns, to give the children experience in adding a column that has gaps.

    3. Do not allow the child to repeat each combination, as "2 and 3 are 5, 5 and 6 are 11." Train him to think "5, 11," etc. Continue to be on guard against counting. If necessary go back to drill on the combinations.

FOUR OPERATIONS WITH WHOLE NUMBERS

4. Emphasize accuracy, not speed. When all the basic habits have been properly formed, speed will take care of itself. To insure accuracy, make checking a fundamental habit with the child. In addition, this should be done by repeating the work, adding in the opposite direction from the way in which the child has been trained. Check up if the original addition is down, and down if the original addition is upward.

5. Do not present examples beyond the realm of the practical. There is no need for addition practice beyond three columns of four or five digits in height.

Subtraction. There is only one new element in subtraction, i.e., borrowing. But the general form should be taught before facing the problem that calls for borrowing, and for this the training we have given the child in the combinations and facts has prepared him.

Begin the work with many examples in which each subtrahend digit is smaller than or equal to the minuend digit just above it. This will give the child training in the general form, and pleasure in applying what he already knows. For obvious reasons, there must be no zeros in the minuend. It will, however, be useful to include examples in which a number is subtracted from the same number, leaving zero.

The teacher will begin with a two-digit line. There is no need to go beyond four digits in each line. It will be important, however, to give experience with examples in which the subtrahend contains a smaller number of digits than the minuend. This will teach the child to understand that the gaps, with which he has already had experience in multiple column addition, represent zero.

Borrowing. Discussions of the methods of borrowing, and there are four of them, tend to become metaphysical and, unfortunately, futile. We shall deal with two, the take-away and the additive method: In the example, $\begin{array}{r}64\\ \underline{46}\end{array}$ the reasoning in each method follows:

(1) 6 from 14 leaves 8. The borrowing has reduced the 6 of the minuend to 5 and 4 from 5 is one.

(2) 6 and 8 (writing the 8 in the remainder) are 14. Add the 1 to the 4 of the subtrahend, and 5 from 6 leaves 1.

We are not impressed by the argument that the additive method is economical in that it makes use of only the addition combinations. We do feel that the take-away method seems more in accord with the logic of the situation and has the distinct advantage of enabling us to check the subtraction by adding the remainder and the subtrahend, a process that would not really "check" where the additive method is used. However, experimental evidence has never shown that either process is superior to the other and we regard both as sufficiently satisfactory.

We do wish to state, however, that whichever method is used should be drilled as a habit rather than elaborately presented as a theory. As stated in connection with carrying in addition, we do not consider it practical or necessary to burden the average child by trying to get him to understand the theories that underlie the operations. The occasional child who cannot be satisfied until he understands why he is doing certain things will demand his explanation.

The teacher will begin with examples of two digits in the minuend and subtrahend, in which the need for borrowing occurs just once. When this has been mastered, the number of digits should be increased to three and four, and the problems arranged so that borrowing occurs more than once.

FOUR OPERATIONS WITH WHOLE NUMBERS 139

The most difficult phase of borrowing concerns the zero in the minuend. This should be taught last, after the other habits have been well established, and should also be presented with a minimum of explanation and a maximum of drill.

In conclusion, we offer the following specific advice in teaching subtraction:

(1) Too much language, even though silent rather than oral, will interfere with speed. Many of the readers of this book will recall the astonishing verbal formulas with which they were taught to do their borrowing. For this there is simply no need. One can increase the number just above and decrease the one to the left of it without ritual.

(2) Subtraction should be checked by addition every time. It represents a valuable habit toward accuracy, and it is good drill in addition. We do not favor the practice of writing down the results of this addition even at the beginning of the instruction.

(3) Employ drill freely at each step. Do not go forward to any step before the preceding one has been mastered. Do not leave the child to himself too long during the process of acquiring a new habit, lest he fall into error and provide the problem of unlearning later.

Multiplication and Division

The Multiplication and Division Facts. As in addition and subtraction, so in multiplication and division, the underlying complementary facts should be taught together. The number of possible multiplication combinations of digits less than 9 is, as the reader may note by turning back to the table of addition combinations, 45. When taught in both directions, as should be done, these provide 81 multiplication facts. If zeros are taught as facts, which we do not deem necessary, there are 100.

There is a tendency in contemporary practice to stop with the learning of these 81 facts, the highest combination being 9 x 9. While most teachers will, in the nature of things, be guided by the courses of study in their own communities, we see no reason for, and some dangers in, abandoning the older practice of continuing the mastery of combinations to 12 x 12, and later adding the 15's up to five or six times fifteen. The practice of carrying the learned combinations to the 12's raises the number to be mastered from 45 to 78.

Whichever number of combinations and facts we adopt, the effort, as in addition and subtraction, must be to secure an instantaneous response *based on habit, achieved by drill*. As in addition, so in multiplication and division, (1) the aim should be to secure an immediate, automatic response, (2) much material for individual work should be provided, (3) the correlatives should be taught together, and (4) the easiest combinations should be taught first.

There is no virtue in running through the Tables logically, as the 2's, 3's to 9 or 12. While there is some evidence regarding the order of difficulty in the learning of the multiplication and division combinations and facts, we hardly think it necessary for the teacher to hold herself to any routine in their presentation. The teacher who individualizes her work, minimizes class instruction, and wastes no time teaching a child what he already knows, will endeavor to determine for each child which of the combinations that child knows and set him to work at those that he still has to learn. In general, it will be advisable to begin with those whose product is less than 10, proceed to those whose product is less than 20, and so on to the end.

FOUR OPERATIONS WITH WHOLE NUMBERS

The division combinations and facts should be taught at the same time as the multiplication combinations and facts. This is important. In the first place, it simplifies both processes and, in the second place, it explains each through the other. Example: 7 x 4 is 28, 4 x 7 is 28, 28 divided by 7 equals 4, and 28 divided by 4 equals 7.

First Step—Multiplication and Division without Carrying. The teacher should present multiplication and division together step by step, always being careful to provide ample drill to fix the multiplication process as a habit before showing how to check in division. This will, obviously, be followed by examples that originate as division, and which teach the child to check this process by multiplication. The habit of multiplying upward should be promptly established.

Before teaching any of the difficulties in formal multiplication and division, indeed, before all of the multiplication and division facts have been mastered, and as an additional method of teaching them, the teacher should present the forms of multiplication and division. *Use the same series of combinations for the multiplication and the division in each unit of the drill.* Example:

$$\begin{array}{cc} 4231 & \overline{4231} \\ \underline{2} & 2/8462 \\ 8462 & \end{array}$$

During this preliminary phase the discussion will be limited to multiplication examples in which the multiplier has only one digit, the multiplicand no more than three or four, *and carrying is not involved.* The division examples will be limited to those which have one digit in the divisor, no more than three or four in the quotient, and involve neither carrying nor remainder. Where the divisor goes evenly into every digit, there is really nothing new to learn, except the form which is good preparation for the next step. In this preliminary drill it will be well to include examples in which the first *two digits* of the dividend contain the divisor, e.g., 4/12.

This type of drill will serve the following purposes: (1) It will continue to fix the response to the combinations. (2) It will give the child the pleasure of applying what he knows. (3) It will teach the forms in multiplication and division incidentally in preparation for later work. (4) It will tend to impress the essential habit of checking: multiplication by division, and division by multiplication.

Second Step—Multiplication and Division with Carrying. Teaching children to carry in multiplication is much the same as teaching them to carry in addition. If this has been mastered, there should be no difficulty here. In multiplication, the child has one more factor to bear in mind. He must multiply and at the same time remember the number he is to carry. After enough work has been done with carrying in multiplication, the pupil should be introduced to examples in division that involve carrying. The examples at this point should involve no remainders, thus providing much drill in carrying without the complication of a remainder. Example:

$$\begin{array}{r} 62 \\ 7/\overline{434} \\ 42 \\ \hline 14 \\ 14 \\ \hline \end{array}$$

Third Step—The Remainder in Division. An excellent way to present the problem of the remainder is by way of a one-digit divisor and a one-digit dividend, thus

$$\begin{array}{r} 2\ \ 1/2 \\ 2/\overline{5}\ \ \ \ \ \end{array}$$ It is obvious that this drill can begin orally, and that we soon move forward to examples involving two

FOUR OPERATIONS WITH WHOLE NUMBERS 143

or more digits in which, without carrying, we have a last digit that involves a remainder, thus 3/25. After the child has learned to handle the idea of the remainder, the number of digits in the dividend should be increased so that they involve more than one in the quotient. The child is still free from the need of carrying, but he has learned the form of working his problems out in detail as follows:

$$\begin{array}{r} 71\ 1/8 \\ 8\overline{)569} \\ 56 \\ \hline 9 \\ 8 \\ \hline 1 \end{array}$$

Fourth Step—Division with Carrying and Remainder. The next step involves much work and drill with examples that have a single-digit divisor and dividends of three or four digits which provide experience with both carrying and remainders. Example:

$$\begin{array}{r} 67\ 3/4 \\ 4\overline{)271} \\ 24 \\ \hline 31 \\ 28 \\ \hline 3 \end{array}$$

Fifth Step—The Zero Difficulty in Multiplication and Division. So long as we limit our work to single-digit multipliers and divisors, the zero presents problems only when it occurs in the multiplicand or in the quotient. As we stated when dealing with addition and subtraction, the best time to teach the significance of zero is when we meet it in a problem. The best way to present the zero in multiplication is to recall the situation in addition and subtraction, where we learned that it had no effect on the results. In division, the problem that involves a zero in the quotient requires very careful attention, for example:

$$\begin{array}{r} 602 \\ 7\overline{\smash{)}4214} \\ \underline{42} \\ 14 \\ \underline{14} \end{array}$$

As the student knows by this time, we do not favor complicated explanations. The essential thing is the right habit. In this instance, the child must learn to *write a figure in the quotient each time he carries one down.* If the divisor cannot be contained in the dividend, then that fact must be recorded by a zero in the quotient.

Long Division First. Most of the readers of this volume, in looking over the foregoing examples, will remark on the fact that we have used the long division form with examples involving single digit divisors, something that is, obviously, not done in adult computation. The explanation is that modern students in this field have reversed the traditional process of teaching short division before long division, contending that the former is a short method and more difficult because it involves keeping in mind quantities which in the longer process are written out. It should therefore be learned later. There is little danger that the pupil will later fail to avail himself of his ability to divide single digits into dividends by the short method. At any rate, this method will be established for him later in his school career.

Completing the Work in Multiplication and Division. We do not propose to discuss multiplication involving more than single-digit multipliers, and division involving more than single-digit divisors. The reason is that these processes are usually deferred to the upper grades. The

FOUR OPERATIONS WITH WHOLE NUMBERS 145

bright child found in the primary grades who should complete the processes will have no difficulty in mastering the additional formal procedure of placing the second and third partial products and adding them, or of estimating the quotient figures.

Concluding Remarks on Procedure in Teaching Computation

A Minimum of Explanation. A contemporary novelist, looking back on his school days, complains in one of his books because he was never told why "if you wanted to divide one fraction by another, you turned the second fraction upside down." Prompted by much the same feeling, the authorities advise the explanation of the several processes, showing the child that addition is a short way to count and multiplication a short way to add, that to divide a number by 4 is to secure a quarter of that number. They advise that we help the pupil to understand the reason for carrying and borrowing by visualization and give him detailed explanations of the problems involving zero.

We consider that these are abstractions, and difficult abstractions, and that comprehension of the reasons for the processes is not necessary except for those children who want the explanations. There is no harm, indeed, much advantage in teaching computation on the basis of habit.

A Maximum of Application. On the other hand, we have no tolerance for the idea of teaching arithmetic as a set of esoteric processes without relation to reality. We would insist on continuous application, step by step, by the method of presenting numberless problems which involve the processes and show the child how and when they apply. That is poor teaching, indeed, which results in the child's actually being able to add, subtract, multiply, and divide, even where many digits are involved, but not knowing why and when to do so. *A minimum of explanation but a maximum of application* of each process is a good rule.

Incidental Introduction to Quantitative Thought. It is hardly necessary to add that we do not favor formal instruction in any of the content here referred to as "concepts of quantity." Incidentally, as a component part of the problems in which we apply the processes of computation as we learn them, and as part of numerous activities with which primary education must be concerned so extensively, these concepts should be met and mastered. They should, however, be learned, informal though the process be, and for that reason they are listed with the other desirable outcomes at the close of the chapter.

Standard Tests to Check Effectiveness of Teaching. This is no place to discuss the theory of standard tests or, as they are also called, achievement or educational tests. We do, however, call the attention of the present and prospective teacher and administrator to the fact that admirable tests have been devised and published and that these are indispensable to the class, the school, and the school system.

These tests, commercially published and sold in quantity for class use, accompanied by manuals of directions and norms, will enable the teacher and the administrator to judge the outcomes of the work of the school, the class, and the individual child. They should also be used constantly for diagnostic purposes to determine the location of class and school difficulties and the needs of individual children. The scientifically devised and standardized tests are infinitely superior to any "home made" or informal method of supervising and judging the achievements of classes and of individual children.

FOUR OPERATIONS WITH WHOLE NUMBERS

Desirable Outcomes [1]

Third Half Year
I. Quantity
    A. Size and measurement
        1. Inch, foot, yard, and their relationship to one another
        2. Cup, pint, quart, gallon, and their relationship to one another
        3. Deep-shallow-depth, high-low-height, full-empty
    B. Time
        1. Minute-hour, day-week, month-year, and their relationship to one another
        2. The clock and the hands around the clock.
    C. Money
        1. Amount, bank, change
        2. Dollar, half-dollar, quarter
    D. Fractions
        1. Meaning of a quarter
        2. Meaning of three-quarters
II. Computation
    A. Notation and numeration
        1. Ability to count, read, and write numbers to 200
        2. Ability to count by 2's, 5's, and 10's to 100
    B. Addition and subtraction
        1. All combinations whose sums do not exceed 9 and up to 39 within a decade, i.e., 23 plus 5
        2. Ability to add single-digit columns of three numbers within the facts so far learned

---

[1] See the introductory paragraphs under this heading at the end of the last chapter.

        C. Meaning of words and phrases; add-addition-sum; subtract-subtraction-difference; column-row-line; equals-are equal to; answer (to a problem or example); the signs + and =

Fourth Half Year
- I. Quantity
  - A. Direction, size, and measurement
    1. Weight, pound
    2. Length, ½ inch
  - B. Time
    1. Hour
    2. Minute
    3. Second
    4. Telling time
  - C. Money
    - Making change involving amounts up to $1.00
  - D. Fractions
    1. Meaning of a third
    2. Meaning of two-thirds
  - E. Roman numerals to V
- II. Computation
  - A. Notation and numeration
    1. Ability to read and write numbers to 500
    2. Ability to read dollars ($) and cents (¢)
  - B. Addition and subtraction
    1. All addition-subtraction combinations
    2. Column addition of three single-digits
    3. Addition by endings within the same and into the highest decade, i.e.,
       16   16
        3   7
       —   —

FOUR OPERATIONS WITH WHOLE NUMBERS

    C. Subtraction: 2- and 3-place figures which do not involve borrowing

Fifth Half Year
I. Quantity
    A. Measurement
        1. Linear: foot, yard, city block, mile
        2. Liquid: cup, glass-full, pint, quart, gallon
    B. Fractions: meaning of a fifth, a tenth, and a twelfth
II. Computation
    A. Technical vocabulary: which costs more; subtracted from; state the sums; take from; which is larger; subtract the smaller from the larger; check your answers; state the missing numbers; one-half, one-fourth, three-fourths; find the total cost; what change should I receive; what is the difference or remainder; equal to or equals, for $=$; add, if the sign is $+$; decimal point, minus; plus
    B. Notation and numeration
        1. Ability to read numbers to 1000
        2. Ability to write numbers to 1000
    C. Addition
        1. The higher decade combinations as facts and an ability to use these facts in column addition
        2. Column addition with 2- or 3-place figures, sometimes indicating money
    D. Subtraction; borrowing, examples limited to 3 figures
    E. Multiplication and division
        1. The multiplication facts whose product does not exceed 45 where they are taught through 9, or 60

where they are taught through 12, i.e., 5 x 9 or 5 x 12
    2. The reverse facts of division
        a. Ability to multiply a three-digit multiplicand by a single-digit multiplier
        b. The reverse in division where no carrying is involved

Sixth Half Year
  I. Quantity
      A. Thorough mastery of all the concepts of quantity listed for the preceding five terms
      B. Roman numerals to XII
      C. Comprehension of the meaning of unitary fractions from 1/2 to 1/12 or more
  II. Computation
      A. Established ability to read and write numbers
      B. Final mastery of all the primary addition-subtraction and multiplication-division facts
          1. Mastery of higher decade addition and subtraction facts which total 39 or above
          2. Ability to apply these in column addition and in multiplication with carrying
      C. Addition
          1. Ability to add single columns of five digits each
          2. Ability to add shorter columns of two- and three-digit lines, involving all the difficulties
      D. Subtraction: up to four-digit lines involving all the difficulties
      E. Multiplication and division
          1. Ability to multiply a three-digit

multiplicand by a single-digit multiplier
2. Ability to divide a four-digit dividend by a single-digit divisor, involving all the difficulties
3. Ability to apply all of the foregoing processes with attention to the decimal system where money is involved

REFERENCES FOR FURTHER STUDY

Broxon, J. P., and Coffman, L. D., *The Teaching of Arithmetic*. Chicago, Row, Peterson, 1925.

Clark, J. R., Otis, A. S., and Hatton, C., *First Steps in Teaching Number*. Yonkers, World Book Co., 1929.

Morton, R. L., *Teaching Arithmetic in the Primary Grades*. Newark, Silver Burdett & Co., 1927.

National Society for the Study of Education, *Twenty-Ninth Yearbook*. Bloomington, Public School Publishing Co., 1930.

CHAPTER XIII

SPEECH—INFORMAL COMMUNICATION

The Influence of Environment. Of all the experiences and accomplishments which the child brings with him on entering the elementary school, he has advanced furthest in the art of speech. Indeed, his ability to understand and make himself understood is so entirely adequate for his needs that we are likely to think of it as completely achieved. We tend to take our point of departure where the environment has left off. It rarely occurs to us to teach the child to speak. He has, it appears, already picked this up.

The beginnings of speech, as we all know, go far back into infancy. Because the learning process begins so early, we have been ignoring the art of speech in school, and limiting our efforts to the structure of language. We are, however, becoming increasingly aware that our failure to do formal work in speech has been an oversight, and a grave one. Commenting on the American voice, one competent author describes it as "composed of spurious sounds, falsely produced and misdirected." There is, obviously, no organic national defect to account for the comparative rarity of pleasant speaking voices. It is a matter of bad habit, just as a pleasant, cultivated voice and clear enunciation are rooted in good habit.

Let us turn to the manner in which most of our children have learned to speak. They have "picked it up." There is, obviously, no objection to this method of acquiring habits, provided we are careful as to the source from which the "picking up" is done. It had better be admitted at once that the history of the settlement of the country, the composition of the population, and the social ideals that are dominant are such as to present for the schools of our country a problem different from, and more difficult than, that of other societies.

"In no subject," says Percival Chubb,[1] "do the forces of social environment against which the school has to strive make themselves so continually felt as they do in English. In arithmetic, or science, or geography, the teacher may sow on virgin soil; the English teacher must sow on soil choked with the weeds of bad habit and must ceaselessly ply the hoe against untiring enemies. Good speech is a habit, a point of social manners. The average English, or German, or French child speaks and writes his native tongue more correctly than the average American child not so much because the teaching is more painstaking as because the standard of social manners is higher."

This statement, in all its implications, is perhaps open to question. It is probably not true that American speech is more harsh and less pleasing than that of other peoples and other countries. It is less pleasing than the speech habits of the better educated and socially superior sections of other countries. To refer to people who speak our own language, it is not true that the slum dweller of London or the peasant in the farming regions of England possesses any superiority in speech over the average American. The difference only holds as between the better educated groups.

In a country which holds to class divisions, the child who has the privilege of belonging to the upper group picks up his speech in an excellent environment. In

[1] Chubb, Percival, *The Teaching of English*. New York, The Macmillan Company, 1902.

school he associates almost exclusively with children of the same social level. We in America are, on the other hand, engaged in living out a cherished dream. We mingle children of all the classes. We mingle children of many races. To add to the difficulty, we suffer from a peculiar interpretation of democracy. It seems to have become priggish to speak one's language with care, so that many who know better hide their shameful superiority behind a mask of *argot*.

It is only with this in mind that we may agree with Mr. Chubb: "We lack linguistic conscience and linguistic pride in this country. We do not attach to illiteracy the stigma that attaches to it abroad,—a stigma that money, dress, ostentation, cannot atone for. Until with us, also, to be a gentleman is, as a first essential, to use gentle speech, we shall not cure, we shall but cauterize, illiteracy."

Whatever the procedure elsewhere may be, our country awaits the generation of teachers who by determined, conscious effort, will improve and beautify the speech of the American people.

The Task of the Teacher. Communication of emotions and of ideas through words has two forms: It is oral and it is written. Each of these forms has two aspects:—the basic mechanics, and the content. Since communication involves at least two persons, each mode of speech presumes two kinds of participation. We listen as well as speak; we read as well as write. In this chapter we shall discuss the mechanics and the content of oral speech. In the next chapter we shall deal with the mechanics and content of written language, and the beginnings of literature in the oral forms in which they must be presented to young children.

"If the normal schools could send out one generation of kindergarten and primary teachers with beauty of speech and voice and with enthusiasm for inspiring the same characteristics with the children in their care, one big step would have been taken in developing a generation of Americans with a deepened respect for oral and written English." This statement, made by one who is well acquainted with the American teacher of early childhood,[2] should serve to help make our first point: This volume deals with method, not content. The teacher's background must be assumed. No teacher who has herself failed to develop her speech to the greatest charm of which her vocal organism is capable will be either interested or able to help the children in her charge to do so.

Our second point is this: Very rarely indeed will the teacher consider it necessary to teach speech directly as speech. The opportunities for indirect instruction in speech during story-telling, dramatization, and other aspects of spoken English will be numerous. The good teacher will, without appearing to do so, develop in her pupils a linguistic conscience, a recognition of the fact that there is a right and wrong usage in language. Finding opportunities to substitute the correct for the incorrect expression that the child has used, she will teach by example, and the power of imitation may be relied on to come to her aid.

Students of the field do not always agree in naming the elements of speech. In her survey of American elementary school practice, to give one instance, Meader [3] defined speech improvement as "specific work toward pure vowels, front utterance, distinct consonants, resonance, voice placing, etc." Since there is no established series of speech elements we shall, for our purpose, gather

---

[2] Hill, P. S., in her introduction to *Language and Literature in the Kindergarten and Primary Grades,* by Eleanor Troxel. New York, Charles Scribner's Sons, 1927.

[3] Meader, E. B., *Teaching Speech in the Elementary School.* New York, Teachers College, 1928.

them into three major classes and state that good speech implies excellence of *voice, articulation, and pronunciation.*

Voice. "One distinguishing feature of the 'American voice'," says Rogers,[4] "is its lack of proper fundamental vibrations caused by the use of only part of the organ of vocal expression;—the superficial and not the fundamental element of voice." In adequate voice production, the vocal chords furnish the fundamental vibrations and the pitch of tone, while the air chambers above the larynx supply the resonance. Both qualities are essential to good speech.

In the best form of speech, a current of air forces a passage through the vocal chords while these are approximated sufficiently to resist and combat its outward passage. This produces the fundamental tone. If the chords remain apart and the current of air passes through the aperture without hindrance, we have the unpleasant voice caused by the absence of fundamental tone.

Breathing Exercises. Changing our vantage point, let us note the charm that we enjoy and associate with a good voice: its range, its pleasing tone; its resonance, its perfect functioning in "front utterance"; above all, its adequacy to vary with the mood of the speaker. By carefully planned breathing exercises, the vocal chords may be liberated, the habits of inertia overcome, and these desirable elements attained to a greater degree than most of us possess them. These exercises, similar to the routine followed by teachers of vocal music, will improve the tone. If, when they have heard the tones which it is possible for them to produce, children are taught consciously to strive for them, habits of finer speech will soon be formed.

[4] Rogers, C. K., *English Diction.* Boston, The Author, 1915.

Exercises for Resonance. For the quality of voice known as resonance, the brightness and vividness of the voice, the nose, as part of the vocal mechanism, must be employed. For one reason or another, many of us speak without the correct use of the nasal chambers. Humming exercises, done in rhythm to heighten the interest, will help the child to become aware of this part of voice production. As resonance, or front utterance, is formed in the mouth and not in the throat, children should be made to feel the humming in the upper part of the mouth, in the front teeth. In addition to formal exercises, melodies may be hummed. The exercises should be so conducted that the breathing will be rhythmic, inhalation alternating with the humming.

Since our object is to give the child the sensation of resonance and fine tone resulting from the use of the nasal chambers, care should be taken that these humming exercises be carried on without any sensation of tension or pressure in the throat. The teacher should, further, avoid striving for volume. The object is to secure well-placed and well-sustained tone. The exercises should be accompanied by a certain feeling of release, relaxation, and freedom. This would seem at first impossible unless the mouth is opened and the throat given free play. It is, however, entirely possible. The mouth should feel relaxed during the exercises.

It is not necessary, nor will it completely achieve the purpose, to limit humming to the consonant "M" or to omit vowels. One should, in fact, use various consonants and diphthongs with different beginning and ending vowels. Children should be taught to listen to the resonance which it is possible for them to produce and to strive consciously for this resonance in their speech.

Articulation. "Articulation," says Rodney Bennett in

his helpful book, *The Play Way of Speech Training*,[5] "is the correct shaping or modification of tone after the vocal chords have made it, and should be distinguished from pronunciation, which means the correct ordering and stressing of the sounds of a given word." Poor articulation means slovenly rather than incorrect speech. It is due very largely to a lack of speech consciousness in the environment that bad habits are acquired without anyone's awareness of their existence. Ultimately these habits set the norm, and good speech comes to appear an affectation. Poor articulation is due to faults of the ear and its inability to hear its own speech and compare it to better standards, to faults of voice, and, obviously, to faulty methods of producing the sounds.

Conversely, therefore, what is necessary to improve articulation is the development of a respect for language, a desire to improve and beautify one's speech, to improve the voice, and, finally, to learn the proper methods of producing the sounds. The most common fault in articulation, according to Rogers, is the habit of forming vowels in the mouth independently of fundamental tone. The primary sound of all vowels should, she says, be made in the fundamental tone by one single impulse. The articulation of consonants is confined to the mouth, but all vocal sounds should be initiated in the larynx.

Another frequent cause of poor articulation consists of "chewing" one's words. The sounds represented by the letters *t, d, n, l, r*, are produced when the tip of the tongue comes into close contact with the hard palate just behind the upper gum. Many people form these sounds with movements of the jaw that simulate eating, whereas it is nimbleness at the tip of the tongue that is needed. An excellent corrective exercise is the following: With

---

[5] Bennett, R., *The Play Way of Speech Training*. London, Evans Bros., 1931.

SPEECH—INFORMAL COMMUNICATION 159

jaws and back of tongue relaxed, concentrate on the tip of the tongue and repeat the consonants with various vowel endings, as *ta, tay, tee, tie, tow*. When carried out effectively, there is neither aid nor response from any other part of the body.

Phonetics as an Aid. Perhaps few teachers will go to the extreme of mastering the basic physiology of speech in order to understand the production of sounds, and fewer still will undertake to master the international phonetic alphabet. Possibly neither of these efforts is really necessary for the teacher who does not plan to become a specialist in speech correction. We shall, however, devote a sentence or two to a description of this work for the teacher who may be interested in going further.

"Phonetics" is the name of a system which analyzes the sounds and other elements of speech regardless of particular languages and records them by means of an international alphabet especially devised for the purpose. To each speech element there is allotted a symbol. Each symbol refers to a given sound, regardless of the spelling or the several spellings by which the sound is ordinarily indicated in written form. For any particular language, all the sounds that occur in it are noted. It is determined by what physical means these sounds are made. With this equipment, the teacher is enabled to train the children to hear and distinguish sounds sharply and to use the organs of speech in such a way as to reproduce what they hear.

Pronunciation. The matter of pronunciation need not detain us. It involves not so much a fundamental speech trait as a habit of being well informed. Pronunciation is more or less arbitrary and implies conformity to standard usage. Most teachers will have sufficient self-respect to discover the accepted standards in questionable cases and to train their pupils accordingly.

Aids Toward Good Speech. We appear to have been dealing rather extensively with technicalities in this matter of speech training, but in actual class work little of the procedure will be technical or direct. Most of the instruction will be incidental to work in spoken English. For these reasons, we present a number of items of specific advice which may prove of use in building habits of good speech.

1. Arouse in the child a consciousness of the need for pride in, and admiration of, good speech.

2. As an aid in the development of this consciousness, pride, and admiration, train the children to hear themselves and to hear others speak. Train them to hear the speech as well as the content, listening to the voice to see whether it is pleasing, and to the articulation to see whether all of the sounds that should be, are actually produced.

3. Once they have learned to appreciate what is fine and desirable, let the pupils learn to speak in a voice that is good to hear, because it has vividness and range and color, and because it flows easily, with correct articulation, and uses the nasal chambers to produce resonance, "forward speech" to produce the consonants in the mouth and the vowels in the larynx.

4. Always relax the jaw muscles before speaking; keep the lips well apart to avoid mumbling and nasal sounds; never close the teeth in speech.

5. Take plenty of time to sound every letter in its turn. Do not hurry over some words or precipitate one syllable over another. Hurrying will melt speech, make it indistinct, blurred, and slovenly.

Correct Usage. The word "speech" has been used hitherto in a technical sense to include voice, articulation, and pronunciation. We must now call attention to the proper use of the mother tongue. Here we begin to insist on the use of the language with standard correctness and the elimination of the numberless errors of enunciation and of usage. We come, in other words, to the choice of the words that make up our current speech, the accurate use of the parts of speech, the concept of the sentence.

Conversation is, of course, the most frequent informal experience offering the opportunity for development in the correct use of English. We do not propose to follow the practice of those text writers who furnish lists of appropriate topics. The teacher who, after her studies of child psychology, her observation, and her directed teaching, cannot discover vital topics will hardly be aided by formal suggestions. The deadliness of the usual topics for written composition is sufficiently well known to cause one to hesitate at the thought of damming the spontaneity of the young child by introducing the same stupid conventionality into spoken language instruction.

Good Conversation. It may not be out of place, however, to point out some of the qualities of good conversation. These are confidences in oneself, fluency, relevance, and consecutiveness. The basic difficulty, if there is any, arises out of the limited and necessarily trivial experiences of the children, which ordinarily narrow the possible range of conversation. To counteract these deterrents of good conversation, we urge upon the teacher the sound advice of Percival Chubb that we draw upon books and the personages who live in books.

"The poverty of family intercourse," he says, in commenting on the poor conversation in our homes, "is due partly to our impoverished exchequer of words, partly to our slender resources of allusion. Most of us go unexpressed. Our best thoughts and feelings never get into currency for lack of the bullion of words out of which they must be minted. Life in its sources is abundantly rich and flowing; but it easily stagnates in the pools of gossip and the newspaper rubbish heap. This need not be while there is the rich vicarious life of books to share in, opening up to us fields of common experience, common circles of friends, and acquaintances."

Whatever topics we discuss, whether the group be large or small, whether we converse informally or give our children the opportunity for somewhat formal presentation, let us bear in mind the cultivation of an agreeable voice, clear enunciation, correct pronunciation, and grammatical accuracy. Let us lead the child to appreciate and to strive for clarity, ease and spontaneity, relevance and consecutiveness, over increasing periods of time and within an ever more inclusive range of topics.

Desirable Outcomes

It is not as easy in speech as in arithmetic or handwriting to make clear-cut statements of desirable outcomes. The results of association with the truly cultivated teacher are not measurable. The elements of variability in capacity, family background, and conditions of the particular locality are probably more effective in making difficult a formulation of outcomes and measurement of achievement than such a formulation would be in the more easily isolated fields of music and art. We have, however, deemed it desirable to present for the teacher what may be regarded as the best contemporary formulation, that of the Committee on Language and Composition of the Department of Superintendence of the National Education Association.

At the End of the First Year
    I. In general, the child should have had conscious practice in

SPEECH—INFORMAL COMMUNICATION

1. Speaking loud enough to be heard by the person farthest away;
2. Speaking slowly enough to be understood;
3. Speaking with a relaxed throat;
4. Sounding beginnings and endings of words distinctly;
5. Articulating each syllable distinctly;
6. Allowing others to complete their remarks without interruption;
7. Being silent and attentive while others are talking;
8. Facing the listeners and including the whole group when addressing them;
9. Observing the proper etiquette when beginning to speak at the same time as another;
10. Waiting until an adult has completed his remarks;
11. Making reports consisting of three or four sentences about interesting observations or experiences such as games, a circus, or processes of construction;
12. Expressing gratitude for favors graciously and sincerely.

II. More specifically, the child should
1. Have had conscious practice in
    a. Using words gained through observation and experience, reading and conversation;
    b. Avoiding slang and foreign phrases;
    c. Using the correct forms of the verbs: see, do, sat, bring, is, come, go, run, sit, give, write, lie, begin, ring, take, sing, break, can, and may;
    d. Using correctly *don't* and *doesn't, was* and *were, it is I, am not* instead of *ain't, haven't any* instead of *haven't no;*
2. Speak in complete sentences when the purpose is to provide drill in sentence-making;

3. Avoid excessive use of *and, but* and *well*. (This does not refer to conversation in which *yes* or *no* or a phrase is a satisfactory answer.)

At the End of the Second Year
I. In general, the child should have had conscious practice in
1. Speaking quietly and forcefully;
2. Speaking in a tone pleasant to hear, avoiding pitching the voice too high or speaking in lifeless, nasal, raucous tones or in a monotone;
3. Conversing about what has been read;
4. Retelling interesting portions of conversations or lectures;
5. Making requests in a polite manner;
6. Observing the courtesies due a host when being entertained as a guest;
7. Using judgment concerning when to speak; refraining from conversation when it will annoy others, as in the schoolroom, auditorium, or sick room;
8. Showing courtesy to anyone entering the group late by inviting him to join the conversation;
9. Telling a short story interestingly;
10. Sounding endings of words distinctly—d, t, p, b, g;
11. Cultivating a composed manner by keeping the hands still, and avoiding such habits as fingering a string of beads, buttoning or unbuttoning a coat;
12. Sitting properly, avoiding a slouching position;
13. Looking at the group and speaking directly to all its members;
14. Allowing others a share in the discussion;
15. Being thoughtful of the feelings of others;
16. Making contradictions in a courteous manner;
17. Assuming a natural position, standing erect and squarely on both feet when addressing a group;

SPEECH—INFORMAL COMMUNICATION

18. Concluding a speech gracefully;
19. Walking on and off the stage in a straight line without an appearance of haste.

II. More specifically, the child should have had practice in
1. Discriminating in the use of words by avoiding needless repetition;
2. Using meaningful adjectives and avoiding overworked ones, as *nice, fine;*
3. Speaking in clear-cut sentences;
4. Arranging sentences in sequence;
5. Using the following forms correctly:
   a. *Verbs*—see, do, eat, bring;
   b. *Attribute complement*—It is I.

At the End of the Third Year

I. In general, the child should have had conscious practice in
1. Breathing from the diaphragm and supporting the tone with the breath;
2. Enunciating words, avoiding sliding vowels or consonants;
3. Pronouncing words, avoiding substitution of sounds;
4. Showing a real interest in the subject discussed;
5. Standing or sitting properly and avoiding getting too close to a listener;
6. Addressing others in a polite tone and avoiding peremptory or rude tones;
7. Giving all members of the group reasonable opportunity for expressing their opinions;
8. Suggesting topics that he can follow up, avoiding unpleasant ones and needless repetition;
9. Keeping to the point under discussion in discussion groups;
10. Being generous and not complaining or talking about himself all the time;
11. Telling good stories, anecdotes, and illustrations

in conversation, and using references and magazines which contain good stories and joke pages;
12. Guiding conversation according to his friend's interest;
13. Introducing his parents to the teacher or a new pupil to the class;
14. Preparing and presenting discussions, making sure the statements are correct, avoiding useless sentences at the beginning and ending;
15. Illustrating the discussion by means of charts, drawings, pictures, or posters if such devices clarify the meaning;
16. Preparing and telling stories, familiarizing himself with the story as a whole, endeavoring to feel the story and make it personal, putting his whole mind on the story and listeners, omitting all unnecessary details and keeping the same point of view throughout.

II. More specifically, the child should have had conscious practice in
1. Improving the spoken vocabulary by using words gained through observation and experience, wide reading, conversations, and lectures;
2. Using the following forms correctly: *is, come, go, run,* and *am not* instead of *ain't*.

REFERENCES FOR FURTHER STUDY

Bennett, R., *The Play Way of Speech Training*. London, Evans Bros., 1931.

Chubb, P., *The Teaching of English*, New York, The Macmillan Company, 1902.

Cross, E. A., *Fundamentals in English*. New York, The Macmillan Company, 1926.

Driggs, H. L., *Our Living Language*. Lincoln, Univ. Publishing Co., 1920.

Gullan, M., *Speech Training in the School*. London, Evans Bros., Ltd., 1929.

Klapper, P., *Teaching English in Elementary and Junior High Schools.* New York, D. Appleton-Century Co., 1925.

McKee, P., *Language in the Elementary School.* Boston, Houghton Mifflin Co., 1934.

Sheridan, B. M., *Speaking and Writing English.* Chicago, Sanborn, 1928.

Young, N. J., and Memmott, F. W., *Methods in Elementary English.* New York, D. Appleton-Century Co., 1923.

CHAPTER XIV

SPEECH—FORMAL EXPRESSION

In spite of the mountains of printed matter that surround us today, we have, as a race, been literate for only a little while. Even now, with newspapers, magazines, and books so easily accessible, and in the face of the incredible circulation of which certain journals and magazines boast, many of us seem to prefer oral speech as a medium of communication. Although we are no longer dependent on the bard to repeat the lore that constitutes our culture, we gladly retain the theatre to hear our tongue beautifully spoken, to see the players play the parts. Many of us, perhaps too many, prefer the lecture to the printed page.

Thanks to the inventions of modern science, oral speech is evidently on the verge of regaining some of its lost ground. The telephone replaces the post; the phonograph preserves the cherished voice; the radio may be threatening the newspaper and magazine; the "talkie" begins its wonders to perform. Spoken English is coming into its own, and the need to have it beautiful and worthy of the culture of the race and the refinement of the man is, if anything, of greater importance than ever.

Beyond these general considerations we have the fact that the primary child stands in a class by himself. He is a non-reader and to him the teacher must be the text, the model, and the sole recourse. Her vocabulary, her idioms and constructions, her enunciation, indeed, the very tone of her voice, will be keenly heard and readily imitated. Remembering the age of the child and the terms in which he understands and enters on experience, the teacher should cultivate the art of making her speech graphic, concrete, imaginative.

The Story

Communication, we said in the last chapter, presumes two kinds of participation. We listen as well as speak. In early education it is the privilege of our young illiterate to listen and of his teacher to cultivate the several art forms of speech. Until he learns to read, the teacher must be his minstrel. To prepare herself for this task, Percival Chubb advises that she study the method of the bard who told his stories in the youth of the race, and by a certain dignity elevate her mode of speech above the plane of ordinary talk. When the subject calls for it, let her fill her utterance with symbols and with pictures. Let her reread her Homer and those other epics of the early world to aid her in cultivating the characteristic virtues of the early story teller, and above all, the noble simplicity of his language.

The situations are genuinely similar. In the youth of the race, we gladly gathered to listen to the story that lifted us above and beyond the time and the place in which we lived our daily lives. In the primary room today, the teacher sees about her just as eager and imaginative an audience, ready to forget time, place, and probability for the joyful privilege of entering the land of make-believe.

Qualities of the Good Story. What kind of a story is it that the children like to hear? Let us answer the question in the words of that born story teller, Sara Cone Bryant:[1] "In the stories to which children listen most eagerly something happens all the time. Every step in

---

[1] Bryant, Sara Cone, *How To Tell Stories to Children.* Boston, Houghton Mifflin Co., 1905.

each story is an event. There is little or no explanation, description, or telling how people felt. The stories tell what people did and what they said. The events are the links of a sequence of the closest kind. In point of time and of cause they follow as immediately as it is possible for events to follow. There are no gaps, and no complications of plot requiring a return on the road."

Can we learn from this description of the good story the kind that we should select and the way in which it should be told?

Each event should in turn present a distinct picture to the imagination. These pictures should be made out of very simple elements, either actually familiar to the child or sufficiently analogous to familiar ones to enable him to evoke them. Lifting her speech above the plane of ordinary talk in the manner of the world's early epics, the story teller should give these familiar and recognizable images a tinge of mystery. "Each object and happening is like everyday," says Miss Bryant, "yet touched with a subtle difference, rich in mystery."

The good story teller will bear in mind the flavor to her style that will be added by skilful repetition of scenes, of episodes, of phrases, and even of characteristic designations. Like all good story tellers she will be aware of place, perspective, variety, suspense, climax, and surprise. Like all good bards she will tell her tale with clear, rich intonation, with delicate variations of expression, with faultless enunciation.

The teacher who has cultivated the art of telling the story will be well repaid in the obvious delight that the children are deriving from her performance. She will note with pleasure the relaxation of her group and the easing of school-room tension. She will find herself achieving happy confidential relations with her pupils, and she will be rewarded with the knowledge that she is cultivating for their future advancement the useful abilities of concentration and attention.

The story is the child's introduction to the enchanting realm of literature. It is the best possible preparation for his future recreational reading. In searching through the literature for ready-made stories or material that will lend itself to adaptation for children's stories, it would seem safe to state that most children will respond to the old fairy story, to the well-established nonsense story, to the nature story, and to the well-told historical tale. In this last category we would include far more than the actual story of man and of our own country. Let us by all means remember the treasures of the Bible and the mythologies of the peoples from whom our culture is derived. Their acquisition in early youth assures a wealth of allusion and of intellectual and emotional pleasure throughout life.

List of Stories. While we would have the teacher locate her own material either by working over available stories or finding lists in books that deal with children's literature, it may be of assistance to beginners to note one set of available stories for their guidance. The following from the Denver Course of Study is called "a reliable index of what children enjoy."

During the First Two Years
    Aesop. The Lion and the Mouse
          The Dog and His Shadow
          The Sun and the Wind
          The Hare and the Tortoise
          The Boy and the Wolf
          The Fox and the Grapes
    Bannerman. Little Black Sambo
    Beecher. The Anxious Leaf
    Bryant. Little Half Chick
          The Three Bears

The Elves and the Shoemaker
The Little Red Hen and the Fox
Raggylug
Star Dollars
The Gingerbread Boy
How Brother Rabbit Fooled the Whale and the Elephant
The Poplar Tree
Why the Morning Glory Climbs
Why the Evergreen Trees Keep Their Leaves in Winter
Epaminondas
Golden Cobwebs
The Little Fir Tree
Piccola
The Little Pink Rose

Cook. How the Chipmunk Got the Stripes on Its Back
How the Robin's Breast Became Red
Clytie
The Donkey and the Salt
Golden Rod and Aster
The Redheaded Woodpecker

Dillingham. The Kitten that Wanted To Be a Christmas Present

Harris. Tar Baby

Hoxie. Billy Bobtail

Lindsay. Dust under the Rug
The Little Traveler

Olcott. Why the Snow is White
Forget-me-not

Potter. Peter Rabbit

Scudder. Cinderella

During the Third Year

Andersen. The Nightingale
Arabian Nights. Aladdin, or the Wonderful Lamp

Bailey. The Story of Merrymind
Baldwin. Grace Darling
  The Bell of Atri
  Androcles and the Lion
Ballard. The Mirror of Matsuyama
Bible. Story of Joseph
  Story of David
  Story of Ruth
Bryant. Burning of the Rice Fields
  The Rat Princess
Cather. The Story of a Salmon
Grimm. The Sleeping Beauty
  Little Red Riding Hood
  Snow-White and Rose-Red
Harper. Legend of the Christians
Keller. The Story of Helen Keller
Kipling. The Elephant Child
  How the Leopard Got His Spots
Lyman. The Boastful Bamboo

Qualities of the Good Narrator. We shall close this section with some definite suggestions that should prove of value to the teacher in her effort to perfect herself in the art of telling the story. These precepts are based on those formulated by Miss Bryant:

1. Cultivate your feeling for the story and strive toward increasingly just appreciation. It will be well to try to evoke your own childhood in order to secure the same identification with the characters that the children experience. If you cannot do this with regard to any particular story, do not tell it. Never tell a story you do not feel.

2. Know your story so that it may flow from your lips with the unconscious freedom of a vivid reminiscence. But do not memorize it. Master the plot, and leave the telling free for the spontaneity with which you would narrate a personal experience.

3. Seat the children in close and direct range of your eyes. Where the group is small enough, have them seated in a half circle, taking your place at a point opposite the center of the arc, not in its center.

4. Once the story has begun, do not break into it for purposes of discipline. Try to set the right mood of the tale to begin with, by evoking it and showing it in yourself. Tell it simply, directly, dramatically, with zest. Avoid self-consciousness, affectation, talking down, being grown-up and didactic. Try to enjoy the story in the mood that belongs to it, and tell it to the children in those terms, sincerely, as an equal.

5. Be economical in the use of words, and let face, voice, and gesture serve where the written form may have employed more actual words for purposes of description.

6. Tell the story dramatically. Cultivate brevity, close logical sequence, unhesitant speech. Exclude foreign matter.

7. Remain suggestive rather than illustrative. It is not the purpose of the story teller to play the parts of his story, but to arouse the imagination of his hearers to picture the scenes for themselves.

Dramatization

Listening, even to interesting stories charmingly told is, after all, a passive occupation. If it has been worth while, the child has been stimulated and his imagination has been aroused. Those of us who have experienced the day dream—and who has not?—appreciate how identification with the fictitious characters leads the child into realms of fantasy and unconscious desire to live the story out and be the hero of the tale.

SPEECH—FORMAL EXPRESSION

Here is the opportunity for self-activity, the road toward oral expression. What better content for expression can we provide than that to which children invariably respond with such eagerness—playing out the story? Now that we have heard the tale many times and enjoyed it; now that we know the characters so well, have seen them in action, and have heard them speak in their several situations, let us pretend that we are they and play their parts.

Preparation for leisure, one of the objectives of education, means preparation for play. It means art, and art, above all things, means breaking down the walls of reality and soaring into the realms of fantasy. Dramatization will stimulate the imagination, call out the inventiveness, and develop the language of the participants. Fortunately, there is no need, as in teaching the skills, to bear in mind the demands of the future. We do not want to prepare our pupils to play some other time. Our primary children will, with all their hearts, play now. More than that, they are ready for those innermost essentials of art, make-believe and vicariousness. They love to pretend. They love to imitate.

When the story has been told and the children have truly enjoyed it, the primary teacher who has even the remotest bit of her own childhood memories left can get a joyous and precipitate response to the suggestion that they play it. How the child hails the opportunity to be someone else, to expand, to live out in imitation what he has seen the elders do!

This change of rôle from oneself to a queen or an elf offers incomparably precious opportunities for the cultivation of refined, dignified, carefully enunciated speech. Form and formality such as would appear to the child affected and out of place when describing an incident that happened this morning in the street beyond his own seem meet and proper, coming from the princess or the knight.

In our opinion there is no room in the primary grades for the preparation and presentation of plays in the formal sense, i.e., the memorizing and repeating of the production of someone else. We would limit these younger children to plays made by themselves spontaneously either on the basis of stories which they have heard or read or of experiences arising from other aspects of their school work.

There are valuable outcomes of dramatization beyond those that we have mentioned. The limits of creative ability are soon reached by most of us. But the effort to create represents excellent training for appreciative growth in this as in other arts. "The majority of people," says Corinne Brown [2] in her fascinating book, *Creative Drama in the Lower School,* "are spectators. Let us teach our children to be intelligent observers of the drama, critical but sympathetic, exacting but courteous. It is the duty of the dramatist and the actors to hold the interest of the audience, but that interest amounts to little if it is not intelligently appreciative."

Written Composition

The basic mechanical aspects of written communication are, obviously enough, reading, writing, and spelling, tools to which we have devoted other chapters. There remain for consideration here the grammatical structure of the language and the commonly observed forms. The best preparation for written expression is, undoubtedly, the speech work with which we dealt in the last chapter. "Composition" is best begun with the somewhat lengthy

---

[2] Brown, C., *Creative Drama in the Lower School.* New York. D. Appleton-Century Co., 1929.

SPEECH—FORMAL EXPRESSION

and formal narration by the child of an experience that he has had, a story that he has heard.

While oral work far outweighs writing in relative importance at the primary level, we would make the following suggestions toward the beginning of actual writing:

1. Train the child to think before he speaks. Let him formulate what he intends to say before saying it.

2. Having become clearly aware of the proposed content, let him secure a definite concept of the sentence. The number of adults with a long school record who do not write in sentences is shocking. Insist that the child speak in sentences during the period of preparation before writing has come into question. Help him to acquire the feeling that a sentence is a definite, complete statement with a beginning and an end, and let him demonstrate this in practice, not as academic information.

3. In beginning written work it will be found useful, though by no means indispensable, to follow this order: copy, dictate, compose. There is no need to teach mechanics as such. Copying, when well motivated so that the child knows what he is about, will help establish the sentence habit from the points of view of form and content. Dictation is another approach to the same objectives; it tests the child's grasp of the mechanics and it provides him with model sentences.

4. When beginning the actual construction of original sentences, start with a complete oral statement of the sentence before having the child write it. This is a natural transition from the dictated sentence, and will, if the preceding steps have achieved their aims, reduce the need for correction

to a minimum. Keep the sentences short to prevent the thought from becoming involved.

5. There is no place for extended formal composition work in the primary grades, but children may well be led to go beyond the single sentence to a connected series in any form that seems desirable. This may be a letter, a description, a narration.

6. Be on the look-out for the occasional child of creative ability in this form and, as in music and art, foster this creativeness. There will be children who can compose verse and who, in prose, will employ a wealth of simile and metaphor worthy of note as a special ability. If this aptitude makes its appearance before the child has learned to write, use his oral compositions as blackboard material. If the child can write, help him to express himself correctly, and encourage him to persevere.

An excellent form of creative work in the primary grades is that which involves the whole group in co-operative effort, so that in the end the class, rather than any individual, is the author of the poem or the story. Proceed by calling for suggestions step by step as the composition develops. Criticism of the proposals and adoption of the final form should be an expression of the aesthetic judgment of the group.

7. Let all necessary correction be on an individual basis, with each particular child. As in arithmetic, reading, writing, and spelling, skill in the mechanics and growth in the development of expression are matters of individual variation. Learning will go forward at varying rates of progress. There is little value in class discussion of bad usage or bad mechanics in writing when there are always many children who do not need the particular correction under consideration.

SPEECH—FORMAL EXPRESSION

8. Do not teach the mechanics of written form separately as a subject. Always teach these essentials of written form in application, when the line of verse, the name, or the sentence is being written.

LITERATURE

Memorizing. We advise the teacher to continue the traditional school practice of memorizing. More than ever before are the ears of our children being assailed by unworthy forms of song and speech. With the insistent repetition so well characterized by the jazz rhythm, these songs and forms of speech are forced not only upon our consciousness, but upon our very memories, practically against our will.

More necessary than ever before is the memorizing of beautiful and meaningful verse as a background, a criterion, and a resource for our children. We would store the mind of youth with the treasure of the noblest thought and feeling uttered by the race. Early impressions and recollections, so important in the development of character and personality, should do much to ousting the baser and cruder songs of later years, and lay some basis for taste and literary culture.

The teacher should follow her own taste, her own experience, and the course of study of her own system, in determining which passages to set for memorizing. As a beginning and a suggestion for those who want it, we present the following list which resulted from a ballot taken by The Journal of The National Education Association.

Grade I

   Stevenson—My Shadow
   Taylor—Twinkle, Twinkle, Little Star
   Stevenson—Swing

Field—Why Do Bells For Christmas Ring?
Alexander—All Things Bright and Beautiful
From the German—Sleep, Baby, Sleep
Cooper—Come, Little Leaves
Stevenson—Rain
Rossetti—Wind
Stevenson—Autumn Fires
Tennyson—Bird and the Baby
Brown—Little Plant

Grade II

Longfellow—Hiawatha's Childhood
Ingelow—Seven Times One
Lear—Owl and the Pussy Cat
Cary—Suppose
Stevenson—Wind
Houghton—Lady Moon
Larcom—Brown Thrush
Child—Thanksgiving Day
Field—Rockabye-Lady
Stevenson—Land of the Story Books
Sherman—Daisies
Field—Dutch Lullaby
Kingsley—Lost Doll
Stevenson—Windy Knights
Miller—Blue Bird
Allingham—Fairies
Field—Duel
Coleridge—Answer to a Child's Question
Sherman—Four Winds

Grade III

Longfellow—Children's Hour
Brooks—O Little Town of Bethlehem
Rands—Great, Wide, Beautiful, Wonderful World
Moore—Visit from St. Nicholas
Longfellow—Hiawatha's Sailing

Jackson—September
Hogg—Boy's Song
Krout—Little Brown Hands
Cary—November
Field—Norse Lullaby
Allingham—Wishing
Aldrich—Marjorie's Almanac
Bjornson—Tree
Tennyson—Owl

Reading. In literature as in composition, the preparatory stages must be oral. While we are waiting for the child to master the tool of reading, he listens to stories, retells and dramatizes them. He also listens to and memorizes verse suitable to his stage of development and, under good instruction, he discusses these things with his classmates and begins the development of appreciation, learning to look for the elements that make for beauty.

While some few children will begin a little reading on their own as early as the first grade, literature at the primary level, as distinguished from learning to read, will be mostly oral. In the third year many of the children of average mentality will be reading for pleasure. We do not have the space, nor is it necessary, to print here lists of available books and collections suitable for children of this age. Courses of study such as those of the cities of Denver, St. Louis, and Los Angeles contain splendidly selected and graded lists so extensive as to give any teacher a great deal of scope in her choice. The point to bear in mind is the desirable outcome: a love of literature and the habit of resorting to the reading of beautiful books for comradeship with great minds, for recreation and, indeed, for solace.

If the outcomes for literature are conspicuously absent from the list of desirable outcomes with which we close the chapter, it is because all efforts to state them are necessarily vague, as, for example, these from the St. Louis Course of study: aesthetic pleasure; experience in which the imagination may be developed; enlargement of one's knowledge of human life; recreation; appreciation of the beautiful in prose and poetry; aid in the selection of good literature.

Desirable Outcomes

At the End of the First Year. In written English, the child should have mastered the following use of capitals:

1. His name begins with capitals;
2. Sentences begin with capitals;
3. The word "I" is written with a capital.

At the End of the Second Year. In written English, the child should have had conscious practice in:

1. Using the approved form of the paper in all written work to be handed in;
2. Indenting paragraphs;
3. Using capitals when
   a. Beginning the days of the week, holidays, months;
   b. Writing initials;
   c. Beginning all proper names;
4. Writing notices, making sure to include all necessary information;
5. Writing informal notes, being careful to state the purpose of the note clearly and courteously;
6. The following, which should be established as habits:
   a. Writing his full name with proper use of capitals;
   b. Beginning sentences with capitals;
   c. Writing the word *I* with a capital;
   d. Placing a period at the end of a sentence;
   e. Placing a question mark after a question.

SPEECH—FORMAL EXPRESSION

At the End of the Third Year. In written English, the child should have had conscious practice in:

1. Using one side of the paper only in all work which is to be used as a final copy to be handed in or preserved;
2. Writing on all except the last line of a ruled sheet, and on an unruled sheet leaving at least a half inch at the bottom of the page;
3. Spelling words for this and previous grades correctly;
4. Having good pen and ink at hand always;
5. Indenting paragraphs;
6. Writing to the end of each line except at the end of a paragraph or in an outline, and not crowding the writing at the end of the line;
7. Writing social letters telling items of interest to the receiver, and expressing himself naturally;
8. Using an appropriate informal salutation;
9. Using an appropriate complimentary close;
10. The increasing use of capitals and punctuation marks;
11. The following habits:
    a. Placing a period at the end of a sentence;
    b. Placing a question mark after a question;
    c. Writing the days of the week, holidays, months, proper names, and initials with capital letters;
    d. Using approved form of paper;
12. The following uses of capitals:
    a. Abbreviations of titles and proper nouns;
    b. The first word of every line of poetry.

REFERENCES FOR FURTHER STUDY [3]

Bailey, C. S., *The Story Telling Hour.* New York, Dodd, Mead & Co., 1934.

[3] Books dealing with written composition are listed under this heading at the end of Chapter XIII.

Bamberger, F. E., and Broening, A. M., *A Guide to Children's Literature*. Baltimore, Johns Hopkins Press, 1931.

Brown, C., *Creative Drama in the Lower School*. New York, D. Appleton-Century Co., 1929.

Bryant, S. P., *How to Tell Stories to Children*. Boston, Houghton Mifflin Co., 1905.

Chubb, P., *The Teaching of English*. New York, The Macmillan Company, 1902.

McKee, P., *Reading and Literature in the Elementary School*. Boston, Houghton Mifflin Co., 1934.

Moore, A. E., *Literature Old and New for Children*. Boston, Houghton Mifflin Co., 1934.

CHAPTER XV

MUSIC

The Four Elements of Music

It will hardly be necessary to add to the existing mountain of literature in praise of music, its reason for being, its value to man. All literate persons know that the race has developed a number of recreative arts, and that these at their highest offer man the noblest of all relaxations, his opportunity to create and to share in the expression of beauty and of emotion.

It may, however, be more useful at the beginning of this chapter to present an analysis of the elements of this particular art. If we are to deal with it in our classes and endeavor to introduce our pupils to it, it is essential to know what are the component parts of this form of self-expression which is based on sound.

There are four component elements, each of which is present where there is music as contrasted with other sound, and each of which implies a skill and therefore, for most of us, training. It is quite true that, lacking aesthetic response, there will be no enjoyment of the music in spite of the possession of the skill. Reversing the situation, however, and granting the presence of aesthetic readiness for enjoyment, this will be distinctly limited, sometimes to the vanishing point, if the ear has not been trained to listen and consciously attend to rhythm, tone, melody, and harmony.

Rhythm. "Music," says Giddings,[1] "is made up of

[1] Giddings, T. P., *Grade School Music Teaching*. New York, C. H. Congdon, 1919.

time and tune. Time is the framework upon which the tune hangs." As it happens, rhythm is the one element in music which ties it closest to the other arts. It is a universal element and a moment's thought will reveal to the student its deep roots in our physical being. Rhythm, obviously, is one of the elements in poetry and the dance, and, in a somewhat more subtle way, it is present in the graphic and the plastic arts. It is based on regular time intervals. Most of us fall rather easily into this alternation of stress and release as exemplified in innumerable phases of daily life, such as walking. Training will make the child aware of the existence of rhythm and help him to hold to the regularity of it and to enjoy the elements of balance and proportion which make rhythm so delightful.

Tone. Tone is probably the most unique of the four elements of music, the one that belongs to this art most exclusively. It is tone that makes music out of and distinguishes music from other forms of sound. Tone is a quality of sound that, produced by voice or instrument, makes it appealing to the ear. It is beauty in the realm of sound as color is beauty in the realm of light. The skill implied in connection with this element of musical tonality is the development of a tonal sense, a response to the beautiful quality of sound.

Melody. We have dealt with rhythm, the time element of music, and we have dealt with tone, the quality of beauty in sound. However beautiful tones may be in themselves, they cannot continue to charm us if they are heard at random. They must proceed in gracefully ordered fashion. This brings us to the third element, that of tune.

We have tune or melody when, based on a rhythmic pattern, the tones are arranged in a clearly defined design. The untrained and the unmusical will be satisfied with

MUSIC

designs that are obvious and insistently repeated, indicating musical poverty on the part of the composer. The trained and the musical ear and mind will be delighted when beautiful tones are arranged to form an appealing melodic sequence characterized by subtlety, variety, suitable length, and intricacy.

Harmony. We come to the fourth of the constituent elements of music. Whereas melody consists of tones heard successively, harmony consists of tones heard in combination. These tones are of different pitch and, when combined, are called chords. To any melody may be added harmony, which intensifies its musical value.

THE AIMS OF MUSIC IN THE PRIMARY GRADES

In the following statement of aims, we will to a very large extent rely on the formulation of the Standard Course in Music published by the Music Supervisors' National Conference in its Proceedings in 1921.

Singing. The aim of singing in the primary grades is to give every child the use of his singing voice and the pleasure in song as a means of expression. This activity, which implies individual as well as group singing, should lead to the development of the voice, the enrichment and enlargement of the song repertory along lines appropriate to the taste and expanding powers of children. Hand in hand with this work for most of the group must go corrective work for the few who do not take naturally to music. These are sometimes referred to as monotones, but would better be called defective singers.

Ear-Training. The activity centering around ear-training must be organized to cultivate the power of careful, sensitive, aural attention. This power to listen must be continually extended to new features and lead toward the development of ability to hear and recognize simple phrase groups of tones. Ear-training should also lead toward the development of rhythm and the recognition and enjoyment of rhythmic patterns when these are heard in musical compositions.

Appreciation. This aim implies the cultivation of enjoyment through the hearing of much good music. It implies musical experience beyond the content of the songs that the children themselves sing, and musical delight beyond that afforded by their own singing. The child should be led to enjoyment of music as something heard as well as something expressed.

Reading and Writing. The introduction of the musical staff may occur as early as the middle of the first year or as late as the beginning of the third year. Reading, as the word is used in the primary grades, implies the development of an elementary degree of power and skill in independent sight singing. Writing means almost exclusively the ability to copy the various symbols of musical notation. Simple dictation may, however, be attempted toward the end of the third year.

Instrumental Instruction. This aim is not at the present time regarded as one of the indispensable objectives of public school music. Many schools do, however, so regard it. These schools supply instruments and instruction in small classes. Many children, to whom private instruction would not be available, are in this way discovered to have aptitudes worthy of development. In some instances, it represents the beginning of vocational training.

Creative Work. This phrase, as we employ it here, refers to the desirability of discovering and developing the special musical ability of the few children who may be found to possess it. Such ability should be fostered. Such children should be stimulated to do creative work and given opportunity for it.

Equipment. The desirable equipment for music work in the primary grades would include a key board instrument; appropriate instruments for instruction if such work is carried on; a phonograph and a carefully selected library of records; an ample supply of song books and supplementary material for class singing; charts, a pitch pipe, and a staff liner; blank music paper or music writing books. A player-piano would be of great use and, where the training and the taste of the teacher can be relied upon, a radio would be highly desirable additional equipment.

Procedures

By way of preface to this section of the chapter, we must warn the student against the false idea that just as we analyze the work in music into its several elements, so must the teacher do her work of teaching piece by piece. That would, indeed, be a misfortune. While we, for the sake of coherence, here deal with instructional procedure topic by topic, the teacher will understand that all the elements of music instruction must go forward concurrently. Reference to the statement of desirable outcomes at the end of the chapter will make this point clear.

Ear-Training and Song-Singing. The delights of music are by no means confined to sensory enjoyment. They are infinitely beyond simple physical sensation. But they are none the less primarily available through listening. If, therefore, skill is an essential basis of music, the training of the ear is a fundamental in musical education. Broadly speaking, all music study is ear-trainng, and the various activities connected with training the ear are surely the most important in music education. It is the ear, says Giddings, that keeps the pupil in time as well as in tune. The best ear-training comes from singing songs either individually or in concert. Let the pupil do enough of this in a proper manner and his ear will be well trained.

This brings us quite naturally to singing, with which all work in music happily begins. Children bring with them a means of communication, speech, which serves until such time as they learn to read. Through the same media of voice and ear they are approachable musically. Just as, on entering school, they bring with them a great deal of general knowledge accompanied by curiosity to learn more, so they bring from the pre-school period and out-of-school environment much musical experience.

The parallel may be carried further. Just as differences in alertness, interest, and attack are notable, and are largely attributable to innate differences in general intelligence, so we find a distinct range of differences in responsiveness to music. Some of the children sing the tunes correctly the first time they try. Others will be able to follow the tune rather well, but will find it difficult to stay in perfect tone. A few will have very great difficulty, indeed, the first time they attempt to sing in tune. Nevertheless, it is with singing, as we have said, that the instruction in music begins.

The goal of school music instruction should be the unfolding of the beauty of music in all its manifestations. The child's first step in gaining a conception of beauty in music may well be his own acquisition of a beautiful singing tone. If he, himself, sings beautifully, he will be better able to recognize and appreciate beauty of tone as he hears it.

Singing is as spontaneous and natural a form of self-expression as speech. It trains the ear, the voice, the memory. It captures the child's fancy and appeals to his intuitive feeling for rhythm. It awakens a sense of the beautiful in tonal utterance, in melodic outline, and in formal patterns of balance, proportion, and symmetry. It points the way toward self-expression through the art of musical interpretation.

The literature of music teaching is rich in advice to the teacher in such matters as phrasing, voice quality, attack, release, rhythm, smoothness, sliding voices and monotones. The ambitious teacher who is not acquainted with this literature will never feel satisfied until she has taken the necessary steps to master the advice offered and the techniques worked out by the leaders of music in education.

To state the procedure briefly, singing begins with rote songs. Just as the child, before learning to read, listens to the teacher tell stories to the class, often dramatizes them, securing his introduction to literature in his prereading period by non-reading methods, so he begins his musical experience by learning to sing and to memorize songs without awareness of the existence of notation. In both instances the ear precedes the eye.

The following, from the Denver Course of Study, summarizes rather briefly some of the methods of teaching rote songs and of dealing with that ever-recurring problem, the defective singer.

> The teacher should sing the new song through to the class, exercising care to sing smoothly and with distinct enunciation. Next she should sing the song, phrase by phrase, and have the class repeat each phrase. The children should be able to sing the phrase correctly without assistance from the teacher after hearing it once. Incorrect response is often caused by too long phrases or indistinct articulation on the part of the teacher.
>
> If the phrase is too difficult, it should be divided and each part worked out separately. Then the teacher should combine the first and second phrases, the third and fourth, and so on through the song.

The song should be given an artistic finish by observing all marks of interpretation. The piano should not be used until the song has been learned.

Many children who enter the kindergarten and first grade are found to be comparatively deficient in musical sense. An individual who sings or speaks on one unvarying tone has been erroneously termed a "monotone." The number of such individuals is almost negligible. There are children, however, who do not sing up to pitch and who have difficulty in singing a melody. In most cases this trouble is the result of vocal misuse or aural defect.

These children should be encouraged to participate in all singing except in the learning of a new song, when they may be allowed to whisper the words while the rest of the class sings. The defective singers should be seated near the front of the room. Part of the lesson period should be devoted to individual work. The best singers should help to train the others. In every lesson each defective singer should be given an opportunity for individual singing.

Reading and Writing Music. While trained listening is the primary essential without which there can be no musical enjoyment, the ear alone is inadequate for either the appreciation or the evolution of the art of music. Just as writing made literature and the drama and poetry possible, so the system of notation has made it possible for those who are gifted in musical composition to express themselves at length for the benefit of their contemporaries as well as the generations that follow. No memory, however specialized, could have retained the world's literature of music. More important, its very composition would have been impossible. The reading and the writing of music are "fundamental processes" without which we must remain musical illiterates whose "enjoyment" and "appreciation," to use current pedagogical terms, remain limited.

Strange as it may seem, one still finds leaders in musical education who do not concede this view. "Those children who can best learn music by means of its notation" —we are quoting the editors of a series of books for music teaching—"should be taught to do so to the point of real expertness, while the other children who learn their music through imitation or by following their classmates should develop their powers in these respects to the point where they can learn much music quickly and accurately." Reversing the process of the ordinary method of teaching reading, in which the teacher must guard against the child who memorizes and thus tends to seem to read, these authors actually recommend the development in the class of certain leaders to carry their classmates forward in the learning of a piece of music.

That some children must remain musically illiterate because of inability to learn to read, all would agree. That learning musical notation must be limited to the leaders, presumably few in number, we cannot grant. Rather do we find ourselves in accord with Giddings [2] when he says that we learn to read music for the same reason that we learn to read books—to know the content. "We teach the child to read as soon as he enters school," he says, "and we make him read as early and as well as possible, so that he may know and appreciate literature. A person who cannot read has a very limited knowledge of literature, and we take great pains to make books for even the blind to read. The same principles apply to the reading of music."

We must, however, make a concession to the opposing view. It is probably much more difficult to learn to read

[2] Ibid.

and write music than it is to learn to read and write language. In the latter case, there seems to be the one important element, recognition. To read music, however, the child must be able to keep in mind the key signature, must take in at a glance groups of notes standing for definite pitches, must recognize the shape of each note so as to give each tone its correct time value, and must observe the measure sign and the bars so as to accent correctly. Moreover, he must do all these things at a fixed rate of speed.

There is another, even more important difference. In ordinary reading, the most important element in the earliest stages of learning is recognition. The situation in music is different. Not only is recognition in all likelihood more difficult because the art of writing is more complicated, but the child has to express his recognition by producing the tone. The process of reading music involves the ear as well as the eye. The approach to reading music is sight-singing.

Sight-singing usually begins with the second year of school, after the child has had much experience with rote songs. The approach is musical rather than technical. Emulating the modern practice of teaching "reading" rather than letters and sounds, the music teacher avoids scales and intervals as mere drill, and instead gives the child an opportunity to sing appropriate songs and to learn notation by using it. In the end, without detailed drill as drill but by singing with the teacher, the child learns to sing the words of the song from the printed page, paying attention to the production of smooth tones rhythmically, in correct pitch, with appropriate expression. This method is valuable, but it has its pitfalls. Just as the child may "fool" one by pretending to read what he knows by heart, so he may sing accurately either what he remembers or what he hears the child next to him sing.

MUSIC

The alert teacher will bear this possibility in mind and aim at reading as well as at singing.

What one reads, another has had to write. Music writing will be found an invaluable aid in mastering the theory of notation and in learning to read. More important, it will provide those who may have something to say with a means of expression. After the child has mastered the skill of writing language he is asked to do original work. He writes letters and other "compositions." It should be obvious that this applies to music as well. There may not be a large number of important composers in our classes, but neither is the number of litterateurs impressive. The ideas of most of us may be mediocre, but we are entitled to the privilege of expression.

The equipment for music writing consists of staff paper and pencil, though blackboards may be prepared for this work. The children must, naturally, be taught to make the musical symbols. This is followed by copying melodies. Copying gives the pupil experience in making the various symbols of notation neatly, accurately, and rapidly. Writing from dictation, transposition, and other more complicated aspects of writing must be left for the upper grades, but even at the primary level children can learn to write the symbols as the teacher reads (not sings) them.

It is inspiring to the children of a class to have them invent some simple melody for a line or two of verse and then see the teacher write their own composition on the blackboard. From the earliest moment, the child who shows the desire to invent a melody should be encouraged and assisted to write what he sings. If the writing of his own creation requires more skill than he possesses, the teacher should write it and teach the child to read his composition.

Appreciation. The authors of a recent book dealing with the child-centered school seem much upset by the point of view of "the earnest classical students of music." While some of these conservative leaders actually seem at times to display flashes of insight they tend on the whole to understand the situation no better than the typical conventionalists. The principal objection seems to be the "preoccupation with listening." The appreciative aim of music has, these writers believe, thwarted the realization of music as an art of self-expression. By providing for lessons in appreciation "they brand themselves indelibly as defenders of the theory of education as passive adaptation—listening." The proponents of "creative music" evidently think that listening is worse than reading. They do not seem willing to grant that most of us are destined to "appreciate" and "read" literature, not to create it.

The comparison of early childhood with primitive man is attractive, but misleading. Having no means of record, primitive people do exist on much the same level. The work of the noblest artists is doomed to perish except insofar as it affects the folk-tale or the folk-song. As soon as memory is relieved by a method of writing, differences in creative ability begin to appear. Music, like all arts, is carried forward from generation to generation by the mighty of each age. The literature of music assumes proportions, the art becomes ever more intricate and complicated, and listening becomes far from the easy and passive affair that the "artistic teachers" would contemptuously imply.

Just as in the case of literature all of us can write and few of us are endowed with the gift of being able to "write," so with music. We should all have the facility to express what we may have to say, but few of us will add to the literature of music. In the department of English from the elementary school to the college, the courses in literature as reading are available to all while the courses in writing make the mass of us merely "respectable" and offer the few talented ones training in creative expression. In the same way in music, the bulk of us must be trained to listen and the talent of the few creative ones should be fostered for composition.

The word *creative* is unfortunately being confused in current educational discussion with that good old phrase, *self-active*. Certainly neither we nor any one else in the field of music advocates "passive adaptation" or opposes "pupil activity." Playing and singing individually and as groups represent activities. The truth is that "listening" in the schools came in with the phonograph, decades after children had been singing and advancing musically through singing. Creative effort as a means toward appreciation has long been valued in education, but it remains an unalterable fact that the greatest permanent participation in music for the majority of us must be through the ear as it must be through the eye in literature.

The case for lessons in appreciation is, in our opinion, well put by the authors [3] of The Teacher's Book published to accompany the Universal School Music Series. "The child," they say, "has a right to a larger musical experience than he can ordinarily get through his own performance. While it is true that appreciation comes largely through participation, familiarity with the great masterpieces of music is possible only in a limited way through school singing. Given a phonograph and a player piano, and there is almost no limit to such an acquaintance."

This phase of music instruction is constantly changing. New records are continuously made, and the still unexplored possibilities of the radio may prove of incomparable value. We particularly commend to the student

[3] Damrosch, W., Gartlan, G. H., and Gehrkens, K. W., Universal Music Series. Teachers Book. *Manual of Music Appreciation.* New York, Hinds, Hayden and Eldredge, 1923.

the following books for valuable guidance in this aspect of music teaching: *Music Appreciation for Every Child,* (Primary Grades) by Glenn, Lowry, and de Forest. *Music Appreciation for Little Children,* a publication of the Victor Talking Machine Co., *Listening Lessons in Music,* by Agnes Moore Fryberger, and *Music for Children,* by M. Storr, published in London by Sidgwick and Jackson, Ltd.

Instrumental Instruction. The matter of the use of musical instruments is at the moment receiving more extensive discussion in the literature of "progressive" and "creative" education than we propose to allot to the subject here. To begin with the simpler aspect of the question, class teachers have, in the nature of things, never been expected to have the time, the energy, and the ability to offer instrumental instruction. Some parents, on the other hand, have always secured for their children private instruction in the several instruments. This skill on the part of some of the children, acquired outside of the school, has regularly been used by the schools for recitals and for the organization of bands and orchestras.

More recently the schools in many sections have entered this field to the advantage of the pupils. They have demonstrated the feasibility of small-class instruction for many of the instruments. In this way they have induced private teachers to take classes at a greatly reduced rate per pupil and persuaded parents to pay for the instruction. The schools have arranged the programs for the convenience of these classes in instrumental instruction. In some cases, the Board of Education owns instruments which are either offered the children for a short period of time to determine whether they will continue with the instrument or these instruments are provided during the entire period of instruction.

The more difficult aspect of this question is the recent movement in creative music. There are enthusiastic and competent teachers who not only organize rhythm bands and toy orchestras, but provide "primitive music for primitive people" and insist that "children—musical primitives—should have the opportunity to make their own instruments and their own music."

It is our opinion that the field of public education suffers from excessive generalization. Every time some one with the ability to make himself heard does what is or seems to him to be a good piece of work, the new day dawns and the new gospel is preached to a long-suffering profession. Interesting work too rarely seems to be its own reward. Too frequently it turns out to be every other teacher's challenge. What one person or one school achieves in a particular environment with a particular group of children too frequently turns out to be what every school should adopt.

We find the toy instrument bands and orchestras thoroughly worth while. The making of primitive instruments to be combined into musical groups that play music which the children have composed seems to us fascinating. But we consider it unintelligent to couple with the praise for this work condemnation of those who do not find it possible to carry it on. We consider it unfair to the average teacher to state that she is making a failure of music instruction because she does not use the method of the moment. We believe that there are musical people and musical peoples who have achieved maximum musical appreciation without this particular gospel.

Desirable Outcomes

We shall close our chapter with the statement of expected outcomes formulated by the Educational Council of the Music Supervisor's National Conference. These desirable attainments are stated for each school year of the primary grades as a criterion for the teacher by which she may judge her own work.

At the End of the First Year

    1. Ability to sing pleasingly a repertory of 30 to 40 rote songs appropriate to the grade, including one stanza of "America."

    2. The reduction of the number of "monotones" to 10 per cent. or less of the total number of pupils."

    3. Ability of 90 per cent. of the pupils to sing individually, freely, correctly, and without harmful vocal habits, some 5 of the songs sung by the class as a whole.

    4. Preference on the part of the children for good tones rather than bad, *and the disposition to love the best of the music they have sung or heard.*

At the End of the Second Year

    1. Ability to sing correctly and pleasingly 40 to 60 new songs, 20 of which are to be memorized and which shall include two stanzas of "America." It is also suggested that some of the songs of the first year be kept in the repertory.

    2. Ability of 90 per cent. of the pupils to sing individually, freely, correctly, and without harmful vocal habits 6 to 8 of the songs sung by the class as a whole.

    3. Not more than 5 per cent. of the entire class to be "monotones" at end of year. The other pupils to sing without bad vocal habits, with musical enjoyment, and with good musical effect.

4. Ability by end of year (or by the middle of the following year, according to procedure) to sing at sight with syllables, easy melodies in the usual nine major keys, containing notes and rests, one, two, three and four beats in length, and employing diatonic tones in stepwise progressions and with simple skips.

5. Ability to recognize some 5 or 6 good compositions on hearing the first few measures of each, to follow and recognize a recurrent theme in a new song or new piece of very simple structure; and a tendency to prefer compositions that have real musical merit and charm to those that are weak or common.

At the End of the Third Year

1. Ability to sing correctly and pleasingly 40 to 60 new songs, at least 10 of which shall be memorized, and which shall include the four stanzas of "America." It is also suggested that some of the songs of the preceding years be kept in the repertory.

2. Ability of 90 per cent. of the pupils to sing individually, freely, correctly, and without harmful vocal habits, 8 or 10 of the songs sung by the class as a whole.

3. The "monotone" to be practically eliminated. Individual attention should be given to special cases.

4. Ability by end of year to sing at sight, by syllables, easy melodies in any of the usual nine major keys, these melodies to contain stepwise progressions and skips of 3rds, 4ths, 5ths, 6ths, and 8ths and employing notes and rests at least one, two, three, or four beats in length, and two notes to the beat; and a knowledge of some twelve of the more familiar signs and terms used in connection with staff notation.

5. Ability of at least 25 per cent. of the pupils to sing as well individually, at sight, as the class can sing as a whole.

6. Power that enables the pupils to recognize by sound that which they know by sight, and vice versa; i.e., "see with the ears and hear with the eyes."

7. Increased power to attend to, and give account of, the salient points of design in the music introduced, and increased sympathy for, and pleasure in, those factors that make for charm of musical design and expressive quality; also, ability to recognize and identify some 9 or 10 standard musical compositions when the first few measures of each are played.

References for Further Study

Fryberger, A. M., *Listening Lessons in Music*. Newark, Silver, Burdett & Co., 1925.

Gehrkens, K. W., *An Introduction to School Music Teaching*. Boston, Birchard, 1919.

Giddings, T. P., *Grade School Music Teaching*. New York, Congdon, 1919.

Glenn, M., Lowry, M., and de Forest, M., *Music Appreciation for Every Child:* Primary Grades. Newark, Silver, Burdett & Co., 1925.

Kinscella, H. G., *Music Appreciation Readers*. New York, University Publishing Co., 1926-27. (Six books.)

McCauley, C. J., *A Professionalized Study of Public School Music*. Knoxville, J. E. Avent, 1933.

Mursell, J. L., and Glenn, M., *The Psychology of School Music Teaching*. Newark, Silver, Burdett & Co., 1931.

Starr, M., *Music for Children*. London, Sidgwick and Jackson, Ltd., 1924.

Thorn, A. G., *Music for Young Children*. New York, Charles Scribner's Sons, 1929.

Victor Talking Machine Co., *Music Appreciation for Little Children*. New York, Victor Co., 1920.

CHAPTER XVI

ART—PRINCIPLES UNDERLYING INSTRUCTION

THE FOUR ELEMENTS OF ART

Art, as it happens, is a word used with considerable vagueness, not to say unction, in contemporary life. Unlike music, the word art fails to convey a sufficiently definite concept. We shall have to clarify and sharpen it before we can go forward with the task of this chapter.

As employed in everyday usage, art is an exceedingly inclusive word. We speak, and rightly so, of the art of living. If we narrow the meaning of the word to creativeness and enjoyment in the field of formal aesthetics, we find that music, poetry, fiction, the drama, and the dance, all belong to the family of the arts. In the narrower sense in which we shall consider it here, art is beauty made visible by the hand of man.

The forms of beauty with which we are to deal are sometimes referred to as the space arts. Beauty may be visible in space in one of two ways: It may be a statue or it may be a picture; it may be a building or it may be beautifully formed letters on the printed page. Art, in other words, may be graphic or it may be plastic, shaping matter into form.

We have implied that the space arts involve line, form, and construction, but a moment's reflection will show that we have omitted some of the elements. Let us make good this omission in the expressive words of Henry Turner Bailey: [1] "Color," he says, "is one of the three

---

[1] Bailey, H. T., *Art Education*. Boston, Houghton Mifflin Co., 1914.

passwords to the world beautiful. The second is form, and the third arrangement. The essentials in mastery and progress in art must rest on the development of a keen eye for color, a knowledge of pleasing combinations of color and skill in producing such combinations."

Narrowing them somewhat, as we must in discussing general as contrasted with professional art education, and limiting our consideration to the primary grades, we may say that the elements or fundamentals of art are four in number, i.e., color, drawing, design and construction.

Color. The six pigments which approach most nearly to the red, orange, yellow, green, blue, and violet of the spectrum may, according to Littlejohns,[2] be regarded as "a color alphabet of six letters which will make a far larger number of words than any child can ever hope to be able to use."

Drawing. "As it exists at present," says Sargent,[3] "drawing is the result of an evolution. Its vocabulary has been added to by each generation and embodies the accumulated results of human observations. One imagines that he is expressing himself in terms suggested directly by the object, but this is only partly true. Drawing an object means translating one's perceptions into terms which have been evolved by the race, and which demand careful selection."

Design. Design is the arrangement of parts in an evident order and into a satisfying whole. "Wild-rose petals fallen in the grass," says Bailey, "have no less individual beauty than they possessed when growing upon the rose-hip, but the beauty of the flower they constituted is gone, the beauty of arrangement has disappeared."

Construction. In general, the meaning of this element is

[2] Littlejohns, J., *Art in Schools.* London, University of London Press, 1928.
[3] Sargent, W., *Fine and Industrial Arts in Elementary Schools.* Boston, Ginn & Co., 1912.

PRINCIPLES UNDERLYING INSTRUCTION 205

obvious enough. It is the plastic aspect of art as drawing is the graphic. It calls for the production of things that shall satisfy the sense of beauty. It is often the fruition of previous efforts in drawing and design. It is the visualization in materials of an aesthetic concept. It deals with materials from the point of view of form and color. It carries art from fantasy to utility and practicability.

THE AIMS OF ART IN THE PRIMARY GRADES

"There is no general agreement throughout the country," says one of the most recent students to make a survey of this field,[4] "in regard to minimum essentials of art education, or in respect to actual subject matter content or types of classroom activities which may be supplied under the various topics listed in the curriculum." Under the circumstances, we shall present for the consideration of the student a number of efforts to formulate principles for a course of study in art for the primary grades.

We shall begin with Professor Whitford, who suggests the following classroom activities and experiences for the primary level:

    1. Free creative expression in drawing, design and paper cutting;
    2. Use of line, form, and color in representation and design; graphic vocabulary (drawing of animals, figures, objects, plants, action drawing);
    3. Illustration of stories, games, events of every day life, themes, nature study, etc.;
    4. Study of art in home and clothing;
    5. Study of art in relation to town or city;
    6. Use of simple hues of color in illustration, design, and poster work (simple decorative arrangement);

[4] Whitford, W. G., *An Introduction to Art Education.* New York, D. Appleton-Century Co., 1929.

7. Rhythmic repeats (borders and simple surface patterns);
8. Application to constructed objects (bowl, tile, box, etc.);
9. Picture study;
10. Lettering and printing posters, etc.;
11. Special problems: Hallowe'en, Christmas, Valentine, and Easter cards, favors, posters, etc.;
12. Construction, modelling, and project work of various kinds (pliable materials which do not hinder imagination);
13. Correlation with English, nature study, community life, etc., and all grade projects possible.

Sargent proposes work in representation, construction, and design, with the following specific aims:

Representation:

The most valuable outcome of the work of the first year in elementary school is the formation of a habit of drawing things uppermost in the interests of the children, giving general pictorial expression of things that interest them. Beginning with the second year, there should follow a more careful and detailed description of the objects represented than in the first grade, and an intensive study of a few typical things, to enable the children to draw these particular things well.

Construction:

Activities should include work with the sand table, clay, paper, and blocks. Beginning with about the second year, the work in construction should in part parallel the drawing, as free illustrative construction, and in part represent the beginning of well-planned work which requires careful measurements and exact delineation of patterns. This calls for the beginning

PRINCIPLES UNDERLYING INSTRUCTION 207

of working drawings, involving in part the making of patterns, and introduces the use of the rule.

Bookmarks, tags, weather signals, flags, pinwheels, valentines, covers, envelopes and folders, illustrative diagrams, such as plans for school gardens, are some of the projects that may engage the children toward the end of the primary period.

Design:

After informal experiences that lead to a sense of rhythmic arrangement and to familiarity with the most easily recognized colors, such as red, orange, yellow, green, blue, and violet, there should follow problems involving the planning of simple forms to be constructed and decorated with suitable ornamentation.

Holiday greetings and souvenirs, bookmarks, valentines, covers for school papers, and borders are some representative projects. Toward the end of the primary period children should be able to distinguish several steps in the different values of a given color, using collected samples and colored crayons.

While the following formulation of aims, presented by R. R. Tomlinson,[5] apply to the entire elementary school and are somewhat general in character, we consider it one valuable approach to the problem of goals:

1. To encourage children to express their conceptions in a variety of ways and materials.
2. To seek pleasure through creative achievemnt.
3. To enable them to see correctly and to represent and make what is seen and conceived, thus to train the hand, eye and mind, for which purpose art is correlated with handwork.
4. To teach the basic principles.

[5] In his introduction to Littlejohns' book, referred to in a footnote on page 204.

5. To train the aesthetic sense, that is, to develop the power to appreciate beauty in nature and art.

Materials. It is not necessary to list all possible material. Perhaps it will not be possible to secure all the material listed. We have endeavored to indicate in brief space the most commonly used and approved equipment in primary art instruction.

Paper—Manila and white drawing paper, and construction paper in colors in sizes 9″ x 12″ and 12″ x 18″ or larger.

Paints—Poster paints are desirable but expensive. Calcimine or cold-water fresco paint is a cheap substitute. The colors should be pure colors of the principal hues. Semi-moist water-colors, eight colors to the box, are frequently used. The technique of handling water-colors is more difficult.

Tools—Large camel's hair water-color wash brushes. Scissors, paste, rulers, clay, etc.

Pencils—Soft drawing-pencils about 3B.

Crayons—Soft chalk-crayons are best for little children.

Procedure

The Approach. "Drawing," says Professor Waddle,[6] "is an activity almost as universal in childhood as speech or play. Only play, of which in some respects spontaneous drawing is a form, reveals more of the inner nature of childhood. In drawing, as in play, the real child 'comes out to meet the world'." This implies that during the first years of experience in art expression we must not only provide a great deal of scope for spontaneity, giving the child joy in his work, but foster creative effort. Formal

---

[6] Waddle, C. W., *An Introduction to Child Psychology*. Boston, Houghton Mifflin Company, 1918.

instruction and imitative work are out of place in these first experiences. With a little encouragement, children will express themselves in drawing and painting in ways that frequently amaze.

When all this has been agreed upon, it remains true that in the arts of expression as in the other fundamental processes there are basic skills to be mastered. The child is a primitive. At best, he can only begin where the race began. But civilized man has developed basic principles of form, color, and arrangement, which must be transmitted to youth.

There are those who would carry the free painting and drawing, with which the best primary teachers begin, so far as to deny children the privilege of benefiting by what the generations have learned and invented. They seem to believe in teaching nothing at all. The proponents of this view seem deeply impressed by what they consider the resemblance between the products of untaught young children and the art of primitive peoples.

> "It was natural that some should begin to mark the resemblance between the art of children and that of the race's childhood. The vigor and freshness admired in one came to be prized in the other, and the great day of creative self-expression of children in art was ushered in. So today, an exhibit of the artistic efforts of children in the progressive schools resembles in its boldness and originality of treatment, in its frank use of primary colors, and its charming lack of accurate proportion or finished technique the qualities found in a collection of Indian, Negro, Maya, Egyptian or Igorot art." [7]

We confess ourselves less than expert in Igorot art. Just why it should be preferable to our own we do not

[7] Rugg, H., and Shumaker, A., *The Child-Centered School*. Yonkers, World Book Co., 1928.

know. Why lack of accurate proportion or finished technique should be so charming we find it equally difficult to grasp. We prefer the attitude toward originality expressed by Sargent. Good design, he thinks, is not the chance output of an uninformed mind. A young child may produce something original in the sense that it is a fortuitous arrangement of shapes that never existed before. Such a result, however, is not necessarily a design because it is original, nor is there any value in the fact that it did not exist before. If it is not good enough to be in itself a reason why it should exist at all, or if the experience involved leads to no better production in the future, it has not been worth doing.

We would call two important facts to the attention of those who go to such lengths in their belief that our unhampered children may produce work comparable to the best products of primitive peoples: In the first place, the primitive examples which appeal to them so much are probably the work of gifted and unusual members of the community. In the second place, this excellence is certainly attributable to early training. This would hardly warrant the assumption that all children are creative and that no training is necessary.

Let us view the same contention from another angle. For the creation of visible beauty, these two things are essential: manual dexterity and creativeness. By creativeness we mean those rare and precious qualities— originality, imagination, inventiveness. But facility in drawing and in the use of color may exist apart from true creativeness. The child who shows an aptitude for technical skill may fool the teacher with his glibness and serve as an example of the creative method. The mark of creativeness is not manual dexterity, but imagination and inventiveness. How numerous are the drudges whose easily attained facility with brush and pencil would have gained them renown in the progressive schools and who, because entirely lacking in creativeness, are earning their keep by making copies of works of art in the galleries.

On the other hand, the naturally creative child with a real talent for expression in the graphic and plastic forms may be overlooked because he lacks facility and must learn the techniques ploddingly. Numerous studies have shown that there is a distinct lack of correlation between high endowment and manual dexterity. Some of the children who have the greatest amount of initiative, imagination, invention, and originality may look rather unpromising in their first approach to the medium. They may be overlooked in favor of the less creative but more facile child whose dexterity lends itself to the production of work that can be exhibited to make the point of the new school.

We believe in an exactly reverse procedure. We would teach those skills and approaches that are established and known, to serve as a means of expression. On the basis of these firmly established abilities, let each express that which he has within him in his own way. Skill does not come suddenly by inspiration. Skill rests on habit and, as Bailey so well puts it, "develops slowly, through doing things with reference to some standard of excellence."

General Principles of Instruction. In the next chapter we shall present, under the several headings that correspond to the components of plastic and graphic art, detailed methods of teaching the skills and the elements of drawing, construction, color, design and appreciation. From this method of presentation the student should not draw the conclusion that we advocate teaching each of these elements in isolation. While we have felt it necessary to analyze the work into its component parts in order to emphasize the essentials in each, we find ourselves in agreement with Bailey, who advises that "from the very first, drawing, designing, and coloring, should eventuate in construction."

We would be glad to see all of the work in art carried on as activities or projects, always provided that each project is educative in this particular sense, and eventuates in advancement in the several elements of art which we have discussed.

By way of preface to the details of the next chapter and, as applicable to all of the instruction in art, we close this chapter with the following general principles underlying instruction:

(1) Avoid emphasizing excellence of the finished product. Whatever may be true of other subjects in the curriculum, in art we should adhere to the principle that only that should be taught which can be shown to be of value to the child now. As in music, our work should be done on the child's level, and serve as a means toward attaining his purposes. We must avoid adult standards and improve the taste of our pupils and create on their part a demand for excellence now.

(2) The school should avoid exhibitions of the children's work, particularly for the parents and other members of the lay community. The danger of the exhibition, as of the children's play or other entertainment, is that the teacher, bearing in mind adult standards, will be tempted to be too insistent on finish. The average layman will not understand the usefulness of crude work in the development of the child.

(3) Let us avoid imitation as far as possible. We should not set tasks arbitrarily, as, for example, telling the children what to draw and how to draw it. It is best to begin with their innate desire to express themselves graphically, and provide them with opportunities for expression.

This may seem to the student in contradiction to our

PRINCIPLES UNDERLYING INSTRUCTION

discussion of "creative education" in a previous section. This is, however, not the case. It is obvious that instruction in various skills must begin at various levels of maturity. We cannot teach reading at age three or philosophy at age ten. In art it has been found best to begin with "free work" and defer precise instruction and standards for a year or two after the entrance to school.

More than music, art lends itself to individual self-expression. In the realm of music we seek release and emotional outlet, but we usually sing the songs we have learned. Very few indeed are the musically creative. In graphic and plastic art, however, invention comes more readily and for this reason our work should proceed by way of encouragement of direct self-expression.

(4) There is no need for formal drill. The child should learn by doing, but not what he is told to do. Neither imitation nor dictation is in order. "In successful composition work," says Klapper, "the lesson proceeds because the child has something to say rather than because he has to say something." This is a sound principle that may well be applied, as he does apply it, to successful work in art.

References for Further Study

Bailey, H. T., *Art Education*. Boston, Houghton Mifflin Co., 1914.

Boas, B., *Art in the School*. New York, Doubleday Doran & Co., 1924.

Jacobs, H. W., *The Drawing Teacher*. New York, Binshey & Smith, 1928.

Littlejohns, J., *Art in Schools*. London, University of London Press, 1929.

Mathias, M. E., *The Beginnings of Art in the Public Schools*. New York.

Nyquist, F. V., *Art Education in Elementary Schools*. Baltimore, Warwick & York, 1929.

Sargent, W., *Fine and Industrial Arts in Elementary Schools.* Boston, Ginn & Co., 1912.

Sargent, W., and Miller, E., *How Children Learn to Draw.* Boston, Ginn & Co., 1916.

Charles Scribner's Sons, 1924. *Art in the Elementary School.* New York, Charles Scribner's Sons, 1929.

Todd, J., and Van Gale, A., *Enjoyment and Use of Art in the Elementary School.* Chicago, University of Chicago Press, 1933.

Whitford, W. G., *An Introduction to Art Education.* New York, D. Appleton-Century Co., 1929.

Whitford, W. G., Liek, E. B., and Gray, W. S., *Art Stories—Book One.* Chicago, Scott, Foresman & Co., 1933.

Wiseltier, J., *A Program of Art Education for Connecticut.* Hartford, State Board of Education, 1933.

CHAPTER XVII

ART—INSTRUCTIONAL PROCEDURES

Drawing

That "learning to draw is learning to see" is an old way of saying something that is exceedingly interesting. When he begins to represent what he sees, the child looks at his environment with an enhanced clarity that stimulates his entire consciousness. Gradually he learns to analyze and interpret visual impressions, to recognize and select the characteristic and the significant features from the bewildering multiplicity of details.

Drawing is a motor outlet for the imagination. The child who draws from imagination finds in it a means of exercising his mental imagery by expressing it in visible form. Though the child may, in the beginning, draw only for his own amusement, he eventually comes to wish that the result shall represent the ideal well enough so that in addition to recalling the thought to himself, it shall also express that thought intelligibly to others.

Sargent considers that under effective instruction the most valuable outcome of the work of the first year in drawing is the formation of the habit of drawing things uppermost in the interests of the children. He urges the teacher to avoid too much or too insistent criticism. He would limit technical instruction to incidental advice as the occasion arises. He would have the teacher work with and for the children at times, so that they may see better ways of obtaining results.

The toys and games of the children, their experiences,

whatever happens to be vividly in their minds and holds interest in their conversation are appropriate subjects for pictorial expression during the early stages of school experience. Since children at this age show little interest in accurate representation and are not ready for such accurate and elaborate drawing, they should be allowed the free and rapid expression that seems so natural and delightful to them. In the beginning of their experience, young children draw what they know about an object rather than what they see at any given moment.

There is no need to hurry children through this stage. The best preparation that can be made for the next stage of the work is the facility that a child gains by drawing in his own way, with the aid of encouragement and good example. This serves the purpose of having the child become accustomed to express his ideas by drawing before the age of self-consciousness and hesitation is reached.

As he grows older, the child changes his attitude toward the results of his efforts. He becomes dissatisfied with mere activity and develops an interest in quality, i.e., the truth of the representation. Now he wants knowledge and seeks adequate means. At this point he should be taught to make a more careful and detailed study of objects. At this stage it is well to center on a few typical things and to draw these well. The child must be led to eliminate some of the crudities and to make the kind of observation that leads to correct impression and accurate recording.

Parker and Temple,[1] in their admirable book, "Unified Kindergarten and First Grade Teaching" present the following valuable advice to the beginning of instruction in drawing:

[1] Parker, S. C., and Temple, A., *Unified Kindergarten and First Grade Teaching*. Boston, Ginn & Co., 1925.

ART—INSTRUCTIONAL PROCEDURES

(1) The subjects selected for drawing should be interesting in themselves and, if possible, should be significant to the children because of recent pleasurable association.

(2) The objects to be drawn should be suitable from the standpoint of the child's skill.

(3) The teacher should stimulate the children by drawing for and with them.

(4) Children may be helped to observe form by having their attention drawn to the distinct parts of an object and their shape and size with reference to the function which they perform.

(5) It is well to examine all the drawings with the class, encouraging the children to note the excellent features in one another's work and to discuss some of the glaring deficiencies.

(6) It is often advisable to discuss with the children their plans for drawing before distributing the material.

CONSTRUCTION

Expression in graphic and plastic art always requires a medium. As the child secures ever greater control over materials and becomes ever more responsive emotionally to form, color and arrangement, he partakes more and more of man's joy in beauty. "Through repeated attempts to gain satisfactory form," says Mathias, "the race has accumulated valuable experiences concerning the use of materials."

Construction is another opportunity for the employment and enjoyment of form and color, this time produced in plastic rather than in graphic form. Those children are few indeed who have not endeavored to make things before coming to school. Since pupils like to play with constructive materials, the capable teacher will not find it necessary to assign tasks. Taking her point of departure from the child's delight in playing with and modifying the form of materials, she will endeavor to improve his manual skill, help him to work purposely toward previously conceived ends, and to plan the processes which will accomplish them.

As in drawing, so in construction, the school experience should begin with the free use of materials. These materials should be so easily manipulated that the child will be able to secure quick results for his efforts without the use of tools and with little skill. There is readily accessible a wealth of opportunity for construction, infinite in variety. Clay for modeling, pasteboard boxes and wood for larger structures, materials for weaving, papers for cutting and tearing, cloth and crêpe paper for costumes, are always desirable in the primary grades.

Beginning with sand and building blocks, the teacher will easily find commercially prepared or home-made opportunities to serve as an outlet for the child's constructive imagination. Not all materials will do, and of those available some will serve better than others. Mathias [2] proposes a valuable set of criteria for determining the usability of materials in the primary grades which will guide the teacher better than would an actual listing of things that may be employed. The materials used should, she states,

(1) Provide for free bodily activity through large work and discourage little, intricate work that inhibits free movement;
(2) Promote the condition of satisfaction;
(3) Allow the child to begin where he is and utilize his native equipment;

[2] Mathias, M. E., *The Beginnings of Art in the Public Schools*. New York, Charles Scribner's Sons, 1924.

ART—INSTRUCTIONAL PROCEDURES 219

(4) Provide problems the solution of which will lead on to further growth;

(5) Provide for quick results.

When the child first enters school we should avoid too much instruction and too many tools. We should refrain from insisting on skills. We should not require complicated processes. Such instruction and such demands are likely to limit the imagination. Toward the end of the primary period, however, we may begin to pay some attention to technical procedures and introduce pupils to some of the simpler instruments of precision, such as the rule and compass. At this point, children should begin to see that materials must be shaped according to a predetermined form. They should be led to abandon the primitive methods of arriving at results by trial and error. They should gradually learn that there is a language of construction involving mathematics, patterns, and plans.

The following specific suggestions are taken from "Unified Kindergarten and First Grade Teaching": [3]

1. Allow children to experiment freely with such materials as they are to use in order that they may satisfy their curiosity, become somewhat familiar with the qualities of each material, discover some of its possibilities, and gain some power in handling it.

2. When suggesting things to be done, be sure that they are activities which are worth spending time upon and that they will make a strong appeal to the interests of the children. Only thus is it possible to secure the concentrated attention and effort necessary in developing skill.

3. Provide for repetition and practice by allowing the children to make a variety of objects which

[3] See preceding footnote.

involve the same process instead of limiting them to the repeated making of the same objects.

4. Help children to form clear visual images of the desired results through observation of real objects, toys, and pictures, and the comparison of their own products with some that are superior.

5. When a child cannot discover for himself how to do a thing, it is better to show him than to depend on verbal directions.

6. Develop standards of good work through comparison of children's efforts and through wise praise.

7. Select materials and problems with reference to the ability of the children so that they may not lose confidence through failure, but maintain a hopeful attitude toward their work.

Color

We all respond to color, and the child has had experience with color and been delighted by colors long before he entered school. He must now begin to distinguish between colors, values, hues. But this need not be taught as abstract knowledge. The ultimate goal should envisage for the child ability to use color truthfully and with good taste, and to appreciate good color effects in nature and in art. Color appreciation will develop in children when they have chosen and combined tones and manipulated pigments. Beginning with general consciousness of color sensations, the child will gradually learn to discriminate fine color qualities, find pleasure in harmoniously related tones, and learn to harmonize given colors. Methods of achieving these ends are almost as numerous as resourceful primary teachers. A number of students in this field have definite procedures of their own.

Sargent would acquaint the children with the more prominent color tones, such as red, orange, yellow, green, blue and violet, by collecting samples or separating into color groups samples already gathered. He suggests placing two given colors, as yellow and green or green and blue, a little distance apart and arranging samples so as to form a graded series of intermediate tones between the two. He also advises making a series of lighter and darker tones of single colors by means of samples.

Bailey suggests this interesting procedure: Beginning with the spectrum, use a glass prism and throw on a sheet of white paper on the wall, "the richest and purest color unit known." From this as the point of departure, have the children collect examples of the rainbow colors and learn to distinguish five typical colors by name—red, yellow, green, blue, purple. Teach the children to see that these five colors may be arranged in a circuit in the spectrum order and to think of them in such a relation. By means of natural objects, colored papers, crayons, and water colors, teach the five typical colors, their names, and their spectrum order as the alphabet of color. Lead the children to choose the most pleasing tone of each, to discover that the most intense colors are not always the most pleasing, that subdued or "middle" colors are found most frequently in nature and in common objects and that the brilliant colors are usually found in small quantities only.

Teach the children to recognize different values of one color, lighter and darker, and how to produce them by the thinning of the pigment with water, by adding white for the light values, or by mixing black with the pigment for the dark values. Teach them to recognize and to produce the middle red, yellow, green, blue, and purple, and a light and dark value of each. Let them discover the most pleasing combinations of two values of one color in a given design, and that the two values must not seem too near alike, nor too sharply different.

Finally, lead the children to see that the typical colors are seldom seen in nature, that varieties of a color are called its hues, and that there are combinations of hues of color which look best when combined in a given design. Let them learn by experience that the hues must not be too much alike or very greatly different, and that the nearer colors are in hue the more they must differ in value.

Design

We come to one of the most useful and applicable aspects of instruction in art. Art differs from music in that it need not be taught as an isolated activity calculated to furnish harmless enjoyment or to provide opportunity for the worthy use of leisure. While music may be divided into the two aspects of creating or performing, on the one hand, and appreciating, on the other, the work in art leads to that indescribably important third element, application.

The child who has really been affected by the work in art will retain a heightened sense of beauty and an intensified dislike of ugliness. He will see and enjoy beauty in the landscape. He will choose his apparel and arrange his environment with discrimination and good taste. "Taste," says Bailey, "develops gradually through the making of choices with reference to some ideal."

"The only way to learn to design," says Littlejohns, "is to learn to make." He advises the teacher to commence with easily manipulated materials, such as colored buttons, peas, or marbles, dropped on to a base of sand. Other possibilities are cutting paper to be pasted on a background, or stitching colored wools or silks on cloth. Clay, raffia, wood and paint suggest still other possibilities. The point is that in design, as in every other phase of art instruction, progress is made by doing, not by knowing. The child will advance in design by endeavors to create, not by memorizing or even by understanding verbal instruction. The teacher who cannot do cannot teach.

Definitions of design are as elusive as definitions of good taste. From the point of view of arrangement, it has been described as "an evident order in the parts which constitute the whole." In addition to being evident, the arrangement must be satisfying. But the words *evident* and *satisfying* are themselves elusive. It is probably true, as Mathias puts it, that in order to be completely satisfying, the whole must afford both utilitarian and aesthetic satisfaction. Assuming that the genuine usefulness of any article is readily determinable, we must still inquire what are the elements in an arrangement that afford aesthetic satisfaction? Mathias [4] lists these interestingly as follows:

1. Rhythm—movement gained by orderly repetition
2. Balance—equilibrium established by an equal division of weights
3. Emphasis and subordination—accenting certain parts of a composition and subduing others
4. Proportion—spacing that pleases

Bailey makes the stimulating suggestion that design be taught by emphasizing the intimate relations of its basic principles to those of music. He points out that a monotonous order is the most elementary. The accented orders, he shows, are essentially three—the double movement, the triple movement, and the pentuple movement. All

[4] Mathias, M. E., *Art in the Elementary School.* New York, Charles Scribner's Sons, 1929.

other "times" are derived from these or are similar to them in their manifestations. To this principle he would direct the attention of the children, "that they may see the music of nature."

He would begin work in design with the principle of repetition. In the endeavor to give children a sense of the regular recurrence of the elements, he suggests the possibility of emphasizing this recurrence by working to music. With colored crayons, for example, the children might repeat to the accompaniment of music the elements that go to make a border, thus securing the sense of regularity, uniformity, and perfect order.

Coming to repetition with accent, he would again employ music to teach the child the relationships between the loud and soft, and long and short of music and the bright and dull of color. In the same way, he would introduce the other rhythms, leading the children to produce the several patterns with crayons and to discover that these rhythms occur in one direction, forming borders; in two directions, forming surface patterns; and around a center, forming rosettes.

Appreciation

It is difficult to define appreciation as one of the phases of procedure in graphic and plastic art. Unlike music, in which appreciation essentially means listening, and literature, where appreciation essentially means reading, appreciation in art may, among other things, actually mean expression. Inevitably one lives in the terms of color and line and arrangement that he knows and feels to be beautiful and satisfying. In the realm of art instruction, the philosophy of Rousseau comes to its full fruition: Art is life.

In the most complete sense of the word, effective

instruction in art should result in altered behavior in certain aspects of life, and this changed behavior is definitely appreciation. Appreciation of visible beauty may express itself particularly in two ways, as selection and as aesthetic contemplation. Contemplation, again, has two aspects—enjoyment of natural beauty and enjoyment of the fine arts.

In its aspect of selection, art appreciation can hardly be distinguished or separated from design. Instruction in design is instruction in appreciation. The person who has been really influenced by his work in design will, in the making or the purchasing of things for his daily use, make his selections in terms of the adequacy of the object in question, the refinement of its essential parts and proportions, the grace and fitness of the decorative parts.

In its aspect of aesthetic contemplation, art appreciation may, as we noted above, express itself as enjoyment of nature or enjoyment of formal art. "The primary significance of art in education is the development of aesthetic attitudes toward the visual world," says Nyquist.[5] But the visual world is not all man-made. Visible beauty gives joy, whether it be the work of man or of nature. Of what avail is the sunset to him who, having eyes, sees not? The direct outcome of the work in art appreciation will be heightened enjoyment of the contour of the hills, the form and the color of the leaf, the graceful curve of the tree bent by the wind.

Aesthetic contemplation also concerns the enjoyment of the fine arts: the architecture, sculpture, painting, and printing of every class; formal design, and all else that is art in the usual restricted sense. It is possible, in the graphic and the plastic arts as in music, to speak of formal appreciation and to enlarge the scope of aesthetic

[5] Nyquist, F. V., *Art Education in Elementary Schools*. Baltimore, Warwick & York, 1929.

experience far beyond the creative capacity of any group of children.

We know little indeed about effective formal procedure for appreciation except insofar as the effort to create teaches respect and admiration for fine work. Approaches are numerous and obvious. Art galleries and beautiful examples of sculpture and architecture, reproductions and art history, detailed analysis and comparisons—these suggest themselves and are frequently employed. Even in the primary grades the capable teacher will find ways and means to point out to her pupils such aspects of formal painting as fine spacing, interesting composition, color harmony, and rhythm of lines and masses. At the very outset of school, some children may be encouraged to begin the collection of copies and of reproductions.

Desirable Outcomes

The leaders in art education have not, unfortunately, been able to present organized principles in this field on which they can agree and which they are willing to sponsor. After examining courses of study in art representing a considerable number of cities, we have come to the conclusion that one of the soundest formulations of outcomes is still that of Walter Sargent, presented in his "Fine and Industrial Arts in Elementary Schools" [6] in 1912. The following statements are based largely on his work, although we have added some further elements concerning which there seems to be substantial agreement:

At the End of the First Year

    (1) A reasonable standard of accomplishment in drawing has been reached if the children have

[6] Sargent, Walter, *Fine and Industrial Arts in Elementary Schools*. Boston, Ginn & Co., 1912.

ART—INSTRUCTIONAL PROCEDURES

developed a habit of expressing their ideas with pencil so that drawing seems to them a matter of course.

(2) A reasonable standard of accomplishment in construction has been reached if they have gained ability to handle simple material such as paper, clay, sand, and blocks so that such materials assume desired shapes.

(3) A reasonable standard of accomplishment in design has been reached if they have gained some ideas of good spacing and arrangement under guidance of the teacher, and have begun to enjoy the rhythmic spacing of forms. They should know which color combinations are pleasing, and the dark and light of each color.

(4) A reasonable standard of accomplishment in color has been reached if they have discovered the general distinctions of color and know the names of these five colors: red, yellow, green, blue and purple.

At the End of the Third Year

(1) A reasonable standard of accomplishment in drawing has been reached if the children, in addition to increased facility in drawing, have added to their resources of expression a somewhat definite knowledge of a few typical objects, gained by successive lessons on the same topic, and have fixed in mind certain fundamental geometric relations, such as vertical, perpendicular, horizontal, and parallel, not as definitions but as means of comprehending and expressing form.

(2) A reasonable standard of accomplishment in construction has been reached if they have de-

veloped their ability to embody ideas in materials not only as the result of increased skill of hand, but also because of the added power given by some command over such an aid to accuracy, foresight, and economy as a foot-rule.

(3) A reasonable standard of accomplishment in design has been reached if they have better ideas of good spacing and proportions and an increased pleasure in ability to distribute forms over a surface in consistently related measures.

(4) A reasonable standard of accomplishment in color has been reached if they can distinguish between hues and values, mix and name intermediate colors in paint and crayon, obtaining bright and dull colors, and understand that intensity is in part a matter of relation.

CHAPTER XVIII

THE NON-SKILL OBJECTIVES

A Brief Preface to Three Chapters [1]

In dealing with the six fundamental skills, our chapters naturally divided themselves into certain sections. We dealt with the content appropriate for children, presented in a series of units in a sequence which practice has taught the profession to be appropriate, accompanied by a more or less detailed outline of teaching procedure and a statement of desirable outcomes.

Prior to beginning this non-skill division in which we propose the method of the project, the student would find it profitable to examine a number of works devoted to a description of this instructional plan. In examining these works on progressive education, the reader may or may not find a formal description of the content or the type of mastery that represents the goal of the particular phase of education. He may or may not find a statement of desirable outcomes against which to check the effectiveness of the teaching. One element, however, is missing in all of these treatments, and one element is always present.

The sections of our chapters devoted to the fundamental processes referred to above as teaching procedure organized step by step, will not be found in these books, since that is precisely what the "new" educators object to. Instead, the student will find a comparatively small proportion of the pages of each book devoted to a restate-

---

[1] In connection with this and the three chapters that follow, the student would do well to review Chapter IV.

ment of the general theory of the curricular program, and the bulk of the work devoted to a record of the actual work of particular classes, typical activities, and typical units of work.

To the general project procedure we have endeavored to introduce the reader elsewhere. For those who would enter the discussion at greater length and see the activity program presented with perhaps greater enthusiasm than we have been able to command, we have provided bibliographies. Typical units of work or projects we shall not, however, present. Did we favor specific procedures in the division of primary education which we are about to consider, we would outline such procedures because we would regard them as universally applicable. Examples, however, remain examples. As we have said elsewhere, that which was effective in the hands of one teacher at one time, in one place, and with one group of children may be hopelessly out of place in another situation. We consider it preferable to indicate the content and, where possible, to set up desirable outcomes. With this equipment let the teacher face her task, her children, her community, and endeavor to achieve in her situation that which others have been able to achieve in theirs. Let her originate real activities, not set up imitations.

To serve at all times as a test of the effectiveness of a school activity, let us recall Stormzand's enumeration of the characteristics of the project:

(1) It is a definite and clearly purposeful task.
(2) It can be set before a pupil as seeming to him vitally worth while.
(3) It approximates a genuine activity such as occupies people in real life.

The task before us is to deal with the five "other objectives" as outlined in Chapter Four, i.e., ethical char-

THE NON-SKILL OBJECTIVES 231

acter, worthy home membership, citizenship, health, and leisure. It is, however, not practical to organize our discussions in exactly these terms. There is one objective, leisure, which covers so large a range of school activity that it cannot be isolated for discussion as a special topic. On the other hand, there is one phase of school work, nature study, which cannot at the primary level be conceived of as tending toward the achievement of one particular educational objective.

Education for leisure is an important aim of education. We dealt with it when we discussed music, art, and literature. We shall be working toward worthy use of leisure when we discuss physical education, nature study, and hand work. When all the work that we outline is carried on effectively there is no place for a specific discussion of the objective of leisure in primary education. On the other hand, there are activities which decidedly belong in primary education and which are difficult to associate with the formulated objectives: handwork other than construction in art; the introduction of the child to his social environment; and his introduction to the phenomena of the natural environment. It is possible to contend that the child's introduction to his community meets the objective of citizenship. Of nature study we might say that in a sense it is preparation for a fundamental process, science, to be studied later. On the other hand, in view of the necessarily unorganized character of the work we might call nature study education for leisure. Not only do some of its aspects certainly represent education for health, but those who organize curricula in nature study point to its ethical values. When we consider gardening and the cultivation of the love of flowers we might well claim to be training the children for worthy home membership.

In the three chapters which follow, we shall assume that leisure is fully covered without specific discussion. In the first of the three we shall deal with citizenship, ethical character, and worthy home membership as training for character. In the second we shall deal with health, and in the third we shall discuss the environment.

CHAPTER XIX

TRAINING FOR CHARACTER

CHILD AND ADULT

"Well, and this boy will make a good merchant, and I will take him out of school and see if he can be apprenticed in the grain market. It will be a convenient thing to have a son where I sell my harvests and he can watch the scales and tip the weight a little in my favor."[1] So said Wang Lung to his heart in that delightful story of Chinese peasant life, "The Good Earth." So saying, he illustrated very well the first point that we desire to make in this matter of character training, i.e., that it cannot be confined to school.

"Is that what they teach you in school," seems to be the reproving cry of the adult that echoes down the ages, each generation in turn paying the school the high compliment of assuming that it has the power to mould morals and manners which will withstand a hostile environment. It is fully time that the adult world take responsibility and change the rhetorical question to read: Is that what you have seen me do? Is that what you have heard me say? Is that point of view implicit in the behavior of your father and mother, your relatives, your fellow citizens, and the men entrusted with leadership and authority?

Even the school is not strong enough to mould character according to preconceived ideals when opposite

---

[1] From *The Good Earth* by Pearl S. Buck. Published by the John Day Company. Copyright, 1931, by Pearl S. Buck.

standards of conduct are apparent in private and in public life. "Educational experiences," says Bobbitt,[2] "must take place where they can be normal. Frequently this is not at the schools. In most fields of training there are some of the culminating activities that transfer to the schools with entire ease; there are others which transfer with difficulty; there are still others which will not transfer at all." Unlike arithmetic and penmanship, ethical character and citizenship training cannot be confined to school activities.

Character and the School

The adult who wants to know whether that is "what they teach you in school" makes another interesting mistake. He forgets that he himself received little or no instruction in *morals and manners*. This phrase is a "dead letter" in many a state law and school course of study. In its instructions to the Character Education Committee, the Commission on the Curriculum of the Department of Superintendence of the National Education Association declared that "training in right conduct is one of the chief objectives of the public school." But the Committee reported in the fourth yearbook of the Department, published in 1926, that "it is impossible to discover any body of settled convictions as to the experiences and subject matter which should be productive in large ways of character results." This, after a survey covering three hundred American cities! "There is little evidence," says the Committee, "of carefully thought out, well-tested techniques of procedure which may be employed in securing character results."

The situation is comprehensible enough. Morality, ethics, or the behavior of the individual in social situations and relations has been in the consciousness of man

[2] Bobbitt, F., *The Curriculum*. Boston, Houghton Mifflin Co., 1918.

as long as he has been man. The sanctions governing his conduct and providing his motives have been numerous, ranging from superstitions, uncomprehended traditions, and unfounded fears to the heights of rational philosophy. Sometimes the motives for morals have been definitely related to religion and sometimes they have not.

For many centuries, however, the civilization of which we are a part has based morality on the teachings of religion. Moral and religious instruction have come to appear synonymous. It has been the duty of the church to provide the codes of morals and to furnish instruction and training therein. Where the church is part of the state establishment, moral instruction is, without discussion, entrusted to its care. Where the church is formally and rather suddenly disestablished, we witness a system of education left without "morals." Such a situation was met in the Republic of France, to take one interesting instance, by the actual construction of a code of civic morality for educational purposes.

The public schools of America have been grounded is non-sectarianism, and religious instruction has been zealously excluded from their procedures. This secularism has not been one of hostility, but the motive has been the desire to live together and maintain the schools together in an atmosphere of religious equality and liberty. Religion is, in our practice, a matter of private concern. The school has carefully avoided moral instruction for fear of being charged with teaching religion. The assumption has been that moral instruction is provided by family and church outside of school. It now seems to be agreed on all hands that the system has not turned out well. For many years the schools have been stretching the words *civics* and *citizenship,* words that imply only political relations, to include neighborliness, obedience to parents, and other obvious virtues of the man rather than the citizen. More recently, however, the need has become frankly recognized, as evidenced by the formulated objectives of "ethical character," and "worthy home membership." At the moment there is open and insistent demand that something be done in character education. We therefore face the problem, in this chapter, of indicating three things: (1) What is the trend in the direction of curriculum? (2) What is the trend in the direction of method? (3) Is it possible to deal with desirable outcomes?

Course of Study

It would be difficult for the ordinary child to fail to benefit by the example of the fine men and women with whom he comes in daily contact. It would be difficult for the well-meaning teacher to fail to take advantage of the opportunities that occur so frequently to "point the moral." The daily group activities of the class and the school, the varied relationships of the playground, the assemblies, the social occasions, the civic activities that the school occasionally joins in, the numerous annual celebrations, the very content of the several subjects—all these inevitably represent incidental character training.

But incidental instruction, someone has aptly said, is accidental instruction, and the schools are quite rightly on the way toward the organization of a formal curriculum. A number of American cities now report such courses of study. It will be noted that the presentation of a course of study implies the formulation of a code of conduct, ethics, or morals. Such formulation is now in process in the United States. A number of cities are either working on or have completed codes of their own. Several plans have become nationally known.

TRAINING FOR CHARACTER

While we cannot discuss some of the best known plans, we must at least mention them for the assistance of those students who may desire to follow this topic in further detail elsewhere. The Character Education Institution sponsors the *Code of Morals* formulated by William J. Hutchins. This institution also publishes the *Iowa Plan*. *The Pathfinders of America* is an organized plan of character training sponsored by an organization of the same name. The City of Detroit has its *Children's Code of Morals for Boys and Girls*. A formulation intended for boys, but not primarily for schools, is the Scout Law which sets up ideals of conduct for the Boy Scouts of America.

Japan is a country in which morals and religion have perhaps retained greater independence of one another than in the Christian countries of the West. It is a country, moreover, renowned for its controlled conduct, and its attention to morals and manners. Finally, Japan is a country with a well-organized system of education. The education authorities of Japan publish a series of booklets covering training in character, year by year. This is not a detailed course of study. Rather is it a formal statement of topics to be discussed, or desirable traits to be implanted. For each topic there is an appropriate picture and, as the children learn to read, a story. The teacher presumably takes her point of departure from the picture or the story for a discussion of the particular trait that it is desirable to instill.

It will be interesting to compare this detailed outline of conduct found in the official Japanese publication with the Scout Law, a code carefully formulated for the guidance of American youth. Representing as they do the concepts of ideal morals and manners of two peoples apparently so far apart in historic evolution and contemporary culture, the absence of basic differences will serve to show that the course of study is not so far from completion as some of us think. It will, we believe, make clear the fact that in character training *willing* is more important than *knowing,* so that the problem of the teacher is not so much one of discovering *what* to teach as *how to do so.* Method is more important than content.

In the following comparison, the Japanese material has been summarized and re-arranged. The Scout Law [3] is quoted verbatim.

I

Japan	*America*
Do not lie. Be honest. Keep your word. When you have done something wrong, acknowledge it at once.	A scout is trustworthy. A scout's honor is to be trusted. If he were to violate his honor by telling a lie, or by cheating, or by not doing exactly a given task, when trusted on his honor, he may be directed to hand over his scout badge.

II

Be loyal to your family and your home. Honor, obey, and respect your parents. Be helpful to them as well as to your brothers and sisters. Be loyal to the emperor, to the imperial family, and to your country. Never forget a debt of gratitude.	A scout is loyal. He is loyal to all to whom loyalty is due; his scout leader, his home, and parents and country.

[3] Reprinted through the courtesy of the Boy Scouts of America.

TRAINING FOR CHARACTER

III

Be alert to help where help is needed. Don't make trouble for others. Don't ask of others that which you should be able to do for yourself. Be self-reliant. Be patient. Be inventive and learn to make things. Do your part in all community undertakings. Don't lose your head in an emergency, but remain calm.

A scout is helpful. He must be prepared at any time to save life, help injured persons, and share the home duties. He must do at least one good turn for somebody every day.

IV

Cultivate friendship. Be neighborly. Be sympathetic and kind towards others. Be generous. Look at the faults of others with a lenient eye.

A scout is friendly. He is a friend to all and a brother to every other scout.

V

Never be impolite. Observe good manners under all circumstances. Do not boast. Do not quarrel.

A scout is courteous. He is polite to all, especially to women, children, old people, and the weak and helpless. He must not take pay for being helpful or courteous.

VI

Be kind to animals. Be kind to those who wait on you. Be kind to older people. Help the poor and needy.

A scout is kind. He is a friend to animals. He will not kill nor hurt any living creature needlessly, but will strive to save and protect all harmless life.

VII

Be a good citizen. Obey all the laws laid down for your guidance. Be respectful to your teachers.

A scout is obedient. He obeys his parents, scoutmaster, patrol leader, and all other duly constituted authorities.

VIII

Be punctual. Don't be lazy. Always be co-operative. Do what is to be done with vim and vigor, with zeal and eagerness.

A scout is cheerful. He smiles whenever he can. His obedience to order is prompt and cheery. He never shirks nor grumbles at hardships.

IX

Be thrifty. Handle your own property carefully, with neatness and order. Respect the property of others.

A scout is thrifty. He does not wantonly destroy property. He works faithfully, wastes nothing, and makes the best use of his opportunities. He saves his money so that he may pay his own way, be generous to those in need, and helpful to worthy objects. He may work for pay but must not receive tips for courtesies or good turns.

X

Don't be a coward. Meet every situation with courage.

A scout is brave. He has the courage to face danger in spite of fear, and to stand up for the right against the coaxings of friends or the jeers or threats of enemies, and defeat does not down him.

TRAINING FOR CHARACTER

XI

Be healthy. Do not follow the bad example of others. Be studious.

A scout is clean. He keeps clean in body and thought, stands for clean speech, clean sport, clean habits, and travels with a clean crowd.

XII

Revere and respect your ancestors. Be reverent at the shrine of the emperor's ancestors. Observe the nation's holidays.

A scout is reverent. He is reverent toward God. He is faithful in his religious duties and respects the convictions of others in matters of custom and religion.

METHOD—CONVICTION OR HABIT?

Method, we said above, is a more difficult problem in character education than is the question of content. First there is the controversy between those who would carry on "direct" and those who contend for "indirect" instruction. Some propose rather formal and, one is tempted to think, formidable plans, such as the *Five Point Plan* and the *Iowa Plan,* providing varied procedures, tests, and records; others would wait for the appropriate occasion to arise and then strike the iron while it is hot.

The truth is that the possible differences in method are not well described by the words *direct* and *indirect.* Whenever any one plans or intends to teach character, the method is *direct* regardless of whether he deals with morals on Monday, manners on Tuesday, and thrift on Friday, as is done in the schools of Elgin, Illinois, or whether he deals with these subjects when the occasion seems propitious. Insofar as the instruction is planned, it is direct. The controversy, if one there be, had better be designated as one between two extreme points of view: some would teach character by words, through reading and discussion, employing illustrations in literature and life, all leading to *conviction;* others would have the child act first and think afterwards, resting on *habits.*

The core of the one method is the pattern found in literature, such as Washington and the famous cherry tree, a pattern that furnishes points of departure for discussing the several virtues. While no experienced educator would favor this method exclusively, it is one that many would rely on primarily. On the other hand, we have those who would proceed by action rather than by word, provide vivid experiences, and foster habits, letting the theory come after the fact.

The first of these methods would be far the easier. In our opinion, it would also be the less effective. The fundamental question is this: *Shall we try to translate thought into action or action into thought?* On this point William James offers wise counsel:

> "There is no better known or more generally useful precept in the moral training of youth than that which bids us pay primary attention to what we do and not to care too much for what we feel. Action seems to follow feeling, but really action and feeling go together. You should regard your professional task as if it consisted chiefly and essentially in training the pupil to behavior."

The danger of the method of discussion is that it may lead to verbalism instead of to action. Too many of us know the right answers but go on performing the wrong deeds. It is surely not a lack of knowing the right that leads so many of us into doing the wrong. So little is as yet known of the deeper motives of life, hidden as these are from our very selves, so few persons and so few situations are clear and uncomplicated, that the plans which are being currently proposed appeal to one as rather naïve.

The Bible has it that "as a man thinketh in his heart, so is he." That is doubtless true, but in the process of achieving this synchronization it is our opinion that being so precedes feeling so. Character education is a problem of *personality,* not of *pattern.* More important than "the deeds of great men" will be actual daily experience on the real plane of activity, in forming the good man. While availing ourselves of every sort of aid, we would still emphasize the need for behavior far more than the need for comprehension or consent. Too many of us in contemporary life consider it wrong to compel children to act in the way that the adult world knows to be right. Too many of us feel it an unwarranted invasion of personality. We must explain the reasons, it seems, and when the child understands them he will conform to our desires. With James we feel that it would be wiser to insist on the act and let the philosophic sanction follow. *Spare the rod and spoil the child,* may be extreme counsel, but it is not entirely false.

Here, then, is a phase of education ideally suited for the project method. Let the children do something involving behavior. Let them live and behave in accordance with accepted standards. Let them control their impulses in difficult situations. Let every aspect of formal instruction arise out of a preceding behavior situation. *First do the right thing; then think about it.*

Desirable Outcomes

To the teacher who would like to observe an able colleague at work, we heartily commend Amelia McLester's "The Development of Character Traits in Young Children."[4] It is from her book that we quote the following list which would be better called a check list than *desirable outcomes*. It should prove helpful as a list against which to check behavior and from which to select material. It is worded and illustrated in terms more specifically suitable for primary children than the more general codes presented in preceding paragraphs.

The ideally socially adjusted child, says Miss McLester, tends to act in the following ways:

1. Good manners:
   Says please; thank you; excuse me, or I'm sorry; good morning; and goodbye, as occasions demand.
   Closes doors quietly.
   Does not always take the largest and best things for himself.
   Keeps his hands off other people.
   Does not do rude things to attract attention, especially before guests or in public places.
   Is polite to guests and sees that they are made comfortable.
   Is courteous in speech and manner to every one, including servants.
   Does not push to get ahead in crowds.
   Covers his mouth when he coughs, belches, or sneezes.
   Keeps his fingers out of mouth and nose.
   Does not play with handkerchief.
   Has clean hands when he comes to table.
   Sits up straight at the table.
   Does not talk when mouth is full.
   Keeps mouth closed when he chews his food.
   Does not make a noise when he eats or drinks.
   Keeps his hands off other people's food.
   Does not play with his own food.

[4] See references at end of chapter.

TRAINING FOR CHARACTER

2. Fairness, generosity, and unselfishness:
   Is willing to wait turn in playing games.
   Is willing to continue to play after he has had his turn at being 'it'.
   Shares his own possessions and school equipment with other children.
   Does not take things from other children without asking for them.

3. Co-operation and kindness:
   Is willing to do his share of work when a group is working together.
   Assists others when they need help.
   Refrains from teasing or annoying other children.
   Is careful not to hurt others in play.
   Is friendly toward all, especially new, younger, and timid children.
   Is kind to pets and animals.

4. Self-control:
   When hurt, tries not to cry.
   Does not complain about assigned tasks.
   Does not tease to be allowed to do things.
   Takes corrections without sulking and endeavors to profit by them.
   Takes defeat in games well.
   Does not make undue demands on teacher's time and attention.
   Waits his turn to talk.
   Is clean in his language.
   Is clean in his conduct with other children.
   Does not tattle on other children.
   Tries to settle difficulties without appealing to adults.

5. Respect for property:
   Takes good care of his own clothing and property.

Takes good care of the property of others.
Does nothing to mar the beauty of a public place, or public property.
Does not waste common property—paper towels, etc.

6. Neatness and orderliness:
Keeps hands, face, nails, and body clean.
Uses his handkerchief properly.
Keeps clothes clean and in good order.
Hangs up hat and coat properly, and takes care of all his possessions, keeping them in their proper places.
Keeps desk and locker in good condition.
Replaces school equipment when he finishes using it.

7. Obedience:
Obeys willingly the rules of the group.
Obeys willingly those in authority—either members of the group, or adults.

8. Reverence and patriotism:
Is reverent at prayer, during reading of the Bible, and when sacred matters are discussed.
Stands when national hymn is played or sung.

9. Perseverance and industry:
Keeps busy and does not waste his time on useless activities.
Concentrates on task at hand.
Finishes one job before starting another, as a rule.
Is not easily discouraged; sticks to his job in the face of difficulties.

10. Initiative and independence:
Thinks through and executes his own plans, without relying too much on guidance and assistance from adults and other members of the group.

11. Reliability:
    Does what he is told without being watched, i.e., acts in absence of supervision as he would otherwise.
    Remembers his tasks without being reminded of them.

12. Honesty and thoughtfulness:
    Plays fair, and is fair in his work.
    Acknowledges when he has done something wrong.
    Returns or reports found articles.
    Does not take things that belong to another person.
    Does not appropriate common property for his own permanent use.

13. Promptness and punctuality:
    Is prompt at school.
    Is prompt in responding to signals, requests, and orders.
    Takes wraps off and puts them on without undue waste of time.

14. Miscellaneous traits:
    Is regular in school attendance.
    Does not make sport of others' afflictions or discomforts.
    Is not hasty in judging others.
    Is generous in criticism of others.
    Does not ask for special privileges.
    Does not take undue advantage of permanent or temporary handicaps.
    Has high standards of work, and puts his best effort into that which he undertakes.
    Sticks to his point when he is convinced he is right.
    Does what he can to keep himself physically fit.
    Does not take undue risks to appear smart.

References for Further Study [5]

Germane, C. E., and Germane, E., *Character Education.* Newark, Silver, Burdett & Co., 1929.

Heaton, K. L., *The Character Emphasis in Education.* Chicago, University of Chicago Press, 1933.

McLester, A., *The Development of Character Traits in Young Children.* New York, Charles Scribner's Sons, 1931.

National Education Association, Department of Superintendence, Tenth Yearbook, *Character Education.* Washington, D. C., 1932.

Neumann, H., *Education for Moral Growth.* New York, D. Appleton-Century Co., 1923.

Trow, W. C., *Character Education in Soviet Russia.* Ann Arbor, The Ann Arbor Press, 1934.

---

[5] Character Education Institution, Washington, D. C., sponsors publications which should be consulted by students planning to make further and more detailed studies in this field.

CHAPTER XX

TRAINING FOR HEALTH

Scope of Primary Health Work

In dealing with character education we set down the principle of procedure that action should precede reflection, that the child should be led to do the right thing first and think about it afterwards. We insisted that character education, particularly at the primary levels, should be founded on habit rather than on theory. While the codes of conduct to which we referred are naturally formulated on the basis of reflection, our "desirable outcomes" were not stated in terms of ethical ideals, but of behavior. With even greater force, if possible, do these principles apply to the "teaching" of health. Here we have a supreme example of the pedagogical doctrine that instruction is educative only insofar as it results in altered conduct. Knowledge of some of the laws of health is indeed important, but knowledge as such, untranslated into action, is of little avail. Particularly does all of this apply to the primary grades. Health work at this level must be directed toward the establishment of sound habits. Explanations, insofar as necessary, may come later.

"Health and Physical Education, as an administrative department," we read in the *Fourth Yearbook* [1] of the Department of Superintendence, "includes logically these three phases: health service, health education, physical education."

[1] Published by the National Educational Association at Washington, D. C., in 1926.

Health Service. "Health service," to follow the Committee further, is a convenient term to cover the various protective measures adopted by the school to conserve and improve the health of the children. These measures and procedures in health service do not primarily depend upon, or involve the knowledge, responsibility, or activity, of the pupils themselves. In view of the fact that this phase of health work belongs primarily to the administration rather than to the teacher, we shall not deal with the details of the routine health examinations; the follow-up program that is an outcome of this examination, leading to the correction of remediable defects; school sanitation, and hygiene, immunization against infectious and communicable diseases; the child feeding program; the provision of first aid and nursing service, and other phases of the general plan for school health.

Physical Education. "Physical Education," to quote the Committee again, "includes the big brain-muscle activities which are valuable in the growth and development of the child. It is the contribution made to the complete education of the child in preparation for life by the fundamental psychomotor activities including play, games, athletics, gymnastics, dancing, pantomime, dramatic activities, swimming, hiking, camping, scouting activities, and similar programs."

This list of activities for out-door and gymnasium to be directed by the teacher implies the possession by her of knowledge and of skills such as most well-trained teachers possess. Where a teacher happens to be unable to direct such work, exchanges with other teachers are frequently effected. Those teachers who have missed this training in the directing of play activities would hardly gain from a listing here of the various games and a detailing of the procedures in each. There are some things that can be learned only by "doing." It would, therefore,

TRAINING FOR HEALTH

be unnecessary for the teacher who already has the skills, and futile for the one who has not, to enter into details here.

To the teacher who possesses the general skills and understands the general atmosphere of the primary children's playground, but is interested in a review or in learning about stimulating new activities, we heartily commend Myers and Bird's "Health and Physical Education." [2] Here she will find a discussion of the supervised playground, its equipment, suitable activities, athletics and informal calesthenics, and lists of games graded year by year as adapted to the several ages of the children in her charge.

Course of Study

We come to the field of health education, and the questions of content, of method, and of desirable outcomes. In the paragraphs below we shall summarize, in much more condensed form than is customary in works devoted exclusively to this subject, the usual content or course of study of the best American city schools. In effect we mean by the term *course of study* primarily the habits which it is desirable to establish, and secondarily that knowledge to be gained and those attitudes to be cultivated which will tend to support the establishment and the retention of sound health behavior.

1. *Cleanliness*. The body must be kept clean. Detailing this for little children, the precept applies specifically to face, neck, ears, hands, wrists, nails, hair, and teeth. It implies clothing that is clean and in order. In terms of habit it means a full bath at least twice a week; brushing the teeth twice daily, before bed and after breakfast; hair that is clean, combed and brushed; nails that are tended and

[2] See references at end of chapter.

clean. It implies a bowel movement recurring at the same time every day. It implies carrying a clean handkerchief, washing one's hands before eating or handling food and after going to the toilet.

2. *Food.* Good food habits mean eating only at regular stated times, the right quantity, and the right constituents. Children should avoid tea and coffee, drink a quart of milk a day, some at each meal, and at least four glasses of water daily. They should eat fruit and vegetables every day, including at least one leafy green vegetable, and cereals such as whole wheat, bran, graham, rye, and toast. Some meat or eggs should also form part of the diet daily. Children should be accustomed to regularity of meals; they should avoid eating between meals, chew their food thoroughly, and eat candy only after meals.

3. *Rest and sleep.* Children should sleep from eleven to twelve hours a day. The best conditions for sleeping are out-of-doors or with windows open, an individual bed, no pillow or one that is flat.

4. *Posture.* The habit should be cultivated of standing with chest up, chin in, waist flat, weight on balls of feet. In sitting, the feet should be flat on the floor in front of the chair, the end of the spine against the back of the chair.

5. *Exercise and play.* The child should engage in vigorous exercise and activities for four or five hours every day, involving the use of big muscles. As far as possible this should be out-of-doors. He should acquire the habit of breathing deeply through the nose. He should be made to understand the value of sunshine and the need for ventilation. He should learn that the best indoor temperature is between 65° and 68° F.

Method

As in character training, so in health education, national organizations have interested themselves in the subject. These organizations have sponsored interesting and important research and publications, and they have from time to time devised plans for the aid of the schools, such as the Modern Health Crusade. These schemes seem related to our national penchant for mass organization. They have some values and leave some residual good. Where, however, an effort is made to follow them out in a formal manner, the schools find too much machinery and too little actual accomplishment. In health, as in character, so much of the basic behavior occurs outside of school bounds and outside of school time that it is beyond the scope of inspection and the possibility of record.

This brings us to a second consideration: Since the scope of daily health habits is so much greater than the possible scope of school activity, the co-operation of the home must be secured in order to attain the best results. After convincing the child of the need to practice certain habits and teaching him the actual method of performance, as, for example, the proper way to brush the teeth, it will be desirable, where possible, to secure the aid of the home. It is the parents who can set the atmosphere in which the regular practice of desirable health habits is encouraged, and it is they who can, at specified intervals, report the consistency with which the child lives up to the goals that have been set for him by the school.

"In the primary grades," say Myers and Bird in their excellent volume to which we have already referred, "relatively little attention need be given to making the child conscious of the reasons why certain health habits should be acquired. The instructional emphasis in these early school years should be given primarily to establish proper health habits, and to develop in the child a feeling of responsibility for his own health conduct." They would, in fact, set aside no period for "recitations in health," relying rather on making maximum use of the numerous opportunities for instruction offered by other aspects of the day's activities and work, and in connection with the other phases of the school health pragram, such as the playground, the nutrition work, if any is carried on, and the several aspects of the health service provided by the general school administration.

In the last three paragraphs we have made three points regarding method in health instruction:

(1) There is no generally accepted and universally followed royal road to health. Conditions differ too much and the non-school environment is too influential to enable the teacher to rely on organized procedure such as she follows in teaching penmanship.

(2) For the best results, the parents should be informed of the program, should be given instruction where necessary, and be induced to co-operate with the school in cultivating certain habits and in responding to the periodic inquiries from the teacher calculated to determine how well these habits are being established.

(3) Formal instruction is out of place. Theoretical instruction is of little value. What instruction is given had better be incidental, in connection with general activities. The goal before the teacher must be habit rather than knowledge. To achieve this she must in some instances teach the "skill," and in all instances keep on checking to see that, in accord with the well-known laws of habit-formation, the child is growing in sound health behavior.

Daily Inspection and Periodic Check

There is one sound practice that is universally applicable. We refer to the daily inspection and the periodic check, which tend to remind the child of the conduct that is expected of him and to induce him to act in accordance with these expectations. The best primary teachers begin every school day with the health-habits inspection. Those who have had the opportunity, from the vantage point of the home, to observe the response of the beginning school child to this daily inspection will testify to its wonder-working effectiveness.

This examination should be objective in character, covering only such practices as are observable. Here are the principal points that can and should be covered by the daily routine inspection. Does the child have

>a clean handkerchief?
>clean face and hands?
>hair neatly combed?
>clothing that is clean and in order?
>shoes that are clean?
>finger nails that are properly cared for and clean?

Where practical, a periodic check is highly desirable, covering those health-habits that are necessarily practiced at home, beyond the ability of the teacher to verify by observation. Such a check will tend to prod the negligent parent and to support the struggles of the conscientious one. Here are the principal points that can and should be reported on in response to the periodic inquiry from the school. Does the child unfailingly

>brush his teeth twice daily?
>sleep in a room with windows open?
>abstain from tea and coffee?
>sleep eleven or twelve hours a day?
>wash his hands before eating?
>avoid eating between meals?

Desirable Outcome

In the following "desirable outcomes" which we have compiled largely on the basis of material found in the Tentative Outline of the City of Cleveland and the Course of Study of the City of Oakland, California, we are doubtless duplicating the content of preceding paragraphs and perhaps stretching the meaning of the word *outcomes*. It seems to us, however, that the detailed list which follows will help some teachers not only in securing a picture of the health behavior of their own pupils, but in the business of persuading the parents of these pupils.

I. *Cleanliness*. Does the pupil habitually
- wash his hands, face, neck and ears with warm water and soap every day?
- take a full bath at least twice a week?
- prevent chapped hands by washing and drying them thoroughly?
- wash his hands before meals, and after going to the toilet?
- keep his nails clean and refrain from biting them?
- trim and file his nails?
- wash his hair once a week and comb it daily?
- use and care for an individual towel, comb, brush, and tooth brush?
- have a regular time for elimination?
- keep hands and objects away from his face?
- bring a clean handkerchief every day and use it properly?
- use the drinking fountain properly?
- use the washbowl and toilet properly?
- keep his clothing clean and neat?

II. *Clothing*. Does the pupil habitually
- wear proper wraps and, when necessary, rubbers, removing them when indoors?

TRAINING FOR HEALTH

remove damp clothing promptly?
wear different clothing at night?

III. *Food.* Does the pupil
eat whole grain bread and cereals?
eat three regular meals daily, particularly breakfast?
eat little or no candy, and only as dessert?
eat properly, slowly, sit down while eating, chew his food thoroughly?
drink milk at each meal, totalling a quart a day?
eat fruit and vegetables every day, including a green, leafy vegetable?
drink at least four glasses of water every day?
wash all fresh fruits and vegetables before eating them?

IV. *Fresh air and sunshine.* Does the pupil
know that rooms should be well ventilated and act on this knowledge?
breathe with the mouth closed?
spend some time every day out-of-doors?

V. *Posture and exercise.* Does the pupil habitually
hold his body in good posture while standing, sitting, and walking?
avoid twisting the body to the left when writing or doing desk work?
choose active games and avoid excessive exercise?
play for at least four hours every day?

VI. *Sleep, rest and relaxation.* Does the pupil
sleep out-of-doors or with windows open?
go to bed at the same regular hour every evening?
rest some time during every day?

VII. *Safety.* Does the pupil
cover his nose and mouth with a clean handkerchief when coughing or sneezing?
keep away from others when ill?
avoid drinking water from strange sources?
keep screens on doors and windows closed?
know that self-control is necessary in case of injury?
know that he should go to an adult for aid when injured?
know that crowding around an injured person should be avoided?
know that open wounds should be kept clean, not be covered with salve, not cleaned with water, but painted with Mercurochrome or its equivalent?
know that nosebleed may be stopped by lying flat on one's back and putting cold applications at back of neck and on the forehead?
know that in case of burn it is well to apply oil or grease or baking soda?

VIII. *Height and weight.* The school can, obviously, do comparatively little toward the attainment of desirable standards in height and weight. In schools where a health service has not yet been developed it may, nevertheless, be of use to the teacher to know what are the norms in these matters. The Weight-Height-Age Table below follows the Tables prepared by Drs. Baldwin and Wood, and published by The American Child Health Association.

TRAINING FOR HEALTH

Height (inches)	BOYS Age					GIRLS Age					Height (inches)
	5	6	7	8	9	5	6	7	8	9	
38	34	34	..	..	..	33	33	..	..	..	38
39	35	35	..	..	..	34	34	..	..	..	39
40	36	36	..	..	..	36	36	36	..	..	40
41	38	38	38	..	..	37	37	37	..	..	41
42	39	39	39	39	..	39	39	39	..	..	42
43	41	41	41	41	..	41	41	41	41	..	43
44	44	44	44	44	..	42	42	42	42	..	44
45	46	46	46	46	46	45	45	45	45	45	45
46	47	48	48	48	48	47	47	47	48	48	46
47	49	50	50	50	50	49	50	50	50	50	47
48	..	52	53	53	53	..	52	52	52	52	48
49	..	55	55	55	55	..	54	54	55	55	49
50	..	57	58	58	58	..	56	56	57	58	50
51	..	..	61	61	61	..	..	59	60	61	51
52	..	..	63	64	64	..	..	63	64	64	52
53	..	..	66	67	67	..	..	66	67	67	53
54	..	..	..	70	70	..	..	..	69	70	54
55	..	..	..	72	72	..	..	..	72	74	55
56	..	..	..	75	76	..	..	..	..	76	56
57	..	..	..	..	79	..	..	..	..	80	57
58	..	..	..	..	83	..	..	..	..	..	58

Weight-Height-Age Table for Boys and Girls in the Primary Grade

In determining height it will be found practical to use a measure, such as a firm paper tape, fastened to the wall. Outdoor clothing, coat, and shoes should be removed. The child should stand erect with his back flat against the wall, heels and head touching the wall. Using an empty chalk box, hold it flat against the tape and lower it until it touches the child's head. For weighing, have the child remove all wraps, sweaters, and shoes. In making comparisons with the norms, take the age to the nearest birthday, the height to the nearest inch, and the weight to the nearest pound.

REFERENCES FOR FURTHER STUDY [3]

Easton, D., *A Practical Guide for Teaching Healthful Living in the Lower Elementary Grades.* Boston, Badger, 1926.
Keene, C. H., *The Physical Welfare of the School Child.* Boston, Houghton Mifflin Co., 1929.
Myers, A. F., and Bird, O. C., *Health and Physical Education.* New York, Doubleday, Doran & Co., 1928.

[3] The following associations publish material that should be consulted by students planning to make further and more detailed studies in this field: American Child Health Association, National Child Health Council, National Safety Council, Joint Committee of the National Education Association, and the American Medical Association.

CHAPTER XXI

INTRODUCING THE CHILD TO HIS SOCIAL AND NATURAL ENVIRONMENT

The universe and all it holds are ever new to the young. Youth is ever pressing on to discover a world fresh and unknown, seeking to take in the wonders of nature and the works of man. The world constantly belongs to the young. It is theirs to take and to inherit. It must be unfolded for them in every aspect: the social, economic, and civic organization; the flowers, the sunshine, the seasons, the mountains, the streams, and the great plains. Children must "observe" their environment and the life about them in the broadest possible interpretation of that word. They must meet the world with every available sense.

I. THE WORLD OF THINGS

It should be regarded as fundamental in education that there is no one road to development. Some children are more readily reached by way of intellect, others by way of emotion. Some minds are better reached through the ear, and some through the eye. Some children are better served by handling materials and by personal observation than by reading the reports of such observations made by others. The use of the hands to make things and to learn by doing is certainly deep-rooted and pedagogically sound. Children differ in their manual zeal and dexterity, but every effort should be made to give them scope.

Work with the hands represents one opportunity for creative expression, possibly the only form of self-expression open to some of the children. It will help give all of them useful practical skill; it will help to develop their judgment; it will give them useful comprehension of tools.

These experiences lead to the development of good judgment of materials, to the discovery of new and hitherto untried or unsuspected interests. Work with the hands will minimize the danger of too artificial, too limited and narrow an approach to life. It will cultivate social understanding. It will give mentally limited children something they can do well, keep them occupied, and help them to a sense of belonging to the group in which they find themselves.

The teacher who has not acquired some little dexterity in the handling of tools and materials will find herself handicapped in the effort to give her pupils the maximum opportunity for growth. The teacher who has some skill in almost any medium will find ready use for it. In dealing with the work in graphic art, we referred to construction as a form of that work. Many other forms of crude but educative effort are available, any of which will be found useful. Out-of-doors, children can be interested in gardening, or in caring for a domestic animal or a pet. They can be led to engage in large, crude construction, making play houses, houses for pets, etc. Indoors, children may build and furnish doll houses, engage in modelling and pottery, fashion and paint wood into toys or useful articles, engage in weaving and in basketry, or use paper and cardboard to make things.

In planning and supervising work with the hands, take the child's point of view and emphasize the thing he is trying to make, not the process by which he is making it. Forego precision and accuracy. Don't insist on design before construction, on drawing before cutting. Let him follow his impulse to do "free hand" work. Place your

SOCIAL AND NATURAL ENVIRONMENT

intention on the outcome and let the process take care of itself. Help the child when he asks for it, but do not turn his attention from the thing he is trying to make to an insistence on skill in making it. Let him do large, crude work.

II. THE WORLD OF MEN

The schools of Germany are now required to take a weekly trip. All over the country one sees pupils accompanied by their teachers, out to learn by travel and direct contact. These trips range all the way from the walk of a mile by the first grade to a week's tour to a distant city or a foreign land by the senior class of the *Gymnasium*. Excursions and observation undoubtedly represent one excellent approach to the comprehension of one's world.

The environment in which we live is of two kinds: On the one hand we have the community organization, the social and economic efforts of man, and the physical results of his labor. On the other hand we are surrounded by the environment that nature provides, whether left in its original form or influenced by the labor of men. Experience with the first of these environments has come to be referred to in school as the "social studies."

In the later school years the social studies comprise a grouping of history, geography, civics in the narrow political sense, elementary economics, and so on. At the primary level the attempts in the realm of social studies are quite properly left unorganized and allowed to vary with the circumstances.

It has been well said that the purpose of the work in social studies at this level is the beginning for the child of a "systematic insight into contemporary life and civilization." We need hardly stress the fact that we make at this early age a simple, informal beginning, and that there is no organized procedure.

Nearly all of the work that has been published in this field presents typical projects. Such projects are of great value in stimulating pedagogical thinking. On the other hand, these publications would represent a definite danger to that teacher who felt that other teachers' procedures and achievements were good models for her to imitate.

Professor Storm,[1] defines social studies at the primary level as "those experiences which are provided by the school primarily for the purpose of extending the child's social understanding." From this statement of purpose we may deduce two principles for our guidance: (1) The introduction to social life must center in the child's own environment. Little of it will become available to him for the first time, but we will endeavor to have him observe it with new eyes, to see things or "into" them in a way that will extend his social understanding. (2) We must endeavor to attain our ends by means of experiences, not by direct instruction.

The Content. Even when we divide environment into its two aspects, social and natural, and confine our attention to the former, the phrase *social environment* implies far more diversity than uniformity. If we are to approach our aims by way of experience and not by direct instruction, it becomes obvious that in a country like ours the procedures will be diverse, not uniform. Each school, perhaps each teacher in different years, will organize unique procedures.

The home is one of the exceptions to diversity of social environment. It is one social institution that most of our children have in common. It will invariably be one of the topics for the cultivation of social understanding. But what a range of differences even here! How many kinds of homes there are! The children and the teacher will

---

[1] See references at end of chapter.

discuss the relationships; the work of the different members of the family; the duties and loyalties, the love, the unselfishness, the understanding, appreciation, and tolerance that go to make the perfect home, the "worthy home member."

Urban children will have access to such manifestations of social organization as shops and services. They will have their chance to know the grocer and the plumber. They will be able to learn by direct contact something of the fire department, the library, the post office. They will be able to make observations of urban transportation problems and methods.

Many of these things will probably be accessible to rural children as the result of school excursions or of stimulated observation on such occasions as they go to town with members of the family. By this same method city children may gain occasional insight into the social organization of the small village and the open country which belong more to the rural child, i.e., the farm and all that goes on there, the blacksmith, the rural mail carrier.

There are schools and teachers who leave the immediate environment and send the child's imagination on travels into remote places or into remote times. In connection with literature and stories they help the children to learn about Indians and Eskimos, about life on deserts or in snow-covered mountain ranges. Beginning with our neighbors who have come here from other lands, we may well go back to study their old homes in far-away places.

Possibly more interesting to young children than remote places are remote times, presented as the story of how our own present came to be. What opportunities there are in America to have the children learn about the history of their own locality, its settlement, its early privations. How interesting, when possible, as it still often is, to hear of these things from the early settlers themselves.

It is right and it is ennobling to endear their childhood homes to our children by supplying their later years with "fond recollections." Not only the history that belongs uniquely to the locality is of precious value. Everything that is unique, be it an industry, a crop, an annual celebration, a ruin, a relic, or a local tradition, should be carefully observed, noted, or visited, as the case may be. These things should be dwelt on and explained, so that we may store the mind with memories of youth that shall be happy, consoling, and proud.

It may not be amiss at this point to summarize the paragraphs that have dealt with the scope of the social studies. In leading the child to an understanding of the social world in which he lives, the teacher will provide opportunities that will enable him to come into contact with and learn from observation, experience, and discussion, at least the following things:

> that various buildings serve various purposes, such as residence, worship, government, business;
> that people work to earn a living and that various occupations represent an interchange of the result of effort;
> that we have means of keeping the community safe by police protection, traffic arrangements, fire protection, lighting, health service;
> that we have various methods of communication, such as the telephone, the post office, newspapers;
> that we have various means of transportation, such as automobiles, railroads, ships, street cars, airplanes.

The Method. So much for "content." What of method? We must repeat here what we have already said about art

SOCIAL AND NATURAL ENVIRONMENT 267

instruction during the early years. When the child enters school at the age of six, he is ready for specific instruction in some subjects, as, for example, number, but not for others to which we wish to introduce him. In this latter case the work is naturally "free" or unorganized. Science and social studies are admirable examples. As study they belong in high school. In the primary grades they begin as "free work" and are appropriate for activities.

Let us avoid *teaching*. Let us proceed by experiencing. The information listed above as a minimum of what is desirable has, obviously, always been available to the child. But we often fail to see what we look at. Formal observation, inquiry, and discussion will arouse curiosity, quicken observation, open the inner meanings, arouse sympathetic comprehension, organize the world for the child, help to make him a citizen.

All of this work would best be carried on by way of projects. Let every step of the introduction to social life be an activity. But not all activities are in themselves pedagogically sound. Let ours be invariably interesting to the children. Let them be only such as the children are eager to engage in. Let these activities be, from the point of view of the teacher, purposeful, planned to achieve clearly envisaged, definitely educative outcomes.

Participation is one excellent form of activity. It has interest; it has the sense of reality; it involves planning and co-operation; it concludes in definite achievement. We refer to the celebration of the several holidays of the year, an excellent opportunity to cultivate understanding and love of country and of home. We refer to civic participation such as is involved in helping the Junior Red Cross, the Parent-Teacher group, or local undertakings. Understanding, willing co-operation, sympathy and altruism, extension of the sense of responsibility—these are the desirable developments of personality at which we should aim, and it is never too early to begin.

In a field in which we are endeavoring to introduce children to social life, our activities should have desirable social atmosphere and sound social relationships. The children should be self-active members of the group, not passively receptive. They should be free agents, not dutiful observers of imposed regulations. The activities in which the children engage should be calculated to release initiative and creative effort.

It may, at this point, not be amiss to translate the general counsel of the preceding paragraphs on method into rather more specific advice:

1. Make use of the instincts underlying play. Let the children imitate and "play" farmer, policeman, fireman, grocer, as they please.

2. Let children use their constructive impulses. Let them give motor expression to their experiences. Let them make things. Let them use material to make houses, clothing, tools, vehicles, machines, to illustrate their experiences.

3. Take many purposeful excursions that are stimulating and enjoyable. Go to the parks, the public buildings, the library, the store, the cobbler's shop, the railway station, the farm. Let the children observe many things and ask many questions.

4. In all of these activities, refrain from forcing children. Endeavor to appeal to them. Do not impose instruction or abstract explanations. Let them experience things. Let them "taste life."

5. Never allow an extended experience like an excursion to remain an undigested and unorganized mass of vague memories. Endeavor to reap the harvest that may be yielded by having the class talk

over the experience. Induce reflective thinking, help organize the impressions.

THE WORLD OF NATURE

Lack of Organized Curriculum. "Nothing else which the schools try to teach," says Dr. Sheldon E. Davis,[2] with regard to nature study, "seems to have so successfully resisted inclusion in textbooks and well-organized courses of study." In an endeavor to become acquainted with the present practices in elementary science, Gerald S. Craig studied several hundred courses of study, handbooks, sourcebooks, teachers' syllabi, and the professional literature. He interviewed supervisors, administrators, and teachers. After exhausting every available means of inquiry into present practice, he concluded that the outstanding characteristic of the nature study and science programs is "total disorganization."

This lack of definiteness of program is comprehensible. In the first place, there is no more room in elementary education for the sciences as contrasted with science than there is for economics and sociology as contrasted with social studies. In the second place, the informal procedure that is most appropriate for primary grades depends on environment rather than on books, and the environment is almost indefinitely variable. The group of studies which later comprises physics and chemistry, botany and zoology, and the other work in science, is at this level left unorganized and allowed to vary with the circumstances of the locality, the season of the year, and the interests of teacher and children.

Nature spreads her wonders before the child. His teacher, taking her point of departure from the character of his curiosity, his ability to understand, or the season

[2] Davis, S. E., *Teaching the Elementary Curriculum.* New York, The Macmillan Company, 1931.

of the year and the location of his home, helps him in his attempts to grasp the meaning of mountains, valleys, streams, oceans; seasons and weather; trees and flowers; ice, frost, and snow; animals and plants, domesticated and wild; temperature, rainfall, food, clothing, and shelter; aquatic life, minerals, and celestial bodies.

The Elementary Science and Nature Study Committee of the Department of Superintendence of the National Education Association made an exhaustive study in order to learn what teachers are actually doing in various parts of the country at various age levels. The result is perhaps the most complete published report of this phase of elementary education. The activities taken from this report and listed below are obviously beyond the possibilities for any one group of children. We do not propose it as a course of study. It is intended as a list of possible activities, some of which may not occur to the teacher unless called to her attention.

I. *Batrachians*

> Watching frogs out-of-doors, in the frog aquarium or terrarium.
> Finding frog tadpoles out-of-doors, watching them.

II. *Birds*

> Watching pigeons in the street or in school.
> Bringing pet pigeons to school.
> Visiting pigeon lofts to see activities of pigeon family.
> Listening to stories of carrier pigeons.
> Feeding winter birds.
> Watching birds common to the school neighborhood, finding their pictures in books, listening to bird calls, imitating these calls.
> Watching the building of nests.
> Watching and possibly caring for a hen and chickens.

SOCIAL AND NATURAL ENVIRONMENT 271

Caring for and watching a pet bird in the school room.

Making a summer report of birds seen, the places where they were observed, and the activities that were observed.

Keeping a bird calendar and discussing what becomes of the birds who leave in winter.

Watching the migrating flock, noting which birds remain, discovering and observing deserted nests.

Watching birds return in the spring.

III. *Fish*

Helping to make an aquarium for goldfish or some fish common in the neighborhood.

Observing and feeding goldfish.

IV. *Insects*

Collecting caterpillars for an insect cage. Feeding them and watching their activities. Noting their decrease in numbers from the time that school opens in the fall.

Looking for bees, watching them out-of-doors.

Discovering and observing cocoons and chrysalids, watching to see what comes from them in the spring.

V. *Other invertebrates*

Watching water snails in the aquarium.

Watching a spider make its web, feeding it in the schoolroom cage.

Collecting thousandlegs for schoolroom observation, watching and feeding them.

VI. *Mammals*

Watching squirrels and chipmunks out-of-doors, and feeding them.

Bringing pet rabbits to school, and caring for them.
Visiting a farm, the zoo, and the circus to see the animals.
Observing young animals and their mothers' care of them.
Making a collection of animal picture books for the schoolroom.

VII. *Reptiles*

Looking for turtles out-of-doors, caring for and watching one in school, finding out how his shell helps him.

VIII. *Wild plants*

Taking a trip to see wild flowers of the vicinity, gathering those which it is permissible to pick.
Watching for the first spring wild flowers.
Noting the colors of wild flowers, preserving some specimens, learning to recognize some of them.

IX. *Cultivated flowers*

Visiting the garden or the park. Learning to recognize some of the flowers.
Observing the effect of wind and insects on flowers, learning about pollination.

X. *Plants in general*

Collecting and sprouting seeds to see young plants come out.
Learning to recognize different vegetables, visiting a garden to see where they grow.
Learning what plants need in order to grow.
Trips to look at vines, shrubs, trees, flowers without woody stems, grasses, and water plants.

SOCIAL AND NATURAL ENVIRONMENT

XI. *Trees*

Gathering tree leaves and seeds; sorting them according to color and shape; grouping leaves and the tree seeds that go with them; sprouting tree seeds to see the young trees come out.

Collecting sprays with winter buds on them, watching the buds.

Taking walks to see and learn to recognize the trees of the neighborhood and to observe the autumn coloring and foliage.

Planting and watching a tree.

XII. *Gardening*

Observing bulbs, planting them in bowls and in window boxes, watching the plants develop.

Observing seeds and sprouting them to see little plants come out.

Buying seed packets and planting them in the garden in school and at home, caring for the growing plants, cultivating and watering them.

Gathering seeds for next year's garden, drying them and putting them up in packets.

XIII. *Sky and weather*

Learning to look for the signs of the coming seasons.

Observing snow crystals through a magnifying glass.

Noting March winds and April showers and their effects.

Observing the decreasing and the increasing length of the day.

Noting the change of temperature from week to week.

Looking at clouds to note color, shape, and size.

Looking at the color of the sky at different times of day and comparing it for days of unlike weather conditions.

XIV. *Star study*

Looking at the stars, finding the Milky Way, the Big Dipper, the moon in its several phases.

Learning to find the Pole Star by means of pointers in the Big Dipper.

Problems of Method. In view of the complete informality of this work there is nothing to be said about method in general. We must, however, refer the student who may find a particular interest in this field to the outstanding work of Gerald S. Craig. The result of his investigations is published by Teachers College, Columbia University, in the form of four pamphlets. The first of these is entitled *Certain Techniques Used in Developing a Course of Study in Science for the Horace Mann Elementary School.* The other three are the course of study itself, covering the six grades of elementary education. In these pamphlets Mr. Craig provides a splendidly outlined course in thorough detail, with sound pedagogical procedure that can be adapted to any situation. He provides an excellent background of scientific facts for the teacher in need of this help and advice on specific method. He furnishes lists of available books for teachers and pupils, and offers this consoling encouragement to the teacher untrained in science: "Much of the material listed in the primary section has been successfully taught by teachers without training in the fields of science."

Desirable Outcomes in Nature Study. Where there is neither formal curriculum nor sequentially organized method, there can be no statement of outcomes. Nevertheless, to aid the particularly interested or ambitious teacher to a realization of what primary children can master under excellent instruction, we have turned the "specific objectives" of the Horace Mann Course of Study for the first three years into "desirable outcomes."

SOCIAL AND NATURAL ENVIRONMENT 275

First Grade

The pupils have
1. Become aware of the great modification of the appearance of the environment with the change of seasons;
2. Observed some of the ways in which trees and shrubs make changes with the seasons;
3. Observed the adjustment of plants other than trees to the cold of winter;
4. Discovered where many of the birds go in autumn;
5. What insects do in the autumn, winter and spring;
6. How the birds that remain in the north in the winter adapt themselves to the winter conditions;
7. Ways in which other animals prepare for winter;
8. That seeds start new plants of the same kind;
9. That water needs more room when it changes to ice;
10. That weather greatly influences what man does;
11. That there is water in the air;
12. That air surrounds man at all times;
13. That a fire must have air in order to burn.

Second Grade

The pupils have learned
1. Some of the ways in which plants pass the winter;
2. That man prepares for winter;
3. How insects survive the winter;
4. That many birds go to warmer climates during the cold months;
5. Some of the ways in which animals survive the winter;

6. That ice forms at the top of water;
7. To observe changes of weather, some of the effects of weather, how to read the thermometer;
8. That water can be turned into ice and steam;
9. That the room is filled with air;
10. That there is dust in the air;
11. That we receive heat and light from the sun;
12. That light is necessary to plant life;
13. That iron nails and tacks are picked up by a magnet;
14. Some of the activities of spiders;
15. Something concerning the activities of moths and butterflies.

Third Grade

The pupils have learned
1. Some of the ways in which animals protect themselves;
2. Some of the ways in which animals care for their young;
3. Some of the ways the plants have of scattering their seeds;
4. That if there were no plants, animals would starve;
5. That man is dependent on plants and other animals for food and clothing;
6. That there are tiny particles (spores) in the air which are like seeds, and that they start to grow whenever they fall upon a favorable place;
7. That the magnet needle points (nearly) north and south;
8. That the warm, moist air drops the water that it carries when it strikes cold objects or cold air;

SOCIAL AND NATURAL ENVIRONMENT

9. That plants give off water into the air in several ways;
10. That the surrounding air exerts force and can be used to do work;
11. That air breathed out of the lungs is not the same as the air breathed into them;
12. The principle of floating objects;
13. That plants which have green leaves must have light in order to grow;
14. That sunlight is made up of many colors;
15. That the earth rotates, causing day and night.

REFERENCES FOR FURTHER STUDY

Bonser, F. G., and Mossman, L. C., *Industrial Arts for Elementary Schools*, New York, The Macmillan Company, 1923.

Dobbs, E. V., *Primary Handwork*, New York, The Macmillan Company, 1924.

Linnell, A., *The School Festival*. New York, Charles Scribner's Sons, 1931.

McKee, J. W., *Purposeful Handwork*. New York, The Macmillan Company, 1922.

National Society for the Study of Education, *Thirty-first Yearbook*, Part II, *A Program for Teaching Science*, Bloomington, Public School Publishing Company, 1932.

Reed, M. M., and Wright, L. E., *The Beginnings of the Social Sciences*. New York, Charles Scribner's Sons, 1932.

Storm, G. E., *The Social Studies in the Primary Grades*. Chicago, Lyons and Carnahan, 1931.

Trafton, G. H., *Teaching of Science in the Elementary School*. Boston, Houghton Mifflin Co., 1918.

CHAPTER XXII

About Our Profession

The familiar essay is almost the only form of literature in which the author of a book and his reader seem to establish some form of relationship. Usually, and especially in a professional work like this, the author must, in the nature of things, address all of his readers as a group, deal with all of the problems in general. Yet the reader is always one of such a group, and the reader's hopes, plans, and ideals are always specific. We have decided to address this chapter to you, the readers who in all likelihood are either teaching now or hope to teach later. Other readers, be they parents or professors in teacher-training institutions, are not really invited to this discussion.

Is teaching a profession? How frequently have we not heard this question? It seems to be a favorite of the institute and assembly speakers when other inspiration fails. The answer is almost always in the affirmative and the reasoning which proves that teaching is a profession is almost always labored and aggressive.

If teaching isn't a profession, the orators tell us, that is because the salaries aren't large enough; the training doesn't last long enough, the attitude of the general public isn't respectful enough, but we must make teaching a profession. Did you ever hear lawyers or physicians or architects debate the question as to whether or not their work is a profession? Does a small income make the clergyman or the country doctor less of a professional man? If the years of training are not long enough for effective preparation, can that not be remedied? But the respect of the general public—can that be commanded?

Horace Mann, one of the most devoted educators and educational pioneers of our country, answered all of these questions magnificently in words which all of us ought to remember: "If the title is not sufficiently honorable now, then it is clearly left for me to elevate it." Let us make up our minds once for all that we can neither command nor demand professional status any more than we can command love or respect. We must earn it by our lives and by our work.

The work of the elementary school and, perhaps more particularly of the primary grades is, we think, the most fascinating of all the stages of instruction. It is certainly the most technical. The easiest way to deal with one who seems to take it for granted that anyone can teach little children because the content is so rudimentary is to offer him the opportunity to receive thirty or forty six-year-old children at the beginning of the school year and let him proceed to teach them reading, writing, spelling, arithmetic, music, art, and supervise their playground activities. The content is indeed rudimentary but the general culture demanded is, for the ambitious and conscientious teacher, never adequate enough to satisfy her. She can always make use of all of her intellectual resources.

Fascinating and technical as the work is, we must nevertheless bear in mind that the elementary school has come down to us from humble origins and therefore bears an humble tradition. The school was established for the purpose of giving rudimentary instruction, and rudimentary instruction only, to those children who were not to go on to higher education. These children of the ordinary people were to enter apprenticeship for some trade after a few years of elementary instruction. For this reason, the teachers for these schools were not chosen from among the educated, the graduates of the universities, but rather from among the people themselves. Too often were these teachers inadequate even for the task of teaching those famous R's, really four in number: reading, writing, arithmetic, and religion.

The progress toward adequate training was very slow indeed. The colleges and universities of the land, with few exceptions, still consider the task of the professional training of elementary teachers outside the proper circle of their activities. The first step toward improvement consisted of the organization of Institutes of Instruction for teachers already in service. These institutes usually lasted a number of weeks and were intended to improve the instruction of those who had somehow gotten into teaching, often with limited capacity even in the curriculum content.

Then, in due course, normal schools were organized for the training of elementary teachers, a special institution for the teachers of a special school, you see, side by side with, and presumably inferior to, the colleges. At first, the normal schools really were inferior, since they admitted their students directly from elementary school, without the intervention of a period of secondary education. It was rule-of-thumb training, practice without theory, such as is given to a motorman who knows how to "push the button" but does not know "what makes the wheels go round." It was practice without theory.

Improvement, as with all else in the last hundred years, has been continuous. The normal schools began to demand high school preparation; they began to lengthen the term of training until today those with the highest standards have become colleges—Teachers Colleges which demand graduation from high school as a prerequisite for admission, four years of training, and the sort of ability and performance that warrant the granting of the degree.

But there still is, as you perhaps know, a great distance between the degree-granting Teachers Colleges and those training institutions furthest to the rear. It is possible in some places to secure a teacher's certificate on the basis of county examinations without any professional study whatever. There are still states in which some of the elementary teachers have been trained by a faculty of one during a post-graduate year at a local high school. There are, of course, normal schools which require only a year or two of training.

But even the leading institutions still have some distance to go. In almost all cases, if not in all, the Teachers Colleges grant a general elementary certificate which entitles the holder to teach and therefore assumes that she has been trained to teach all of the subjects in all of the years, and frequently the kindergarten as well.

The institutions in the forefront of teacher-training ought to begin to require specialization of prospective elementary teachers; these colleges ought to limit the field of competency for which a teacher can be adequately prepared even after four years of training and the taking of the degree. They ought to establish majors. Students might well be required to specialize in such fields as early childhood education, covering the nursery school and the kindergarten; the primary grades; and the upper grades. For those who plan to be certified in the upper grades a further specialization within that area might well be desirable. In other words, the teacher who has prepared to teach in the upper grades might be certified as having general training for this work with particular competence in English, or music, or art, or the social studies. When that day of greater specialization comes, the textbooks which our children use will be prepared by teachers who know the child as well as the subject, rather than by college professors who are scholars in the field of content but have little experience in the field of elementary school instruction.

But let us return to you. We sincerely hope that, faced with an opportunity like yours, to work with the youth of the race, to represent organized civilization and culture in the task of introducing youth to its heritage you will not meet it as a slave who works because he must. We hope that, entrusted with the task of education, than which there surely can be no nobler, you will meet it as a challenge and an opportunity. Representing organized parenthood you are in possession of the privilege of working effectively toward a worthy end. There are few pleasures in life greater than that of creative effort, than work that is truly worth the doing, work that is self-directed. To make education a profession and yourself a member of it we recommend to your attention two things: pride and craftsmanship.

If you face your task with sincere and high intentions, you are entitled to pride in your chosen work because as a teacher you are or will be entrusted with the most precious possession that any society owns. There is no greater trust reposed in any group anywhere than that reposed in the school by the parenthood of society. In the hands of the teacher lies the one greatest power for carrying forward progress in social, political, economic, and cultural betterment.

And now, what of craftsmanship? If there is any one thing in the field of education that is incontestable it is that the teacher's preparation is never complete. Whatever she experiences that is worth while or interesting, when she reads, travels, or associates with stimulating people, she is enriching her background. Ultimately some of her riches will be multiplied in the lives of her pupils.

General culture, then, in every sense of that word, with every variety of taste, skill, and growth that the words imply, will help make a better teacher of the primary grades. No teacher of little children can possibly be too well-read, too well-traveled, or too well-trained for this task.

From preparation in general we come to an examination of some of the details of early education. In this book you have been presented with an outline of the special knowledge and the special skills that are either indispensable or can well be employed to improve teaching. But surely no student can avoid the realization that this task of making oneself adequate for teaching little children can never be completed. Your intellectual, emotional, and spiritual life can never be too fine because it is to you that parents confidingly entrust their children. It is to you that the school beginners turn with such enthusiasm and complete confidence. To them you represent ultimate authority and to them you are the arbiter of all that concerns good taste.

In the realm of aesthetics, there are music and art which need only be mentioned here. There is, however, an interesting movement in early schooling about which we have said little in previous pages but which is most attractive. We refer to rhythm as such and the rôle that it may play under the guidance of the competent and enthusiastic teacher. You will find teachers who, with rhythm as a center, carry on conventionalized dancing, dramatics, pantomime, and free play, all of the greatest aesthetic value.

Concerning the opportunity for growth in the realm of speech little need be added. Are you well read? Do you know well the immortal literature of your mother tongue? Have you developed a critical taste? Do you have an effective and attractive speaking voice? Can you carry on easy, graceful, and interesting conversation? Have you achieved the art of telling stories interestingly to children? Do you bring the spirit of play and gayety into the dramatization?

The use of tools and general skill in doing things with the hands is a part of general competence that many of us have neglected. Yet these are almost indispensable in carrying on work with little children. First there is the construction that represents a part of the work in art. Then there are the numberless crude things that children love to make and in which they need direction in connection with the general projects that so many teachers encourage. Again, there are delightful things to be done with the hands in connection with good work in nature study. Caring for pets or the cultivation of a garden, with a tiny plot assigned to each child, represent delightful work. Weaving and modelling are among the other types of craft work that enlarge the scope of experience and the effectiveness of teaching.

For explaining the phenomena of nature even to little children, many of us find our background inadequate. Even the immediate environment of plant and animal life is an almost closed book to too many of us. What a delightful opportunity and what a rewarding task it is to study in detail about the world of nature! What opportunities to combine pleasure and professional growth during the long summer vacations! In connection with this phase of primary education as well as social studies we urge you to cultivate the art of the school excursion. There are countries in Europe where the excursion is used much more extensively than here as a method of instruction. It is a happy road toward the understanding of environment. It is living. It is stimulating. It leads to vivid response in words and in graphic expression.

There are, finally, current lines of thought and effort

ABOUT OUR PROFESSION

which are not absolutely related to primary edu[cation] but which may give you pleasure and a sense of g[rowth]. The movement for parental education which is sponsored by the students of the nursery school and the nursery school itself deserve your attention. Visits to these schools and an examination of the literature concerning them and their procedure will be rewarding. The primary teacher can, naturally, learn much in the kindergarten from which some of her own pupils come to her classes. It will be interesting to visit excellent kindergarten teachers. Much of their work and certainly the general atmosphere of their classrooms can be translated for your own use.

We dealt, in one of the chapters, with the problems of transition presented by those children who are of first grade age but do not yet possess first grade ability. These are pre-primary children. Some of these children are mentally retarded and open up for the ambitious teacher that whole phase of the field of psychology which deals with the significance and the diagnosis of individual differences. Some of these children come from foreign parentage and foreign environment. This opens interesting economic and sociological problems to the inquiring mind. Visits to the homes of these children may well prove rewarding.

The members of every profession must carry forward as well as carry on. Every generation of teachers, as do members of all the professions and arts, receives a rich heritage to which, as the result of experimentation, research, and careful observation, each generation adds its own modifications, qualifications, and contributions for the future. In the field of education there are many books. To some of these we have referred extensively in this volume. But work will go on, and you will want to keep informed and abreast of the best practice. You will want to know what other workers are doing, how others are meeting problems and situations like your own. For these purposes there are professional journals.

The teacher, like the physician or other professional worker, sometimes finds herself isolated in the sense that there may be a limited number of persons with whom she can discuss her professional interests intelligently, to whom she can outline her opinions, plans, or studies. It is a dangerous and a discouraging situation. It may lead to loss of interest, to a feeling that one is working alone. The remedy for this is the reading of professional journals. These bind the members of the profession; help them to share their interests, their enthusiasms and their effort; help the individual to hold to that necessary feeling that he is part of a large and important group of workers.

Three things in particular you will secure from the journals and each of the three is important. The first is news. Nearly all journals contain important items of news which will keep you informed of important happenings and of the activities of the leaders in your field. The second item for which you may rely on your professional journals is announcements and reviews of new books. It is most important to know what is being published in your field of interest. The third important item for which you may look to the journals consists of articles which almost always present new studies and new practices by your fellow workers. These articles may well stimulate and encourage you to effort toward professional improvement.

The last topic in this chapter and in this book will concern these journals. It is quite hopeless to attempt to list them all, and we shall of course not do so. It is equally impossible to evaluate them all and this we shall certainly not attempt. We shall mention some professional journals with the understanding that we make no claim that they are the only or the best journals. If you are interested in more exhaustive information you must seek it in the various indices of the well-equipped library. One type of journal in particular must be specifically omitted. We refer to the publications of the numerous professional associations and to the many local journals that are published in this country.

Of professional journals general in character, we shall mention three: *The Nation's Schools* is published by the Nation's Schools Publishing Company, Chicago. *School and Society* is published by The Science Press, Lancaster, Pa. *Progressive Education* is published by the Progressive Education Association, Washington, D. C.

In the field of elementary education we refer to *The Elementary School Journal*, published by the University of Chicago.

The specialist in primary education may well be interested in *American Childhood,* published by Milton Bradley Co., Springfield, Mass., and in *Childhood Education,* published by the Association for Childhood Education, Washington, D. C.

The five following journals deal with special phases of elementary school education. *The Elementary English Review* is published by the National Council of the Teachers of English, Detroit, Mich. *The Quarterly Journal of Speech Education* is published by the National Association of Teachers of Speech, at Ann Arbor, Michigan. *School Arts Magazine* is published by Davis Press Inc., Worcester, Mass. *The Journal of Health and Physical Education* is published by the American Physical Education Association at Ann Arbor, Michigan. *The Music Supervisors' Journal* is published by the Music Supervisors General Conference at Chicago.

INDEX

Activities in primary education, 45
  see also *Projects*
Adams, J., 46
Age for beginning institutional education, 13, 19
American Childhood, 287
American Child Health Association, 258
Appreciation
  procedures in general, 43 ff.
  in art, 254
  in music, 188, 195
Arabic number system, 8
Ayers Penmanship Test, 97

Bailey, H. T., 203, 204, 211, 221, 222, 223
Bennett, R., 157
Bird, O. C., 251, 253
Bobbitt, F., 234
Bonser, F. G., 50
Boy Scouts of America, 237
Brown, C., 176
Bryant, S. C., 169, 170, 173

Character Education Institution, 237
Childhood Education, 287
Children's Code of Morals, 237
Chubb, P., 153, 154, 161, 169
Cleveland Course of Study, 256
Coleman, S. N., 10
Commonwealth Spelling List, 93
Conversation as part of oral English, 161
Craig, G. S., 269, 274
Creative work in primary grades, 46, 188
Curriculum
  in primary education, 37
  principles of construction, 36
Cursive writing compared with manuscript, 87

Davis, S. E., 269
deForest, M., 198
Denver Course of Study, 181, 191
Department of Superintendence of the National Education Association
Character Education Committee, 234
Committee on Language and Composition, 162
Committee on Spelling, 92, 93
Elementary School and Nature Study Committee, 270
Detroit
  character education in, 237
  Intelligence Test, 30
Dictionary, instruction in use of, 117
Dramatization, value of, 174
Drill
  place in primary education, 39
  procedures, 40

Education, definition of, 3
Elementary English Review, 287
Elementary School Journal, 287
Equipment and materials for
  art instruction, 208
  music instruction, 189

Fern, E. B., 11
Five Point Plan, 241
Forest, L., 17
Freeman, F. N., 106, 107
Freeman Penmanship Test, 98
Froebel's kindergarten principles, 27
Fryberger, A. M., 198

Gesell, A., 15
Giddings, T. P., 185, 193
Glenn, M., 198

Handwork in the primary grades, 261
Height-Age-Weight Table, 259
Hill, P. S., 155
Horace Mann Elementary School, 274
Horn, E., 93
Houston Penmanship Test, 98
Hutchins, W. J., 237

Individual differences among entering children, 24
Individual instruction
  in arithmetic, 128
  in Winnetka, 42
  need for, 42
International Kindergarten Union, 25
Iowa Plan for Character Education, 237, 241

James, W., 242
Journal of Health and Physical Education, 287

Kilpatrick, W. H., 45
Kindergarten, 17, 27
Klapper, P., 213

Left-handedness and penmanship instruction, 91
Literature
  in the primary grades, 179
  list of suitable books, 181
  see also *Memorizing* and *Dramatization*
Littlejohns, J., 204, 222
Los Angeles
  course of study, 181
  transition classes in, 32
Lowry, M., 198

Mann, H., 279
Manuscript writing
  as an aid in teaching reading, 63
  as a form of penmanship, 87
Materials for instruction. See *Equipment.*
Mathias, M. E., 217, 218, 223
McLester, A., 243, 244

Meader, E. B., 155
Memorizing
  list of poems for, 179
  values of, 179
Modern Health Crusade, 253
Monotones, 192
Monroe, P., 46
Monroe's Timed Sentence Test, 99
Morrison, H. D., 7, 22
Music Supervisors' Journal, 287
Music Supervisors' National Conference, 187, 199
Myers, A. E., 251, 253

National Education Association, The Journal of, 179
  see also *Department of Superintendence*
Nation's Schools, The, 287
Nature study, 269 ff.
New England Primer, 28
Non-readers
  definition of, 81
  diagnosis, 82
  remedial instruction, 82
Nursery School, 14
Nyquist, F. V., 225

Oakland Course of Study, 256

Parker, S. C., 216
Pathfinders of America, 237
Phonetics in speech education, 159
Phonics in reading instruction, 76
Pre-primary children, 30, 32
  see also *Transition classes*
Primer, qualities that constitute excellence, 70
Progressive Education, 287
Projects in primary education, 45, 49
  see also *Activities*

Quarterly Journal of Speech Education, 287

Readiness for school
  ascertainable by test, 25
  other methods of determining, 30, 33

Reading
  children who are not ready to read, 66
  psychology and pedagogy of, 53 ff.
  see also *Transition classes*
Reading Readiness Committee Report, 25
Rhythm bands, 119
Rogers, C. K., 156
Rugg, H., 209
Russell, B., 14

St. Louis Course of Study, 181, 182
Sargent, W., 204, 206, 215, 221, 226
School and Society, 287
School Arts Magazine, 287
Scout Law, 237
Shumaker, A., 209
Silent reading
  defined, 55
  in later primary period, 80
Social Studies, 264 ff.
Speech
  as part of the curriculum, 11
  significance in social evolution, 3
Stanford Achievement Test, 99
Stinchfield, S. M., 4
Storm, G. E., 264
Stormzand, M. J., 45, 230
Storr, M., 198

Story-telling in primary education
  qualities of the good story, 169
  qualities of the good narrator, 173
  list of suitable stories, 171
Teachers College, Columbia, 274
Temple, A., 216
Terman, L. M., 24, 25
Tests in
  arithmetic, 146
  penmanship, 97
  reading, 72
  spelling, 97
Thorndike Penmanship Test, 98
Tomlinson, R. R., 207
Toy instruments and orchestras, 99
Transition classes
  need for, 30
  procedures in, 32

Vandewalker, N. P., 31

Waddle, C. W., 208
Watson, J. B., 16
Weight-Height-Age Table, 259
Wells, H. G., 5
Whitford, W. G., 205
Winnetka, individual instruction in, 42
Wooley, H. T., 16
Writing, significance in social evolution, 5